Getting Reading Right From the Start

▶

Getting Reading Right From the Start

Effective Early Literacy Interventions

Edited by

Elfrieda H. Hiebert
University of Colorado–Boulder

Barbara M. Taylor
University of Minnesota

Allyn and Bacon
Boston • London • Toronto • Sydney • Tokyo • Singapore

Series Editor: Nancy Forsyth
Editorial Assistant: Christine Nelson
Cover Administrator: Linda Dickinson
Manufacturing Buyer: Louise Richardson
Editorial-Production Service: Spectrum Publisher Services
Cover Designer: Suzanne Harbison

Library of Congress Cataloging-in-Publication Data

Getting reading right from the start : effective early literacy interventions / editors,
    Elfrieda H. Hiebert, Barbara M. Taylor.
        p.   cm.
    Includes bibliographical references and index.
    ISBN 0-205-15407-7
    1. Reading (Elementary)—United States. 2. Literacy—United States.
I. Hiebert, Elfrieda H. II. Taylor, Barbara (Barbara M.)
LB1573.G44   1994
372.41—dc20   93-1891
                                                                           CIP

Printed in the United States of America

10   9   8   7   6   99 00 01

To Charley
and to Geoff, Kristie, and Danny

Contents

▶

Contributors

Barbara M. Taylor is Professor and Chairperson, Department of Curriculum and Instruction in the College of Education at the University of Minnesota where she teaches courses on literacy education, children's literature, and reading difficulties. She has published extensively on reading instruction and reading problems in journals such as *American Educational Research Journal, Reading Research Quarterly,* and *The Reading Teacher.* Dr. Taylor is a former elementary and secondary school teacher and continues to work extensively in elementary schools. For the past 4 years, Dr. Taylor has been working with first-grade teachers in six Minnesota school districts and in five other school districts around the country implementing the Early Reading Intervention program she developed.

Elfrieda H. Hiebert is Professor, School of Education, University of Colorado–Boulder. Her research on how instructional and assessment practices impact literacy acquisition has been published in journals such as *American Educational Research Journal, Reading Research Quarterly,* and *Journal of Educational Psychology.* She has edited *Literacy for a Diverse Society* (1991) and contributed to *Becoming a Nation of Readers.* Professor Hiebert has been a recipient of a Spencer Fellowship awarded through the National Academy of Education and currently serves on the editorial boards of *Reading Research Quarterly* and *The Elementary School Journal.*

Anne McGill-Franzen is an assistant professor in the Reading Department at the State University of New York at Albany. Prior to joining the faculty in 1989, Dr. McGill-Franzen was a classroom teacher, a Chapter 1 teacher, and a special education consultant. She was also a research assistant at the Institute for Research on Teaching, Michigan State University, coprincipal investigator on several externally funded classroom observation projects at SUNY at

Albany, and a Center for Women in Government Policy Fellow at the New York State Legislature. She recently participated in a local community-based effort to improve the City School District of Albany as Assistant Director of the Strategic Planning Committee. Her work with low-achieving children has been published in *Learning Disabilities Quarterly, Reading Research Quarterly, The Elementary School Journal, Remedial and Special Education, The Reading Teacher,* and other journals. She was corecipient of the International Reading Association's Albert J. Harris Award for outstanding research published in the field of reading disabilities in 1990. She is author of *Shaping the Preschool Agenda: Early Literacy, Public Policy, and Professional Beliefs* (1993, SUNY Press), which is based on her dissertation. She is on the editorial board of several scholarly publications. Dr. McGill-Franzen is interested in how public policy shapes the school experiences of poor children and influences their opportunities to become literate. She is currently conducting a longitudinal study of the classroom literary experiences of urban children from 4- to 7-years-old, a project funded through the National Research Center for the Learning and Teaching of Literature at SUNY, Albany.

Connie Juel is the Thomas G. Jewell Professor of Education and the Director of Studies in Learning to Read at the McGuffey Reading Center at the University of Virginia. She works extensively in elementary schools with preservice teachers and other students interested in literacy acquisition. A graduate of Stanford University, she has published widely on literacy acquisition. Dr. Juel is a former elementary school teacher, and has served as Associate Editor of *Reading Research Quarterly,* as well as being an Advisor for Children's Television Workshop for programs such as Sesame Street and Ghostwriter. Since 1989, she has been involved with early literacy intervention as represented by her chapter in this book. Along with colleagues at McGuffey and the Charlottesville schools, she is currently directing a community volunteer tutoring program in local elementary schools.

M. Trika Smith-Burke is a professor at New York University in the School of Education, Department of Teaching and Learning. She has written numerous articles and co-edited two volumes: *Reader Meets Author: Bridging the Gap* with Judith Langer, and *Observing the Language Learner* with Angela M. Jaggar. Her involvement in professional organizations is extensive and includes work in the International Reading Association, the National Conference on Research in English and the National Reading Conference.

In 1988–1989, Dr. Smith-Burke participated in the National Reading Recovery Teacher-Leader-Trainer program at The Ohio State University. Currently she codirects the New York University Reading Recovery Project with Angela Jaggar.

Angela M. Jaggar is Professor of Education in the Department of Teaching and Learning at New York University, where she teaches graduate courses in language and literacy development. She is codirector of the NYU Reading Recovery Project and coordinates project research and development. Currently, she is engaged in a study of the long-term effects of Reading Recovery on children who participate in the program. In another study, she is researching the impact of Reading Recovery on teacher development.

Her publications focus on language use, literacy, and learning. She is coeditor of *Observing the Language Learner*, copublished by IRA and NCTE, a book for teachers that focuses on ways to observe, assess, and interpret children's spoken and written language. She is also co-author of "Oral Language: Speaking and Listening in the Classroom," which appears in the *Handbook of Research on Teaching the Language Arts* published by Macmillan.

Dr. Jaggar has been President of the National Conference on Research in English, a Trustee of the NCTE Research Foundation, and chair of the NCTE Elementary Section Committee. Currently, she is on the Board of Directors of Literacy Volunteers of New York City.

Jean Strait and **Mary Anne Medo** are Ph.D. students in literacy education at the University of Minnesota who have worked with Dr. Taylor on the Early Intervention in Reading program for the past 2 years. Currently, Jean Strait is teaching at Minneapolis Community College and Mary Medo is a reading resource teacher at Clement Avenue School in Milwaukee.

Robert E. Slavin, Nancy A. Madden, Nancy L. Karweit, Lawrence J. Dolan, and **Barbara A. Wasik** are all at the Center for Research on Effective Schooling for Disadvantaged Students at Johns Hopkins University. This group, with others at Johns Hopkins and in the Baltimore City Public Schools, developed the Success for All program and has been evaluating it for several years. Members of the group have done research on many topics relating to effective programs for elementary schools serving disadvantaged students and have produced several books, including *Effective Programs for Students at Risk* (Allyn & Bacon, 1989), *Success for All: A Relentless Approach to Prevention and Early Intervention in Elementary Schools* (Educational Research Service, 1992), and *Preventing Early School Failure* (Allyn & Bacon, in press). The group is currently working in collaboration with the Maryland State Department of Education and the St. Mary's County Public Schools to develop the elementary school of the 21st century, under funding from the New American Schools Development Corporation.

Gay Su Pinnell is Professor of Theory and Practice at The Ohio State University where she teaches courses on language development, literacy, and children's literature. She is formerly a primary school teacher and now teaches children daily as part of the Reading Recovery program, an early intervention initiative to help young children having difficulty in learning to read and write. She is co-author of *Teaching Reading Comprehension* and author and editor of *Discovering Language With Children* and *Teachers and Research: Language Learning in the Classroom*, which she co-edited with Myna Matlin. With colleagues Diane E. DeFord and Carol A. Lyons at The Ohio State University, she has been responsible for implementing Reading Recovery and conducting a research program, which resulted in the recent book, *Bridges to Literacy: Learning From Reading Recovery*. A new book, *Partners in Literacy*, will be published in 1993. Currently, she is coordinating efforts to implement Reading Recovery in California, centering at California State University at San Bernardino. She is principal investigator for the Early Literacy Research Project, sponsored by the John D. and Catherine T. MacArthur Foundation. In addition, Dr. Pinnell has authored numerous articles on literacy and language development.

Andrea McCarrier is the coordinator of the Reading Recovery Program for the National Diffusion Network. For the past 4 years she has been part of a research team at The Ohio State University that developed a long-term staff development model designed to support teachers as they implement new approaches to early literacy instruction in their classrooms. The chapter in this book discusses both the theory and practices associated with the elements of the early literacy lesson that teachers learned during their participation in the staff development course.

Claude Goldenberg is at UCLA where he is an associate research psychologist is the Department of Psychiatry and Biobehavioral Sciences and associate director of the Urban Education Studies Center in the Graduate School of Education. A native of Argentina, he has taught junior high and first grade in predominantly Latino schools serving largely Spanish-speaking populations in San Antonio, Texas, and Los Angeles, California. He began the work he reports in this volume when he was teaching first grade while conducting research with the support of a Spencer postdoctoral fellowship from the National Academy of Education.

▶

Preface

In many places, the days are past when children marked Xs and Os on geometric shapes and matched strings of randomly assorted letters in the name of reading readiness. The last several decades have seen an emergent literacy perspective come into prominence. While many have agreed that an emergent literacy approach was particularly needed with children who have often been failed by conventional approaches, it has only been in the last several years that descriptions have become available of applications of an emergent literacy approach in contexts where a majority of children have had few prior literacy experiences.

As we participated in a growing network of collaborative teams of school- and university-based educators who were working on such implementation projects, we found that we were grappling with similar issues despite disparate contexts. Sometimes, these issues related to instructional methodology like the size of groups in which initially low-performing children could most profitably learn. Other persistent issues of policy and teacher development arose as well. For example, colleagues frequently talked about the need for schoolwide implementation and forms of home-school liaisons. At the same time, a theme ran through the stories of colleagues around the country—children were learning to read and write, and their teachers were enthusiastic about children's accomplishments.

The questions and success stories that were raised in such conversations, we believed, should be shared with a larger constituency. Symposia were organized at two conferences—National Reading Conference (1991) and American Educational Research Association (1992)—so that reports could be shared with the larger educational community. Descriptions had so many common themes and the underlying issues were so pressing that it became clear that these reports should be available to a much wider audience—hence, this volume.

Our hope in sharing the reports of these various projects is that these stories of success will be repeated in many, many more classrooms. Initiation of the activities that cut across these projects—identification of clearcut goals and expectations, instructional activities that involve children in reading and writing, authentic assessment practices, and liaisons within schools and between schools and home communities—can be expected to have high payoffs. At the same time, educators should enter these projects with their eyes wide open—and the reports in this volume describe some of the issues with which teams of educators need to grapple. The reports within this volume illustrate solutions and the processes whereby solutions can be achieved.

There are many who permitted us to extend the conversation of "high literacy levels for all" through this volume. Nancy Forsyth and Christine Nelson at Allyn and Bacon shared our vision. They have added patience to vision—a combination that has supported us in completing this project. We are grateful as well for the many times our staff assistants, Lena Johannessen at the University of Colorado and Audrey Borgstrom, Florence Nehasil, and Marsha Aalseth at the University of Minnesota, have accommodated requests related to this volume. The commitment of the contributors to the possibility of literacy for all was evident in their willingness to meet deadlines and to respond quickly with revisions and additional information. We thank them for their hard work on this volume—and their daily efforts to raise literacy levels in schools around the country. Finally, we thank the teachers, children, and parents with whom we have worked. You have shown us that it is possible for all children to get off to the right start in literacy.

EHH & BMT

▶ Part I

The Context for Current Interventions

▶ 1

Early Literacy Interventions: Aims and Issues

BARBARA M. TAYLOR   ELFRIEDA H. HIEBERT

In this introductory chapter the authors explain the purpose of the book: to demonstrate that early literacy intervention programs with a focus on accelerated learning and on authentic reading and writing tasks can prevent many first-grade children from failing to learn to read. An overview is given of seven different intervention programs which are discussed in subsequent chapters along with implementation issues. These programs are grouped into tutoring approaches, small-group models, and schoolwide restructuring efforts. An overview is also given of the concluding chapter which discusses the importance of early literacy intervention programs and the need to go beyond them to meet the needs of low-achieving readers across the elementary grades and beyond.

Although national tests have indicated that children, in general, are reading as well today as in 1970 (Mullis & Jenkins, 1990), substantial numbers of students in our elementary and secondary schools have difficulties with reading. The National Assessment for Education Progress found that 60% of the 17-year-olds who were assessed in 1988 did not have adept reading skills and were thought to be at risk as they became "adults in a society that depends so heavily on the ability to extract meaning from various forms of written language" (Mullis & Jenkins, 1990).

Also, substantial differences in reading performance have been found at grades 4, 8, and 12 according to socioeconomic status and ethnicity. For example, twelfth-grade students from disadvantaged urban schools performed, on average, below the level of eighth-grade students from advantaged urban schools (Langer, Applebee, Mullis, & Foertsch, 1990). African- and Hispanic-American students performed less well than Caucasian students at all three grade levels assessed.

Additionally, the difference in performance levels between better and poorer readers has been found to remain constant at each grade level (Applebee, Langer, & Mullis, 1988). This suggests that schools have not been successful in their attempts to help lower achieving students "catch up" to their peers. Unfortunately, most children who get off to a slow start in reading remain behind in reading (Carter, 1984; Cooley, 1981; Juel, 1988).

The philosophy upon which this book is based is that children in our schools do not have to fail in reading. Schools can change the education that they provide to children at risk of experiencing reading difficulties so that these children become successful readers. This book focuses on "getting reading right from the start," that is, getting children into reading and writing immediately as they enter kindergarten and first grade with the conviction that almost all children can be successful readers and not have to face years of failure.

This book is about school interventions. Most of the interventions described in the book have a home component, and these home components are seen as valuable. However, they are not the primary focus of these projects. All the interventions are based on the premise that much more can and should be done in schools to support young children's literacy. Many children, particularly from lower socioeconomic levels, do not have sufficient access to good instruction (see chapter 2). The projects in this book all describe what can happen when children have access to good instruction. We are not suggesting that poor or minority children should be the focus of early reading interventions. Indeed, many children who are poor or from minority groups come to school with rich literacy backgrounds and high levels of literacy. What we are arguing for in this book, however, is that all children, especially poor children who might have had insufficient access to high quality school reading instruction in the past, be given access to high quality early reading interventions in school if they are in need of such help.

In recent years there has been a growing interest in and development of effective reading intervention programs for children in kindergarten, first, and second grade. Early intervention programs focusing on authentic reading and writing experiences have been implemented to accelerate the literacy learning of children who enter school behind their peers in emergent reading abilities. These programs have, in fact, demonstrated that most children can be prevented from falling considerably behind their peers in reading and from experiencing a sense of failure in reading (Slavin & Madden, 1989; Stanovich, 1986).

There has been a strong tradition of early childhood interventions that predates recent attempts to accelerate the literacy learning of primary-grade children who come to school with lesser levels of literacy than their peers. However, few of these programs, such as Head Start (Peterman, Stewart, Sinha, Kerr, & Mason, 1991), have focused on fostering emergent literacy at the preschool or kindergarten level because such attempts have been regarded by many as "developmentally inappropriate" (Spodek, 1988). We do not support literacy learning in preschool or kindergarten if it is defined as developing students' reading readiness skills through isolated skill-and-drill type tasks. However, we do believe that more can and should be done in elementary schools to engage kindergarten children, particularly those who enter school with relatively low levels of literacy, in activities like reading stories aloud, sharing big books, and writing in which one specific purpose is to develop students' emergent reading abilities. Chapter 8 provides an excellent example of such a kindergarten program.

Traditional approaches to providing extra help in reading in grades 1 through 6 through special education services or Chapter 1 programs have typically operated from a perspective of providing remedial instruction, as opposed to accelerated learning, for emergent readers identified as having reading problems (Allington, 1991). Observational studies by Allington and McGill-Franzen (1989) and O'Sullivan, Ysseldyke, Christenson, and Thurlow (1990), for example, have characterized Chapter 1 and special education learning disability services for elementary children as pull-out programs with an emphasis on repetition of low-level, isolated skill-and-drill activities as opposed to the reading of connected text. Allington (1991) and McGill-Franzen and Allington (1991) have identified this as the "slow-it-down-and-make-it-concrete" approach to helping poor readers. In general, experts have concluded that such Chapter 1 and special education learning disabilities programs have not been as effective as was hoped (Allington, 1991; Carter, 1984; Glass, 1986; McGill-Franzen & Allington, 1991; Slavin & Madden, 1989).

Allington and McGill-Franzen (1989) argue that what is needed is supplemental, high-quality instruction to accelerate the reading development of students reading "below grade level." Low-achieving readers need more time than they typically receive to engage in actual reading and to participate in reading lessons focusing on connected text.

Various early reading intervention programs implemented in this country in recent years not only provide supplemental instruction to accelerate reading development but also provide quality instruction focusing on the reading of and writing about books as opposed to the repetitive practice of isolated reading skills. Children learn the decoding strategies of contextual and phonic analysis, for example, as they read and reread simple stories, not as they complete worksheets or look at words in isolation on the chalkboard. This emphasis on *authentic reading* is tied to the current movement in the United States toward literature-based, whole-language reading instruction as opposed to reading instruction driven by the mastery learning of specific reading skills. A fundamental belief of this newer approach to reading instruction is that children learn to read, for the most part, by practicing reading, not by completing worksheets on reading skills performed in isolation.

These early reading intervention programs focusing on accelerated learning and authentic reading and writing endeavors are producing exciting results. Leading the way has been the Reading Recovery program. Developed in New Zealand by Marie Clay (1985) in the 1970s and implemented first in this country on a wide scale in Ohio in the 1980s, Reading Recovery is a one-on-one tutoring program for low-achieving first graders. The program has had a widespread effect (Pinnell, 1989) and is now being used in at least 40 of the 50 states (Allen, 1992).

Success for All (Slavin et al., 1990) is a schoolwide school improvement program that also provides early reading intervention through individual tutoring in kindergarten and first grade. This program has been effective in disadvantaged urban schools for which it was specifically intended.

Many other smaller early intervention programs besides Reading Recovery and Success for All have been developed and have proven to be successful in recent years. Some of these programs will be described in this book along with Reading Recovery and Success for All.

Our intent in compiling this book has been, first and foremost, to demonstrate to elementary-grade educators that early reading intervention programs with a focus on accelerated learning and authentic reading and writing tasks can be very successful. Many primary-grade children can be prevented from becoming "reading failures." Many different intervention programs are possible, and hopefully, more and more schools will begin to implement one or more programs that fit their situations, realizing that early reading intervention programs are worth the extra effort and expense that they require.

ORGANIZATION OF THE BOOK

The book is divided into three parts. In the first, along with this overview, is a critical chapter by Anne McGill-Franzen (chapter 2) on the past and current state of school policies and practices created by federal legislation and funding for helping low-achieving readers. McGill-Franzen illustrates how Chapter 1 and special education policies and practices have evolved into the problematic situation in which children must first fail before they can receive additional help in reading. The chapter provides rather discouraging information that highlights the need for a book such as this to encourage educators to implement new approaches in helping low-achieving students.

McGill-Franzen makes a powerful case for the need for early, focused, intentional instruction for children who are at risk of failing to learn to read in first grade. The various other contributors to the book have generated different responses to McGill-Franzen's compelling message. Contributors do agree that interventions should begin early enough to get children off to the right start in reading. Interventions are not meant to take the place of good classroom reading instruction, something that all children need. Interventions have been developed, however, with the realistic understanding that good classroom reading instruction will not be enough to help all children become literate. These interventions, ideally, are interconnected with the classroom reading instruction that children are receiving.

The remaining parts of the book deal with different models of early literacy intervention, including tutoring efforts, small-group efforts, and classroom and school restructuring efforts. We believe that each of these models can play an important part in a school's attempts to ensure that all children become literate.

In part II, the focus is on tutoring and small-group approaches to early intervention. Individual tutoring is typically an effective model for working with poor readers (Slavin & Madden, 1989) and has been found to work well with low-achieving first-grade readers. In chapter 3, Juel describes a unique adaptation of tutoring, where university students who themselves are at risk tutor at-risk first and second graders. Juel offers nine principles that she believes were operating in her successful tutoring program and that should be seen as helpful guiding principles in the establishment of any tutoring program.

The implementation of Reading Recovery in the New York City area is described in chapter 4 by Smith-Burke and Jaggar. They raise significant issues pertaining to their work in schools using Reading Recovery, including the need for print-rich, enticing kindergarten instruction that draws children to books and print and the need for effective primary grade classroom literacy instruction.

An interesting contrast between these two successful programs can be found in the person doing the tutoring. Reading Recovery tutors are specially, extensively trained teachers, whereas the tutors in Juel's project were less extensively trained university students who have themselves been poor readers. In both programs, however, tutors are operating from the belief that these children can become successful readers. In both instances, tutors are responding to what individual children are and are not doing as they are reading and writing.

Many children may need extra help in reading but not require individual tutoring. Two chapters deal with ways of organizing small-group instruction so that children are given the extra boost that they need to be successful in reading. Chapter 5 describes a program developed by Hiebert in which small-group instruction provided by Chapter 1 teachers was restructured to significantly improve the reading performance of low-achieving first-grade readers serviced by Chapter 1. Issues related to sustaining this form of instruction and in helping second-grade teachers build on the successes derived from the first-grade program are addressed. Early Intervention in Reading, a supplemental program administered by the classroom teacher to a group of her lowest achieving first-grade readers, is described by Taylor, Strait, and Medo in chapter 6. Issues related to supplemental instruction for low-achieving readers being successfully and willingly provided by the classroom teacher after the pilot year are discussed.

Although these two small-group approaches may be seen as philosophically different if one asks, "who is supposed to help low-achieving readers?" we do not believe that they should be seen as competing. Classroom and Chapter 1 teachers should be able to work together to help low-achieving readers succeed. Furthermore, both approaches have substantial merit. Teachers providing sound supplemental instruction to low-achieving readers have the potential to substantially affect most children because most children receive daily reading instruction from the classroom teacher. On the other hand, if Chapter 1 teachers, who are hired specifically to help poor, low-achieving readers, can change their instruction to be more effective, they will contribute in important ways, as well, to the goal of helping all children become literate.

Part III presents chapters that look at efforts that go beyond tutoring or small-group instruction and focus on classroom or schoolwide restructuring to increase the level of reading success achieved by all students. In chapter 7, Slavin and his associates have taken a very ambitious approach to eliminating reading failure by restructuring entire elementary schools. A facilitator oversees liaisons across classes, kindergarten is carefully linked to the elementary program, and kindergarten and first-grade children in need of extra help in becoming literate are tutored within their regular classroom. In this chapter Slavin et al. argue convincingly that "reading failure is a curable disease." In addition to tutoring for young children to initially prevent reading failure, Slavin et al. call for improved use of Chapter 1 funds, a policy of "neverstreaming" for children who otherwise may require special education services, and improved classroom instruction in which teachers are better able to accommodate student differences. Although this might sound like a tall order, Slavin et al. are persuasive in their argument that as educators we now know enough for this vision to be realized.

As an outgrowth of their work on Reading Recovery, Pinnell and Mc-Carrier describe in chapter 8 a whole-class kindergarten literacy program that they developed with teachers. The intent of the program has been to use knowledge gained from Reading Recovery to help young children who might potentially be in need of Reading Recovery in first grade with emergent literacy in kindergarten.

In chapter 9 Goldenberg discusses two efforts to improve the early native-language attainment among Spanish-speaking children as well as issues that have not been considered in the schooling of Spanish-speaking children. Like Slavin et al., his concern is also with restructuring an entire school program. However, Goldenberg believes that generic restructuring, such as that proposed by Slavin et al., should be supplemented with concerns related to local contexts.

The book concludes with chapter 10, by Hiebert and Taylor, which argues for the need for early reading intervention programs and, at the same time, extensions of early interventions. No matter how successful, early interventions are probably not sufficient. Successful approaches to accelerating the learning of low-achieving readers across the elementary grades and middle grades are needed as well.

SUMMARY

Each program presented in this book provides a rationale, a description of components, a summary of results, and issues to be considered. Most of the projects emanate from current work in emergent literacy operating from a constructivist philosophy of literacy (Allen & Mason, 1989; Teale & Sulzby, 1986).

A major goal of this book is to convince teachers and administrators that it is extremely worthwhile to develop one or more approaches to early reading intervention within their elementary schools. We hope that elementary-school educators will be excited by the descriptions of early reading intervention programs found in this book. Educators reading the book might want to contact one of the contributors for more information about a particular program. However, perhaps a group of teachers, after reading the book, will be inspired to design an early reading intervention program of their own.

We do not believe that any one particular program presented in this book is "the answer." Perhaps a combination of approaches would work best. For example, a school might use a tutoring model for first-grade children who are the lowest 15% in terms of beginning reading ability and a small-group model for children who are the lowest 15% to 30%.

Although commitment to a particular set of practices is probably one of the benchmarks of a successful program, each of the projects in this book has a different configuration of practices. There are some commonalities, but perhaps the greatest commonality is the belief that almost all children can learn to read well. Sometimes the belief that children can learn to read becomes intertwined with the belief that only a particular set of practices can do the job. Although erratic practices that jump from one set of techniques to another will not do the trick, a variety of practices will probably work if implemented by committed, knowledgeable teachers.

We believe that the discussion of issues is an important aspect of each chapter. Authors were asked specifically to reflect on their efforts and to share concerns that have emanated from this work. Working with children who need careful, reflective instruction to help them become successful readers is not something that works perfectly all the time for all children and in all contexts. We hope that the issues that are raised will help teachers and administrators in their attempts to establish early intervention programs in their own schools.

Most important, we hope that readers will leave this book with the conviction that almost all children can learn to read in first grade. School literacy programs can and must be adjusted so that all first-grade children, including those who enter school with low levels of literacy, will be successful readers by the end of the school year.

REFERENCES

Allen, D. (1992). Making headway against reading difficulties. *The Council Chronicle*, 1, 12.

Allen, J., & Mason, J. (Eds.). (1989). *Risk makers, risk takers, risk breakers*. Portsmouth, NH: Heinemann.

Allington, R.L. (1991). The legacy of "slow it down and make it more concrete." In J. Zutell & S. McCormick (Eds.), *Learner factors/teacher factors: Issues in literacy research and instruction* (pp. 19–24). Chicago: National Reading Conference.

Allington, R.L., & McGill-Franzen, A. (1989). School response to reading failure: Chapter 1 and special education students in grades 2, 4, & 8. *Elementary School Journal, 89*, 529–542.

Applebee, A.N., Langer, J.A., & Mullis, I.V. (1988). *Who reads best? Factors related to reading achievement in grades 3, 7, and 11* (National Assessment of Educational Progress Report No. 17-R-01). Princeton, NJ: Educational Testing Service.

Carter, L.F. (1984). The sustaining effects study of compensatory and elementary education. *Educational Researcher, 13*, 4–13.

Clay, M.M. (1985). *The early detection of reading difficulties: A diagnostic survey with recovering procedures* (3rd ed.). Exeter, NH: Heinemann.

Cooley, W.W. (1981). Effectiveness in compensatory education. *Educational Leadership, 38*, 298–301.

Glass, G.V. (1986). The effectiveness of special education. *Policy Studies Review, 2*, 65–78.

Juel, C. (1988). Learning to read and write: A longitudinal study of 54 children from first through fourth grades. *Journal of Educational Psychology, 80*, 437–447.

Langer, J.A., Applebee, A.N., Mullis, I.V., & Foertsch, M.A. (1990). *Learning to read in our nation's schools: Instruction and achievement in 1988 at grades 4, 8, and 12* (National Assessment of Educational Progress Report No. 19-R-02). Princeton, NJ: Educational Testing Service.

McGill-Franzen, A., & Allington, R.L. (1991). The gridlock of low reading achievement: Perspectives on practice and policy. *Remedial and Special Education, 12*, 20–30.

Mullis, I.V., & Jenkins, L.B. (1990). *The reading report card, 1971–88: Trends from the nation's report card* (National Assessment of Educational Progress Report No. 19-R-01). Princeton, NJ: Educational Testing Service.

O'Sullivan, P.J., Ysseldyke, J.E., Christenson, S.L., & Thurlow, M.L. (1990). Mildly handicapped elementary students' opportunity to learn during reading instruction in mainstream and special education settings. *Reading Research Quarterly, 25*, 131–146.

Peterman, C.L., Stewart, J.P., Sinha, S., Kerr, B.M., & Mason, J.M. (1991, December). *Linking language and emergent literacy: Observation, interventions, and model building.* Paper presented at the annual meeting of the National Reading Conference, Palm Springs, CA.

Pinnell, G.S. (1989). Reading recovery: Helping at-risk children learn to read. *Elementary School Journal, 90*, 160–183.

Slavin, R.E., & Madden, N.A. (1989). What works for students at risk: A research synthesis. *Educational Leadership, 46*, 4–13.

Slavin, R.E., Madden, N.A., Karweit, N.L., Livermon, B.J., & Dolan, L. (1990). Success for all! First-year outcomes of a comprehensive plan for reforming urban education. *American Educational Research Journal, 27*, 255–278.

Spodek, B. (1988). Conceptualizing today's kindergarten curriculum. *Elementary School Journal, 89*, 203–212.

Stanovich, K.E. (1986). Matthew effects in reading: Some consequences of individual differences in the acquisition of literacy. *Reading Research Quarterly, 21*, 360–407.

Teale, W.H., & Sulzby, E. (Eds.). (1986). *Emergent literacy: Writing and reading.* Norwood, NJ: Ablex.

▶ 2

Compensatory and Special Education

Is There Accountability for Learning and Belief in Children's Potential?

ANNE MCGILL-FRANZEN

McGill-Franzen presents disturbing pictures of compensatory and special education programs and the reasons for their ineffectiveness. Chapter 1 intends to provide equal educational opportunity to children regardless of family income. Unfortunately, Chapter 1 programs have been concerned with meeting key statutory requirements instead of making important educational differences for children. Special education has intended to provide all children with the right to learn; but the effectiveness of special education services remains questionable for a variety of reasons. McGill-Franzen makes the powerful point that compensatory and special education have allowed classroom teachers to give up responsibility for their lowest achieving students. In addition, these programs helped to perpetuate low expectations among teachers for their low-achieving students. Although this chapter raises many disturbing questions, it concludes on the hopeful note that successful literacy programs with high expectations for progress, such as the ones described in the remainder of this book, can make an important difference for children who find themselves in at-risk situations.

As teachers, parents, researchers, wage earners, policymakers—indeed, as citizens in a free society—we should be troubled by the idea that children born into poverty in 1992 will probably not be able to improve the circumstances of their lives through education. Poor children, who today are disproportionately children of color, are more likely to fail in school than other children.

SOUTH STREET

For example, in one urban school that I will call *South Street*, 52 children began kindergarten in the fall of 1986. Almost 100% of the South Street population qualifies for free or reduced lunches and more than 90% of the children are African-American. Of the original 52 kindergartners, 18 third-grade children remained in that age cohort to take the state test in reading in 1990. Twenty-six children were retained or sent to transition room; 10 children were referred to special education; and the remaining 16 were unaccounted for in school records. In the past, the state identified South Street as a *deficient school* because more than one-half of the third graders in 1986 (the first year that these designations were made public) had not met the state standard for normal development on mandated reading tests. In 1990, 98% of the children passed the third grade state test in reading. Are South Street children better readers? Probably not.

To fulfill a different state mandate (for developmental screening in kindergarten), the school district administered a nationally normed standardized test to these 52 South Street children in October of their kindergarten year. Their mean percentile rank on the composite score was 15. In May of their third grade year, after 4 years at South Street, the mean percentile rank for the remaining 18 children was 19 on the total reading part of the same standardized test. Presumably, the lowest achieving children had been removed from the cohort through retention, special education, and mobility; and these remaining 18 children represented average or above average readers. Yet, the educational status of the children barely changed at all compared with a national sample of their third grade peers. These children began their kindergarten year in the bottom quartile of all kindergarten learners and the luckiest among them finished their third grade year in the bottom quartile.

I Can't Give Them What God Hasn't

What do the teachers at South Street think about the children and what became of them? Do they feel responsible for the learning or lack of it? One first-grade classroom teacher—I will call her Ms. Smith—described the 26 children in her class as follows:

I find it miraculous that they have survived as long as they have, being 6 years old, with as few abnormalities—emotional, physical, mental, whatever. It's unbelievable that they have survived this long. Many of my children come from drug dependent families, parents [with] either one or the other in prison. I mean I can't prove it, but I would say that many of my children have one or two parents that are either dealing drugs or are hooked on drugs . . . and it amazes me that these kids are as functional as they are considering where they come from . . .Those schools where the children can test well on their own merit are at a better advantage than we are in here. Because we have been cited [as deficient] you know the teachers are lunatic when it comes to testing time. Because they know their children are not going to score well unless they are extremely bright which might be one or two children in your class. So the teachers therefore do one of two things: they teach for a month to the test or they have to cheat on the test. I mean, this is what they do . . . I think testing for areas like South Street [is wrong]. Some of the information and the world of experiences that they talk about in the testing (i.e., one family houses with little picket fences and one car garages and children playing football on the beautiful lush green lawn), you can't teach or have them read about those things here because they've never had that. A beach, an ocean—they've never been there, so a lot of the things that are on the test are not relevant to their world of experiences, and plus, I think testing is wrong anyway. [In first grade] we teach the Iowas in the spring. There's a lot of pressure. And there will be a lot of pressure for me, especially this year, because I have a very low first grade. So half of my class will probably score very poorly. They'll probably score a pre-K kindergarten level. And it's not really my fault because I can't give them what God hasn't.

Special Services

Ms. Smith has 26 children in this class. She estimates that one-third of the children participated in Head Start or some other preschool program for income-eligible families. Based on end-of-kindergarten test scores below the 23rd percentile, 17 children participated in a pull-out Chapter 1 first grade reading group for 30 minutes a day, three days per week—nine children go to Chapter 1 during one time slot, eight during another. Ms. Smith says that "remediation is only beneficial if you have a small group. Some of the remedial classes have seven to nine children in them so you're defeating the whole purpose. Remediation should be done almost on a one-to-one basis." None of her children participated in pre-first, but she feels that "about 10 in this class should have."

There is no mainstreaming at South Street. When children from this school are classified as disabled, they are likely to be assigned to a self-contained special class in another building in the city. The third floor of South Street houses students with disabilities from the intermediate school district. Although there are currently no children identified as having a disability in her class, Ms. Smith has referred several for evaluation. Ms. Smith hopes that by June "three of my 26 will wind up in special ed somewhere—either emotionally disturbed (ED) or learning disabled (LD)." She intends to repeat five or six children at the end of the year, notes that "the children that I want to repeat learn, slowly, but they can learn. . . . The children that I recommend to special ed, I feel might have severe academic lags—just can't make it."

One first-grade teacher candidly shares her beliefs about the children she teaches at South Street and the categories the school or she uses to fit the child with the intervention. Although several of the children are recommended for special education or retention, the majority participate in Chapter 1 reading services, a categorical aid program established by the federal government nearly 30 years ago to help certain categories of children—poor children—compensate for the presumed educational disadvantages of being poor and experiencing academic difficulty at school. At its best, compensatory education (Chapter 1, Head Start, and others) represents a promise of equal educational opportunity, regardless of social class background or family income. It is, unfortunately, a promise that is not always kept.

Special education requires that children be identified as having a disability—a constitutional or organic condition that will permanently impair their learning. Identified as disabled, these children are entitled to personalized instruction; and if these children are mainstreamed into the public school classes, this instruction should enable them to pass their courses and advance from grade to grade (*Rowley v. Board of Education*, 1982). Special education is the closest we have come to granting children the right to learn. Sadly, special education is often the reason for their failure.

CONFRONTING INEQUITIES: A BRIEF HISTORY OF COMPENSATORY EDUCATION

Writing about the educational needs of poor children in a 1965 issue of *American Education*, Helen Mackintosh and Gertrude Lewis set forth a disturbingly familiar argument:

> *The function of American schools is to develop a highly literate people. It has been demonstrated that this cannot be done under present school procedures for what by 1970 may be as many as one-fourth of all children—urban, rural, and suburban. Causes and cures are not all within the school's control. (Bremner, 1974, p. 1818)*

With much fanfare and optimism, the first *education President*, Lyndon B. Johnson, signed compensatory education into being—legislation that was expected to bring children from low-income families into the education mainstream. We apparently expected Great Society programs to close the achievement gap—to accelerate the cognitive development and scholastic achievement of children born into poverty in the 1960s. Shortly thereafter, sociologist James S. Coleman and his colleagues (1966) reported the results of a survey mandated by the Civil Rights Act of 1964. Following on the heels of this country's first urban riots and civil rights legislation, the purpose of the survey was to determine the availability of equal educational opportunities to children of diverse racial, social, and ethnic backgrounds. Rather than looking at equal opportunity in the narrow sense of resources or inputs available, Coleman looked at outcomes. He reported that schools had little impact on children's lives. "The inequalities imposed on children by their home," he said, "are carried along to become the inequalities with which they confront adult life by the end of school" (p. 325).

Within a few years, compensatory education programs were called a failure because gains in achievement were not sustained. Lois-ellin Datta, the national coordinator of the Head Start Evaluation at that time, cited the work of policy analysts Edward and Mary McDill and Timothy Spreche to demonstrate that too much was being expected of the new compensatory programs. According to McDill and colleagues, compensatory education had been asked to deliver results never before expected of educators. "No public school system has ever before been abolished because it could not teach children to read and write. Compensatory programs, aimed at the very children who are going to be losers in the regular school program, are in just this situation" (Bremner, 1974, p. 1827).

Since the enactment of Title I of the Elementary and Secondary Education Act in 1965 (ESEA) [reauthorized as Chapter 1 of the Education and Consolidation Improvement Act (ECIA) in 1981], the federal government has been appropriating funds to "local educational agencies serving areas with concentrations of children from low-income families to expand and improve their educational programs" (ESEA, Title I, Sec. 101). Current appropriations are $6.7 billion and, except for the Reagan years, these appropriations have been increased each year since the program's inception (Stringfield, 1991). These funds are intended to compensate for the economic disadvantages visited on children from low-income families and contribute to meeting their special educational needs.

In the winter of 1991, Mary Jean LeTendre, Director of Compensatory Education for the U.S. Department of Education, wrote that the achievement gains provided by Chapter 1—then in its 26th year of providing extra services to eligible children — still had not been enough to enable Chapter 1 children to "catch up and to keep up" with their peers (LeTendre, 1991, p. 328). This result should not be surprising, not because schools cannot make a difference in the lives of children who are poor, but rather, as McDill and colleagues suggested three decades ago, because we never really expected schools to do so. Until the Hawkins-Stafford ECIA School Improvement Amendments of 1988 explicitly proposed that Chapter 1 children attain grade-level proficiency, Chapter 1 was viewed primarily as a financial aid program to poor districts, not as an education entitlement to poor children. There were no assurances, either explicit or implicit, that ESEA or Head Start would educate poor children to a level comparable to their more advantaged peers. Chapter 1 programs were monitored for compliance with key statutory requirements such as the provision of supplemental education services and the fair allocation of instructional time, materials, and other resources to students who were most in need (LeTendre, 1991). We paid scant attention to whether Chapter 1 programs made an educational difference. Seldom did we ask whether participating children ever caught up to their peers or at least managed to avoid failure. Although Chapter 1 children typically receive reading services, we never asked whether they actually learned to read or how well. Until recently, we could not even describe the educational experiences of children who participated in Chapter 1 programs—what they did in remedial reading, the materials they used, the opportunities they had to participate and succeed in the classroom curriculum (Rowan, Guthrie, Lee, & Guthrie, 1986). We took little notice of the growing numbers of poor children who were being classified as disabled because they did not read as well as their peers (McGill-Franzen & Allington, 1991).

   Head Start, another compensatory education measure that was authorized by Congress in 1965, has as its central mission the development of social competence in preschool children from low-income families so that they are more effective in dealing with their "present environment and later responsibilities in school and life" (Head Start Bureau, 1984, p.1, cited in Chafel, 1992, p. 10). Billed by former President Bush as "a paradigm of kindness and gentleness" (Chafel, 1992, p. 9), Head Start is moving toward full funding to serve all eligible children by the mid-1990s. Judith Chafel, former Congressional Science Fellow in the House of Representatives who researched issues of funding and purpose for Head Start, reported that improving the quality of present services is more important than serving all eligible children. Similar to the Chapter 1 programs targeted for school-aged children, Head Start has maintained popularity, even though participating children have not consistently maintained their initial gains. Like Chapter 1, the monitoring of the Head Start programs emphasizes statutory regulations and inputs, not the educational benefits that accrue to individual children. One exception is the High/Scope longitudinal study of a small number of children who participated in the Ypsilanti, Michigan Perry Preschool project in the 1960s (Berrueta-Clement, Schweinhart, Barnett, Epstein, & Weikart, 1984) . Widely cited by policymakers as an example of what compensatory preschool education can accomplish, the High/Scope researchers reported that the Perry Preschool Program saved taxpayers $6 or $7 for each $1 invested in the project because fewer of the Perry Preschool children required costly special education services or retention in grade. Today, preschool participation might not accrue the same cost benefits as when the High/Scope study was conducted. Even though special education is more costly now than in the past (approximately 2.3 times the cost of per pupil expenditures, Moore, Strang, Schwartz, & Braddock, 1988), special education services, even at the preschool level, are much more available and far more children are identified as being disabled at earlier ages, primarily at 4 and 5 years old (Allington & McGill-Franzen, 1992b; U.S. Department of Education, 1992). Many states require school districts to administer developmental screening tests before entry into kindergarten and Head Start, itself, tests 3- and 4-year-olds before entry into their programs. Children who are not able to perform tasks typically mastered by the norming sample are referred to the special education committee for further evaluation before they have an opportunity to participate in any school experience. Although the selection of tests is a local decision, the tasks usually include print knowledge and understanding of illustrations and narratives. Children usually are required to identify and match numbers and letters, print their names, repeat digits and sentences, label and tell stories from pictures, describe objects or toys in terms of attributes and functions, and, in some cases, handle books appropriately. Children who perform poorly on these tasks become candidates for special education. Because Head Start is a program for poor children, and because it must also serve a certain percentage of children with disabilities in order to maintain funding, it is the children of poor families who are most likely to be labelled as disabled.

Incredibly, the role of prior instruction or experience in children's performance on these preschool assessments is often grossly underrated and a poor showing by the child is usually attributed to low ability and delayed development. The trend leans toward earlier referral for special education, not only because such services are now mandated by law, but because public, primary-grade, high-stakes testing has put enormous pressure on schools to push low-achieving children out of the publicly reported assessment stream (McGill-Franzen & Allington, 1992).

SPECIAL EDUCATION: FREE AND APPROPRIATE, BUT NO RIGHT TO LEARN

Although the education of children with disabilities has been part of public education since the time of the common school, it was not universally available until 1975 when Congress passed the Education for All Handicapped

Children Act (EHA). The EHA did not merely make services available to children; but it entitled children with disabilities between the ages of 5 and 21 years old to "a free and appropriate public education . . . in the least restrictive environment" (PL 94-142, Sec. 3). As of 1987, approximately 11% of the total public school population received special education services, up from 8% in 1976. According to Singer and Butler (1987), almost all the growth in special education was due to large increases in the number of youngsters identified as learning disabled. There were also new school programs for the few children with severe disabilities who had previously been excluded from school. Children with learning disabilities—children who have difficulty with reading—make up nearly half of the total national special education population. Although there are several reasons why the LD category has increased so dramatically, two pertinent ones are (1) the availability of special education funds when Chapter 1 was declining and (2) an incentive to use the relatively cheap cost of LD services to offset more expensive services mandated by PL 94-142 (McGill-Franzen, 1987; Singer and Butler, 1987).

An interesting aspect to the analysis done by Singer and Butler (1987) on the implementation of PL 94-142 as social reform is the little-noted fact that the overwhelming majority of children with physical and sensory impairments appear to come from affluent and two-parent families; whereas children with learning disabilities, like those eligible for Chapter 1 services, are at socioeconomic risk: children whose mothers did not finish high school, children whose families live in poverty, and children from single-parent families or from families with unemployed caregivers. PL 94-142 entitles parents to opportunities to participate in the process of planning their children's education; but parents who are themselves at socioeconomic risk, by virtue of poverty and low education attainment, are unlikely to successfully advocate for their children in school. For example, a mother who graduated from high school (a relatively high level of education achievement for the parent of a child with a mild disability) was five and one-half times as likely to attend her child's Individualized Education Plan (IEP) conference to plan the child's education program and determine the placement. This fact led Singer and Butler (1987) to declare that the PL 94-142 "has conferred predictably different entitlements on middle-class and on low-income children" since low-income children with mild disabilities rarely have anyone to speak on their behalf or hold the schools accountable (p. 146).

The Education of the Handicapped Act (EHA) Amendments of 1986 extended the right to a free and appropriate education to children with disabilities between the ages of 3 and 5 years old. By July 1991, all states were required to have educational services for preschool children with disabilities. Although the long-term effects of this legislation are not known, the states have created strong funding incentives for districts to identify preschoolers as disabled (Singer & Butler, 1987), resulting in a preschool population of children with disabilities of about half of a million children. The total numbers continue to rise with a clear trend toward labeling children at younger ages (U.S. Department of Education, 1992).

However, unlike the earlier compensatory regulations for ESEA and Head Start, the EHA went beyond making services available to identified children: the EHA assured that such education efforts would be effective (Wise, 1979). Although these assurances appear to constitute a duty to teach, they do not as yet constitute the child's right to learn, as Arthur E. Wise (1979, pp. 28–29) carefully documents in his treatise on the effects of legislation and judicial opinion on the schools. When children fail to demonstrate requisite skills, it is usually the children, not the schools that are deemed at fault. When Gartner and Lipsky wrote in 1987 that no one in the federal government could tell them how many children with disabilities had returned to mainstream education, they provided powerful commentary about the fate of millions of children who have participated in services authorized by the EHA.

Defining educational benefit is an issue that consistently has been before the courts. In an early education malpractice suit, a young man, Peter Doe, from San Francisco sued the Unified School District in 1973 for allegedly allowing him to graduate without having taught him to read above the eighth grade level (*Doe v. San Francisco*). The plaintiff lost on appeal because the school's responsibility was not clearly defined in this case (Wise, 1979). This occurred in 1973, and Peter Doe was not a youth with a disability; therefore, he was not entitled to support services that would benefit him educationally. In a recent case, the United States District Court for the District of South Carolina held that the Florence County School District violated the EHA and did not provide Shannon Carter, a young woman who had a learning disability, with a free and appropriate education (United States Court of Appeals for the Fourth Circuit, *Carter v. Florence County School District*, November 26, 1991). Shannon Carter's public school prepared an IEP specifying a long-term reading goal of only 4 months per year with a similar goal for math. Shannon's parents objected to this goal, claiming that 4 months would only cause their daughter to fall farther behind in school; and they insisted on *itinerant LD services* in the regular school program rather than placement in a resource room. Because they were dissatisfied with the IEP and concerned about their daughter's lack of progress and her concomitant anxiety about failing, the Carters placed her in a private boarding school where she did very well, gaining and maintaining at least a year's growth in reading for each year she attended. After Shannon's graduation, the Carters sued the school district for reimbursement of school and travel expenses plus interest. The court agreed with the Carters, citing *Rowley v. Board of Education* (1982), which held that the IEP must provide educational benefits:

When the handicapped child is being educated in the regular classrooms of a public school system, the achievement of passing marks and advancement from grade to grade will be one important factor in determining educational benefit . . . Clearly, Congress did not intend that a school system could discharge its duty under the [Act] by providing a program that produces some minimal academic achievement, no matter how trivial (p. 7a).

In this case and in the appeal by the school district, the court found the goal of four months wholly inadequate for a student such as Shannon and allowed the Carters to recover the full cost plus interest. Clearly, the EHA may have unrealized potential to effect positive change for children, since the case of *Shannon Carter v. Florence County* (1991) may bring the education community's most effective intervention strategies to bear on the reading problems of children who are farthest behind. Parents and advocates must have the knowledge and resources to make the assurances and due process protections of the EHA work to the children's advantage, not the school's. Some schools use the EHA to identify low-achieving children as disabled, not necessarily to accelerate the children's progress, but to make the school look as if it is improving on publicly reported state assessments. By removing the test scores of children with disabilities—which is allowable in most states—schools are able to do two things at once: (1) give the appearance of improved performance on high visibility tests and (2) limit their public accountability for the progress of the lowest achieving, neediest children.

PUBLIC ACCOUNTABILITY: MAKING BAD SCHOOLS LOOK BETTER

Given the present climate of reform and concomitant mandates for higher standards and high-stakes testing, the children are penalized—they are the ones who are not promoted or fail to graduate. When the pressure for school improvement heats up and public scrutiny of high-stakes test scores becomes intense, low-achieving children are at-risk of either retention or special education placement. In some districts, low-achieving children are likely to disappear altogether from the assessment stream into special education, and in other districts, their test scores are counted with younger cohorts through widespread grade retention.

In a 10-year trend analysis of placement practices in New York State (Allington & McGill-Franzen, 1992a, 1992b), where the first high-stakes testing occurs at third grade, there has been a significant increase in the number of children referred to special education each year (from an annual placement rate of 2% of the school population in 1979 to an annual placement rate of 3.5% in 1989) and in the number of children retained before third grade. In contrast, there was no significant increase in the number of children receiving compensatory education services in reading during this time period. In New York, as in many other states, children with disabilities are either exempted from high-stakes testing or their scores are not included in the data that are aggregated for public review. So, the lowest achieving children are removed from the assessment stream. By the same token, retaining low-achieving children in the early grades raises test scores, at least during the short-term (Gottfredson, 1986). For example, Walker and Levine (1988) analyzed the test scores of retained students in the Kansas City, Missouri school district to illustrate this point. They suggest that a typical annual gain score for children who were not promoted was about 7 months on a ten-month scale. By failing such a child, the average score was raised not only in the child's age cohort, of which he is no longer a part, but also in the younger cohort, which he just joined. So, the child's age cohort no longer has to count the child's three-month deficit and the younger cohort gains an additional four months during the 2 years (2 years × 7 months).

School districts and the schools within them vary in their use of retention and placement practices for low-achieving readers (Shepard & Smith, 1989) (See also Table 2-1). My colleagues and I argued elsewhere that retention and special education for so-called mild learning difficulties are suspect placement practices in all cases because children rarely derive educational benefits from these placements (McGill-Franzen & Allington, 1992). Further, these practices are unethical when they are motivated by a desire to improve a district's performance on high-stakes testing. As seen from the profiles in Table 2-1, schools with similar demographic profiles often respond differently to children having difficulty in reading. Schools, such as Orton, with the fewest needy children often have the most resources to expend on innovative approaches that do not isolate children. School communities such as South Street, which I described earlier, often have the most overwhelming needs and the least resources for overcoming them: impoverished families, the sparest of education resources, and children with the least guidance and support for doing academic work. It still shocks the observer that 83% of the children in any particular cohort are already outside the mainstream by the end of second grade. In contrast, schools can resist these practices. Riverton and Towerville, towns with similar small proportions of children from low-income families, respond very differently to low-achieving readers.

Riverton, with a transition room, high annual retentions, and special education placements, has 60% of its 1986 cohort out of the assessment stream before third grade. A National School of Excellence, Riverton's reputation is partially based on high achievement scores. By contrast, Towerville has placed only 13% of its children in classes outside the mainstream, a practice that does not overstate its performance on the high-stakes third grade state test. Although one-third of Towerville's children score in the bottom quartile

TABLE 2-1   Cohort Placement Comparisons (1986–1989)

	Retention (%)	Special Education (%)	Off/Out of Accountability Stream (%)
Riverton (Small industrial town, T-room, <20% poverty)			
K	0	7	
1	36	6	
2	5	6	
	41	19	60
Towerville (Small rural town, >20% poverty)			
K	3	0	
1	4	3	
2	0	3	
	7	6	13
South Street (Urban, T-room, > 90% poverty)			
K	0	0	
1	49	20	
2	6	8	
	55	28	83
Orton (Suburban, <5% poverty)			
K	3	0	
1	0	0	
2	0	0	
	3	0	3

Data from New York State Council on Children and Families, 1988; New York State Education Department, 1989, 1990; and Allington & McGill-Franzen, 1992a,1992b.

on end-of-year kindergarten assessment, by third or fourth grade, the majority of children are performing at grade-level or above—with few retentions and placements for disabled students. What might account for these disparities in placement decisions?

In spite of direct evidence that a few school administrators manipulate placements to maximize achievement gain, we believe that most teachers are motivated primarily by their beliefs about the children's ability to learn and their ability to teach them. In other words, teachers decide where the children will be "better off" (Hyde & Moore, 1988). We believe that teachers' beliefs are shaped by their personal classroom histories and by the institutionally constituted categories (i.e., learning disabled, remedial, repeater, etc.) attached to children.

CREATING AND SUSTAINING BELIEFS

Teacher beliefs have been defined as implicit theories that affect and are affected by teachers' thinking during teaching and during thinking about teaching (Clark & Peterson, 1986). Although there is little coherent research on teachers' beliefs as separate from other kinds of teacher knowledge or "personal theorizing" (Ross, 1992), Nespor (1987) describes one theoretical model of belief systems developed to help ground the research of the Austin, Texas, Teacher Beliefs Study (TBS). In Nespor's view, certain characteristics of beliefs differentiate them from other forms of teacher knowledge. Beliefs treat descriptive statements (i.e., ability, maturity and laziness) as if they were static, objective realities or entities, somehow outside the control of the teacher. Beliefs also embody the notion of an ideal or alternative worlds (Abelson, 1979) and may help teachers to articulate goals and tasks for instruction.

Beliefs may be tied to the personal value teachers assign to particular subject area knowledge and skill (Nespor, 1987). To some extent, teachers' beliefs determine how much of themselves they are willing to invest in any given lesson. Further, beliefs derive power from close association with richly detailed memories of particular events, possibly experienced by teachers themselves or embodied in a story told to her by someone else. This is according to the TBS model and suggested by the lesson images of Morine-Dershimer (1978–1979). Memories of these events and the beliefs that derive from them influence the ways teachers experience their work long after the original events have occurred.

In addition, Nespor holds that there is no expectation that everyone will agree on the accuracy or relevance of beliefs because, unlike domain-specific knowledge, beliefs are not evaluated easily. Like domain-specific knowledge, however, belief systems are conceptual systems that help teachers organize and define their work. Nespor suggests that little is known about how people are socialized into particular belief systems or how these belief systems might be changed.

INSTITUTIONAL MACHINERY AND PROFESSIONAL KNOWLEDGE

In his analyses of special education placement decisions and other constitutive activities, Mehan (1992) and his colleagues (Mehan, Hartweck, & Meihls, 1986) have demonstrated that institutional practices shape beliefs about children. Children cannot be designated *retarded, learning disabled,* or *handicapped* if there is no institutional machinery to classify them, as is the case in some Catholic schools. Conversely, when funds are available and programs are in place, then educators find children to classify and treat according to their classification. During the late 1970s and early 1980s, federal funds for compensatory education for low-achieving, poor children dried up just as money for education for children with disabilities was becoming more available. Many low-achieving children who formerly would have been called *poor* or *educationally disadvantaged* became *handicapped* instead (McGill-Franzen, 1987). Mehan would call these events practical circumstances that are not under the functional control of teachers: yet these events help shape our beliefs about children and what is good for them. In many schools, special education and remedial education have become institutionally sanctioned ways of relieving classroom teachers of the responsibility to teach reading to their lowest achieving students because they believe that they cannot or should not teach them.

In a recent study of the relationship between teacher beliefs and early grade retention practices, Smith and Shepard (1988) found that particular belief systems characterized schools, not just individual teachers. In schools where teachers held remedial or interactionist views of development, the prevailing philosophy was that teachers could *bring children along* and retention rates were low. By contrast, when teachers held nativist views of development, retention rates were high, reflecting the belief that children needed extra time to mature. Teachers can be socialized into particular beliefs about low-achieving children and beliefs about the appropriate school response to such variation in development.

Borko, Livingston, and Shavelson (1990) note that teachers tend to store information about individual students, including appraisals of student ability, effort, and behavior, in a type of cognitive schemata identified as propositional structures. These propositional structures are tapped as teachers need specific student or pedagogical information to carry out a particular script for a particular classroom scene. The same authors point out that student ability influences teacher planning and decision making more than any other characteristic, and experienced or expert teachers have more elaborated propositional structures for describing student learning performance.

In a correlational study of teachers' knowledge and beliefs about children's mathematical knowledge and children's mathematics achievement, Peterson, Carpenter, and Fennema (1989) found a positive relation between teachers' knowledge and children's achievement. The most effective teachers differed from the least effective in the way they thought about children's knowledge and how they used this information in teaching interactions. In case studies of the most and least effective teachers, Peterson et al. (1989) describe qualitative differences in these beliefs about children. The most effective teacher assumed that children came to school with a great deal of mathematical knowledge; she focused on what the children already knew;

she emphasized conceptual understanding. The most effective teacher listened more closely to children's explanations and was able to provide the most explicit and insightful observations of her students' knowledge. On the other hand, the least effective teacher emphasized what the children did not know; rather than allow the children to talk, she explained solutions to problems. Instead of building on the children's knowledge to create elaborate conceptual understandings, the least effective teacher gave the low achievers fewer problems, and these problems focused on rote memorization and procedural knowledge.

Whereas the Peterson et al. (1989) study examined teachers' beliefs about and knowledge of children's mathematical knowledge, the same observations have been made about the beliefs and knowledge of the most and least effective teachers of reading. Lyons and White (1989) described differences in the beliefs of more effective and less effective Reading Recovery teachers and related these differences to qualitative differences in the instructional interactions between the teachers and the children. Although the authors expected to find variation in instruction, they were surprised to find that more and less effective teachers differed dramatically in their expectations for the children's learning and in their beliefs about their ability to become "good" readers. The more effective teachers focused children's attention on text meaning more often than on the visual information.

Although what has been called teacher-expectation research has not usually demonstrated severe effects, it has demonstrated consistent effects, particularly the tendency to sustain preexisting levels of achievement over time (Cooper & Tom, 1984). Expectation effects are more likely to occur in certain subjects such as reading instruction, where teachers can exercise wide latitude in the methodology they use (Smith, 1980). Teacher expectations are probably influenced by actual student performance, and actual student performance tends to be influenced by teacher expectations (Cooper & Tom, 1984).

Listening to Teachers Talk About the Children

To explore how institutional practices might have shaped teachers' personal beliefs about children and their potential to learn, my colleagues and I (Allington & Li, 1990; McGill-Franzen & James, 1990) analyzed the audiotaped interview statements made by elementary classroom teachers, compensatory education teachers, and special education teachers as they talked about the low-achieving readers in their classes. We interviewed 39 teachers, 19 of whom were specialists in either reading or special education, from 6 different school districts. Using transcripts of the interviews, we compared beliefs about remedial readers and readers with disabilities for commonalties and differences across categories of learners, teachers, and institutions (Glaser & Strauss,1967).

Low Expectations for Special Education: Not Average and Not Retarded

Special education teachers believed that their students could not perform at grade level in the regular classroom. This belief is in sharp contrast to the assurances provided by the EHA—that special education services should benefit students so that they are able to pass their courses and advance from grade to grade. Without exception, these teachers believed that special education students could be expected to grow only 6 months for every year they were in school, and classroom teachers shared this belief—"We've done all we could do with him at this point". This does occur, even though these special education students tested from one-half to a year and a half behind, according to their teachers. In some cases, the children were reading at grade level but had other developmental problems, ranging from speech ("His last year's classroom teacher had great difficulty understanding his speech; he was not allowed back up. Socially, he had a lot of withdrawal problems"), to whiny, clinging behavior, to intelligence that was below average, but did not classify them as retarded. Sometimes teachers discounted test scores ("guessing") when special education children achieved scores that approximated normal development ("I ask myself, is she smart? The answer is no"). If special education children repeated the grade, teachers were not impressed with achievement at or above grade level ("All reading is good; her comprehension is good. But you have to remember this is her second time going through it, so she should be doing well").

For assignments such as reading stories, special education teachers say they routinely take 5 days when the regular classroom would take only 1 or 2 days. If they perceive that a child is having difficulty, the special education teachers say that they can take "from now till the end of December just working on telling him or her different ways to add." When texts get too difficult, teachers do not want to push students if they are not ready, so students are moved back to easier material. Even when special education teachers use the same materials as the regular classroom teachers, they believe that they teach it in an easier way: "It's taught in a kindergarten, first-grade teaching approach . . . very sequential, less and less high level thinking."

Special education teachers teach at a much slower pace. Often, the emphasis is on what teachers perceive as the practical or concrete, instead of a focus on academic development, which includes reading and writing. One primary special education teacher talked about what she did during the month of November:

> We did Thanksgiving, the whole month was Thanksgiving, from day one. We began by having invitations, by dictating [invitations], by inviting [people] to our feast. The second week we discussed the issue of what we are

going to serve for our feast. We start by making a grocery list. When making
a grocery list make sure to have all the ingredients for what we are making.
We were going to go down and do the grocery shopping together as a class.
Then we spend a week for preparation, we have costumes, we did the baking
in three days, cut the vegetables. . . . One of our primary academic goals is to
show children the relevance of what they are learning in here. [I might say]
"Gee, if you couldn't read you couldn't do that recipe."

A teacher in regular education might use a holiday theme, such as Thanksgiving, to integrate cultural understandings into curriculum and make it meaningful but would do so without eliminating academic instruction. Opportunities to actually read and write are at the heart of literacy development and, when such opportunities follow at a snail's pace, it is unlikely that the children assigned to these classes will achieve average development.

A classroom teacher called the resource room curriculum in her school more common sense kinds of things: "They run a store and sell pencils and things like that; they made a whole turkey dinner and the Christmas tea. Remedial teachers focus on reading."

Classroom teachers and special education teachers were inclined to repeat resource room children and slow down the instruction. Contrary to interpretation of the EHA put forth in the *Rowley v. Board of Education* case (1982), which defined educational benefit as instruction that would allow a learner with a disability to keep up with the class, these teachers never considered the idea of accelerating literacy development. One teacher wanted to repeat a second grader because " he needs another year to get these skills down pat before he's moved on to third. I don't know if I can repeat him because of his age and also the fact that from kindergarten he went to a special primary class, and then he spent 2 years there before he was moved to the regular first grade." Teachers in another school stressed retaining children and moving into developmental programs for "kids who just aren't making it [who] can maybe pick up what they missed or what they're lacking" the following year.

In many cases, special education teachers developed curriculum without guidance or knowledge of the content areas or grade appropriate development, hardly a situation that would support children's promotion from grade to grade. One teacher who had a number of second graders in her resource room said that these children were referred to special education because they could not handle the second-grade curriculum; but she had no idea what that might be. Another teacher taught language arts to "kids who couldn't even put together a coherent sentence"; but she said, "There was no method to her madness." This teacher had never been exposed to writing instruction and as she "went along" she was "learning more and more about what these kids do not know."

REMEDIAL READING: SO THEY COULD SURVIVE IN ANY CLASSROOM

According to the teachers we interviewed, school district guidelines for becoming remedial readers are always explicit and predictable. Students needed to score below a predetermined cut off score, usually in the 20 to 25 percentile range on a standardized test, unless they were children with disabilities. These children were not typically allowed to be remedial readers, suggesting that these two groups of low-achieving readers might be differentiated among the teachers. This appears to be true. The difference is a belief (or rather, as some teachers said, the "hope") that remedial students will catch up. Remedial readers can and are classified as disabled but only after repeating a grade and still being behind or when they just "can't read no matter what."

As they talked about their Chapter 1 students, remedial and classroom teachers captured much of the original justification for compensatory education—the idea that children had less at home and that through the school's timely intervention the children should be able to catch up. The biggest difference between teachers' beliefs about remedial students as opposed to special education students is that all teachers expected (or as one teacher said, "hoped for") at least a 1-year gain for each year in school. Teachers also expected remedial students to eventually achieve at their grade level ("so they could survive in any classroom"); but like their beliefs regarding special education students, many still believed that instruction should be slowed down, even whole years repeated, and then they locate the problem in the child when the child does not maintain grade-level performance.

Many teachers attributed children's below grade-level performance to family problems:

> *I have a lot of children whose families are in prison because they have killed someone, literally. Many come to school hungry or hyper, because they have eaten candy, or they are ill-clothed.*

Nonetheless, at least one identified inappropriate teaching as the problem ("I am totally convinced that we are confusing our kids and that is why they can't read"). Teachers included social as well as academic goals for the remedial children (They have to learn that "they can't get something for nothing, and it starts in the classroom"). Academic goals are frequently the "basics" or "fundamentals" ("I haven't been able to do anything yet with comprehension because my time runs out before I even finish my Hammondsport [perceptual training] lesson"), but other teachers talked about making Chapter 1 children "lifetime readers."

SUMMARY AND CONCLUSIONS

Some of the beliefs and the practices presented here are consistent with the language of the Hawkins-Stafford Amendments of 1988, which holds that Chapter 1 will enable poor children to catch up and keep up with their more advantaged peers. Some beliefs and practices are also consistent with the assurances of the EHA that specialized instruction will benefit the learner in terms of grade-level progress. Others are not. Some of the beliefs and practices represent the *slow-it-down, make it more concrete* philosophy of remediation and special education; these beliefs would hold that children are limited in what they can accomplish by their poverty, their language, the resources of their parents, and what children know when they start school. Many of our traditional programs for low-achievers perpetuate low expectations for children.

Other programs view children differently; for example, the longitudinal study conducted by Snow and her colleagues on home and school influences on literacy in Massachusetts (Snow, Barnes, Chandler, Goodman, & Hemphill, 1991) and much of the recent research on successful early grade interventions, particularly the studies reported in this volume, demonstrates that schools can be powerful equalizers of children's development. The organization of successful programs, the pedagogy, and the expectations for progress testify to the participants' convictions that all children can participate fully in the literate culture of their schools and communities and that schools are responsible for seeing to it that all children do so.

Earlier studies have shown consistently that good teachers can make a difference in the lives of individual children. The Massachusetts Home School Literacy Project (Snow et al., 1991) provides eloquent testimony to the power of teachers to support the literacy of low-income children. In this longitudinal study of the influences of home and school on literacy development, Snow et al. demonstrate that strong home support in the way of books, reading, writing, high expectations, and predictable routines cannot always compensate for 2 consecutive years of weak instruction in school. Although most children with home support were able to withstand 1 year of inadequate teaching, many children with highly literate, articulate, and supportive parents were not able to keep up with their peers when they experienced 2 years of poor instruction. But—and this is the power of teaching—excellent teaching easily compensated for homes that offered no support for children's literacy development.

This text presents several provocative examples of powerful teaching: early interventions that help children develop literacy in spite of family poverty, language differences, limited education resources, and the intractable obstacles to change in bureaucratic institutions like schools. Each of the studies is a commentary on challenging beliefs—in some cases, the beliefs, expectations, and pedagogies of the teachers who worked with children at-risk changed. In other cases, the university faculty revised their constructs of good instructional practices as they looked closely at the children's learning and the teachers' support of literacy development. In other contexts, the institutions, themselves, dismantled the array of funding streams, resources, and placement practices in an effort to redefine the school's central responsibility to the children it served and to coordinate everyone's efforts toward achieving this essential goal.

Goldenberg (Chapter 9) describes the evolution of his personal theories about what works with bilingual children from a California community where he was teacher and colleague as well as researcher. The most successful early childhood teachers appeared to disregard admonitions not to push children into reading and writing before they were ready, and Goldenberg himself rethought what might be the most appropriate way to support the emerging literacy of the young bilingual children from this Hispanic community who had limited access to books in their native language. In another innovative Chapter 1 intervention, Hiebert (Chapter 5) explores the conflict many teachers felt in violating a popular *whole language* philosophy about not teaching words, even when such prohibition seemed to disadvantage children who were the farthest behind their peers. For teachers who managed to hold such beliefs in abeyance, however Hiebert and her public school colleagues were able to deepen their understandings of beginning reading and create support for teachers to control the curriculum and have an impact on the development of the lowest achieving readers.

The idea that development can be accelerated is counterintuitive for many educators; yet this notion is the philosophy behind Reading Recovery, the most widely known early reading intervention with the longest history of success (Pinnell & McCarrier, Chapter 8; Smith-Burke & Jaggar, Chapter 4). The belief that schools bear responsibility for ensuring that all children catch up to their peers is the radical idea proposed by Slavin and his colleagues to administrators in the Baltimore City schools (Slavin, Madden, Karweit, Dolan, & Wasik, Chapter 7). Success for All, as the Baltimore study is known, reworked the school's ground rules for dealing with low-achieving children. The researchers and the teacher-participants in the program set grade-level reading achievement as the goal for all children within the school's primary grades, and they were able to reallocate the resources of the school in service of that responsibility. The success of Success for All (and other interventions described in this text) symbolizes what we can accomplish when an ethos of possibility and responsibility pervades the culture of our schools. We hope that the practices that contributed to the ineffectiveness of traditional interventions will be replaced with teaching strategies that personalize learning, build on children's strengths, acknowledge their histories, and forge thoughtful communities of learners from the diversity of the participants.

REFERENCES

Abelson, R. (1979). Differences between belief systems and knowledge systems. *Cognitive Science, 3,* 355–366.

Allington, R., & Li, S. (1990). *Teacher beliefs about children who find learning to read difficult.* Paper presented at the National Reading Conference, Miami, FL.

Allington, R., & McGill-Franzen, A. (1992a). Does high-stakes testing improve school effectiveness? *Spectrum, 10*(2), 3–12.

Allington, R., & McGill-Franzen, A. (1992b). Unintended effects of school reform in New York State. *Educational Policy, 6,* 396–413.

Berrueta-Clement, J.R., Schweinhart, L.J., Barnett, W.S., Epstein, A.S., & Weikart, D. P. (1984). *Changed lives: The effects of the Perry preschool program on youths through age 19.* Ypsilanti, MI: High/Scope.

Borko, H., Livingston, C., & Shavelson, R.J. (1990). Teachers' thinking about instruction. *Remedial and Special Education, 11,* 40–49.

Bremner, R.H. (Ed.). (1974). *Children and youth in America: A documentary history* (Vol. III). Cambridge, MA: Harvard.

Carter v. Florence County School District, 950 S. 2d156(4th Cir. 1991).

Chafel, J.A. (1992). Funding Head Start: What are the issues? *American Journal of Orthopsychiatry, 62,* 9–21.

Clark, C.M., & Peterson, P.L. (1986). Teachers' thought processes. In M.C. Wittrock (Eds.), *Handbook of Research on Teaching* (Third Ed.) (pp. 255–296). New York: Macmillan.

Coleman, J., Campbell, E., Hobson, C., McPartland, J., Mood, A., Weinfeld, F., & York, R. (1966). *Equality of educational opportunity,* Washington, DC: U.S. Government Printing Office.

Cooper, H.M. & Tom, D.Y.H. (1984). Teacher expectation research: A review with implications for classroom instruction. *Elementary School Journal, 85,* 77–89.

Doe v. San Francisco, 131 Cal. Reporter 854, 1976.

Education for All Handicapped Children Act. (PL 94-142). (1975).

Education for All Handicapped Children Act Amendments of 1986. (PL 99-457). (1986).

Elementary and Secondary Education Act. (PL 89-10). (1965).

Gartner, A., & Lipsky, D.K. (1987). Beyond special education: Toward a quality system for all students. *Harvard Educational Review, 57,* 367–395.

Glaser, B., & Strauss, A. (1967). *The discovery of grounded theory.* New York: Aldine.

Gottfredson, G.D. (1986). *You get what you measure, you get what you don't: Higher standards, higher test scores, more retention in grade* (Report No. 2a). Baltimore: Center for Research on Elementary and Middle Schools, Johns Hopkins University.

Hyde, A., & Moore, D. (1988). Reading services and the classification of students in two districts. *Journal of Reading Behavior, 20,* 301–338.

LeTendre, M.J. (1991). The continuing evolution of a federal role in compensatory education. *Educational Evaluation and Policy Analysis, 13*, 328–334.

Lyons, C.A., & White, N. (1989). *Characteristics of teachers who are particularly successful in accelerating at-risk first graders' progress in reading.* Paper presented at the National Reading Conference, Austin, TX.

McGill-Franzen, A. (1987). Failure to learn to read: Formulating a policy problem. *Reading Research Quarterly, 22*, 475–490.

McGill-Franzen, A., & Allington, R. (1991). The gridlock of low-achievement: Perspectives on policy and practice. *Remedial and Special Education, 12*, 20–30.

McGill-Franzen, A., & Allington, R. (1992). Flunk 'em or classify them: Contamination of primary grade accountability data. *Educational Researcher, 21*, 19–22.

McGill-Franzen, A., & James, I. (1990). *Teacher beliefs about remedial and learning disabled readers.* Paper presented at the National Reading Conference, Miami, FL.

Mehan, H. (1992). Understanding inequality in schools: The contribution of interpretive studies. *Sociology of Education, 65*, 1–20.

Mehan, H., Hartweck, A., & Meihls, J. (1986). *Handicapping the handicapped.* Stanford, CA: Stanford U. Press.

Moore, M., Strang, E., Schwartz, M., & Braddock, M. (1988). *Patterns in special education service delivery and cost.* Washington, DC: Decision Resources Corporation.

Morine-Dershimer, G. (1978/1979). Planning and classroom reality: An in-depth look. *Educational Research Quarterly, 3*, 83–99.

Nespor, J. (1987). The role of beliefs in the practice of teaching. *Journal of Curriculum Studies, 19*(4), 317–328.

New York State Council on Children and Families. (1988). *State of the child.* Albany, NY: Author.

New York State Education Department. (1989). *A report to the governor and the legislature on the educational status of the state's schools: Statewide profile of the educational system.* Albany: Office for Policy Analysis and Program Accountability.

New York State Education Department. (1990). *A report to the governor and the legislature on the educational status of the state's schools: Statewide profile of the educational system.* Albany: Office for Planning, Research, and Program Accountability.

Peterson, P.L., Carpenter, T., & Fennema, E. (1989). Teachers' knowledge of students' knowledge in mathematics problem solving: Correlational and case analyses. *Journal of Educational Psychology, 81*, 558–569.

Rowley v. Board of Education, 458 U.S. 176, 207. (1982).

Ross, E.W. (1992). Teacher personal theorizing and reflective practice in teacher education. In E.W. Ross, J.W. Cornett, & G. McCutcheon (Eds.), *Teacher personal theorizing: Connecting curriculum practice, theory and research* (pp. 3–18). Albany: SUNY.

Rowan, B., Guthrie, L., Lee, G., & Guthrie, G. (1986). *The design and implementation of Chapter 1 instructional services: A study of 24 schools.* San Francisco: Far West Laboratory.

Shepard, L.A., & Smith, M.L. (Ed.). (1989). *Flunking grades: Research and policies on retention.* Philadelphia: Falmer.

Singer, J., & Butler, J. (1987). The Education for All Handicapped Children Act: Schools as agents of social reform. *Harvard Educational Review, 57*, 125–152

Smith, M.L. (1980). Meta-analysis of research on teacher expectations. *Evaluation in Education, 4*, 53–55.

Smith, M.L., & Shepard, L. (1988). Kindergarten readiness and retention: A qualitative study of teachers' beliefs and practices. *American Educational Research Journal, 25,* 307–333.

Snow, C., Barnes, W., Chandler, J., Goodman, I., & Hemphill, L. (1991). *Unfulfilled expectations: Home and school influences on literacy.* Cambridge, MA: Harvard.

Stringfield, S. (1991). Introduction to the special issue on Chapter 1 policy and evaluation. *Educational Evaluation and Policy Analysis, 13,* 325–327.

U.S. Department of Education. (1992). *Fourteenth annual report to Congress on the implementation of the Education of the Handicapped Act.* Washington, DC: Division of Educational Services, Office of Special Education and Rehabilitative Services.

Walker, J., & Levine, D.U. (1988). *The inherent impact of non-promoted students on reading scores in a big city elementary school.* Paper presented at the American Educational Research Association, New Orleans.

Wise, A.E. (1979). *Legislated learning: The Bureaucratization of the American classroom.* Berkeley: University of California.

▶ Part II

Tutoring and Small-Group Interventions

► 3

At-Risk University Students Tutoring At-Risk Elementary School Children
What Factors Make it Effective?

CONNIE JUEL

Juel describes a fascinating effective early intervention program in which college student athletes tutored low-achieving first-grade students. Many of the tutors came from cultures that were similar to those of the children they tutored. The college students, many who had difficulty themselves learning to read, were instructed in how to be effective tutors in a weekly 2¹/₂-hour class. They tutored children for 45 minutes twice a week during the school year. After describing the program, Juel concludes the chapter with nine principles that she believes were particularly important in making this program successful. In addition to "teaching the system" of how to decode words, tutors developed warm, supportive relationships with their first-grade students. They also effectively communicated to the children that they understood what the children were going through because they too had struggled with reading when they were young.

. . . if I could relive my grade school years I would change some of the things that I went through. For instance, when I needed help it was not available and questions that needed to be asked were not answered. It was almost like no one cared. Just a few encouraging words could have changed my whole view about myself and my abilities. It is lonely and hard to deal with the world and the people around you when no one is helping you when you need help. My past has helped my tutoring because I know what can happen if no one pays any attention to you and no one is there to encourage you. What I tell Felicity now I was not told in grade school. I tell Felicity that she can do anything that she wants to do and I will be there for her if she needs any help. Now she reads with confidence and she is more outgoing than she was at the beginning of the semester. By my experience I have helped her and I can see a noticeable change in her behavior. When we first met she did not have confidence in anything that she did. Now she asks questions and she reads aloud with confidence; sometimes you may be able to hear her reading over all the other kids in the room.

The most successful thing in my tutoring was when I told Felicity to stop using the word *can't*. When I first met Felicity she always said "can't." I would ask her to read a certain passage or word, "I can't," or I would ask her to read a book aloud for me, "I can't." I told her that if I heard her say that she can't do anything, I would not talk to her. At first it was hard and it would slip out every now and then. Now she is doing really well and her reading has improved as a result of it. I think it was successful because she was never told that she can do anything that she wants to do. I want her to be conscious of what she was doing and saying because she might be failing herself before she even tries. She is really improving as the semester is progressing and I am not only proud of her accomplishments, but I am also proud of mine.

I did not think that I could tutor a child, until I met Felicity. I have not only helped her, but she has helped me. We will both look back and say, Thanks. (Bettina, spring 1991)

One-on-one instruction is considerably more effective than instruction given to small groups (Glass, Cahen, Smith, & Filby, 1982). In one-on-one cross-age tutoring, gains have been shown both in achievement and attitude towards learning not only by the tutored children but by the tutors themselves (Cohen, Kulik, & Kulik, 1982; Juel, 1991; Labbo & Teale, 1990).

Bettina (pseudonyms are used in all examples) was one of the tutors in a cross-age tutoring program that I coordinated between University of Texas at Austin students and children at a nearby elementary school. The university students were mainly student athletes who had low scores on the Nelson-Denny reading test, which is administered by the men's and women's athletic departments. Many of the student athletes had considerable academic problems when they were in school, with a large number having been in remedial and learning disabled classes at various times (Juel, 1991). Many reported that they had been channeled into sports in response to either academic or behavior problems in school. In the words of one of my current university tutors at Virginia, "Like most black males who are very spirited, I was channeled into sports" (Donnell, fall 1992). When they excelled in sports, many saw that as their ticket into higher education. Some received remedial academic help along the way. One student reported this:

> When I was a freshman in high school, I was a star basketball player and I did not know how to read. One day, the vice-principal called me into her office and told me that she had a lady who wanted to tutor me in reading. I told her, however, that I did not need a tutor because I could read. Everything was fine until the next year when I started receiving letters from colleges. Then, my coach called me into his office and told me I would not be able to go to college because I could not read. So, I went to look for that lady and asked her to teach me to read. She helped me a lot. I met with her three times weekly until I graduated from high school. This was the worst experience I ever had in school. Because of that experience, I learned the importance of learning to read at an early age, and I have tried to give that message to the children who are struggling with their reading skills at L.L. Campbell Elementary School. (Denny, fall 1991)

Although all the student athlete tutors could decode, their vocabulary and comprehension scores on the Nelson-Denny clustered around the ninth-grade level. They were the products of the "Matthew Effect" (Stanovich, 1986). According to the Gospel of Matthew: "For unto everyone that hath shall be given, and he shall have abundance: but from him that hath not shall be taken away even that which he hath" (Matthew XXV:29). Children who get off to an early successful start in reading like to read, read a lot more in and out of school than their less fortunate peers, and through this reading gain vocabulary, concepts, and world knowledge, which in turn makes them even stronger readers. "But from him that hath not shall be taken away even that which he hath." Many of the student athlete tutors were children who got off to a poor start learning to read, learned to dislike reading, and read less both in and out of school than their more successful peers (several tutors told me that they had never read a book in its entirety). Consequently, they fell even further behind their peers in the reading vocabulary and knowledge that would enable them to comprehend college textbooks and courses.

The men's athletic department was quite aware that they had a number of student athletes who were likely to fail their university courses unless they were provided considerable help. They tried various measures. First, most were assigned an individual tutor. Second, they were instructed to take two developmental reading and study skills courses in their first year. These measures were not always successful and so the men's athletic department agreed to try an experiment. The 15 lowest scorers on the Nelson-Denny reading test were placed in my tutoring class for two semesters, in lieu of the two semesters of developmental reading and study skills. Fifteen other male student athletes, who scored poorly on the Nelson-Denny, would serve as a control group and enroll in the two developmental reading courses. Both groups would have individual tutors for their university courses.

Other students were in the tutoring class besides these 15 students. Other student athletes were welcome in the class. Many, but not all of these, also needed help with reading and writing. During the fall of 1990 36 student athletes were in the class, including eight from the women's athletic department. In the spring of 1991 there were 45 tutors. The majority of the spring tutors were student athletes, but others, mainly minority students, had heard of the class and were enrolled.

Each student was expected to read for 4 hours outside the class each week. The men's athletic department provided funds to buy about 200 paperback books, which were selected by me in consultation with student athletes and others. They represented a variety of reading levels, with the lowest level about sixth grade (e.g., Gardiner's *Stone Fox*, 1980), and a variety of genre (including biographies, fiction, horror stories, romances, westerns, and nonfiction sports stories). The majority of the books were written by African-American authors and concerned the lives of blacks (e.g., *Bloods* by Terry, 1984; *Nigger* by Gregory, 1964). The students could select their readings from these books or from any others available in the university library. All students in the class wrote about their reading in interactive journals, and each week the students handed in their journals to the instructor. The journal contained their reading times, pages read, and their personal responses to the readings. The instructor responded in writing to these weekly journal entries. In addition, the university students tutored one elementary school child in reading and writing for 45 minutes, twice a week. (Some of these sessions were both audiotaped and videotaped for later analysis.)

The children (36 in the fall and 45 in the spring) were first-grade, second-grade, and special education students who had been designated by the principal and teachers as having fallen considerably behind their classmates in reading. The elementary school they attended is an all minority school, about 70% African-American and 30% Hispanic. It is located in one of the poorest neighborhoods in Austin; a neighborhood troubled by drugs, crime, and poverty. Because many of the tutors were minorities, came from low-income families, and had experienced difficulty in school, there was a great deal of identification with the children. One Anglo student athlete wrote this:

> Mirrah and I make a perfect match because there are so many similarities between her and the way I was when I was a child. I was a poor reader growing up, and I still remember the way I used to try to hide that fact. Mirrah was in the same position when we began working together this semester.
>
> She was embarrassed with her reading ability and would do anything to try to either get out of reading, or read something she had memorized. Mirrah would tell me that she had already read a particular passage or that she did not need to because she had mastered the skill the passage was developing. These techniques were the very same as the ones that I used when I was her age and therefore I saw through them and was able to find ways to encourage and motivate Mirrah. (Ted, spring 1991)

COMPONENTS OF THE TUTORING PROGRAM

One evening a week all the tutors gathered at the university for a two-and-a-half hour class. During this class we discussed possible tutoring activities, how literacy develops, books that the tutors were reading, and books that the tutors wrote for the children they tutored.

Each tutor wrote at least two books. We spent several evenings on these in our own version of a writing workshop. Ideas and drafts for books were worked on in pairs or small groups, and edited before a final copy was made. Illustrations were drawn (most often by the tutor, but sometimes with the child), and the book was "published." Most included the child's name as the central character who overcame some calamity or problem. The illustrations were done with incredible care and considerable skill. Many of the tutors told me that this was the first time they had enjoyed writing. Several thought they might want to write or illustrate children's books in the future.

The tutors' written books both were to be read and enjoyed with the children, and used to inspire and encourage the children to write books for themselves and others. Writing was one of seven basic activities that were discussed in the evening class. The tutors were encouraged to use three or four activities in each tutoring session; the choice of which activities was determined by analyzing the reading and writing samples of their children. Diagnosis was based in part on the developmental literacy model outlined by Juel (1990), and in part on the tutor's intuitions. Whereas specific activities were suggested to tutors, the tutors were given considerable discretion as to their delivery. I had learned from the pilot semester of tutoring that instruction was most effective when its implementation was left to the tutor. (For a case study of how and why one student athlete developed his teaching techniques, see Calhoun & Juel, 1991.) The seven basic activities are described in the following.

Writing

Storybook writing was encouraged both by the tutor's books and by themed writing centers that were placed around the tutoring room. The themes in these centers were frequently changed. The centers included books, magazines, and blank writing books that had either construction paper or computer-generated covers with graphics, or were cut into shapes that corresponded to the theme. Typical themes were bears, cookbooks, dinosaurs, insects, space travel, houses, and classic stories such as *The Three Little Pigs*. The children and tutors wrote imaginative new versions of stories, retold stories, and wrote factual texts (e.g., *Bear Facts*).

Seasonal themes often included the making of message books (e.g., valentines, Easter cards). In addition, the children sometimes corresponded with other children or their tutors on "postcards" or to their tutors in an interactive journal. Puppets were available in the tutoring room, and these frequently became involved in plays. Book-making materials were also available for writing use.

Through story writing both the tutors and the children could see themselves as authors and as *meaning-makers* which helped them to understand the reasons for writing (Downing, 1979; Petrosky, 1982). Story writing also increased the children's knowledge of text structures, which can aid reading comprehension (Gordon & Braun, 1982).

Reading Books

There were more than 200 children's books in the tutoring room. These included predictable texts, children's favorites, and expository texts. At the beginning of first grade the tutors asked the children to indicate which books they had seen before. Other than books that had been in the kindergarten classrooms, few children recognized any.

Each tutor was urged to read books to children as one of the activities in each tutoring session. Both tutors and children were expected to gain vocabulary from reading and listening to stories (Elley, 1989; Feitelson, Kita, & Goldstein, 1986). Both were also expected to increase their imaginations, world knowledge, and motivation for reading and writing.

My Book

Reading instruction at the elementary school followed a traditional mode, with the children placed in basal readers and reading groups. The children we tutored were all struggling with the basal vocabulary. One problem with "pull-out remediation" has been the lack of overlap between the materials and experiences in the child's classroom and those in the remedial situation (Johnston & Allington, 1991). To link these experiences for the children we tutored we created "buildup" readers (Guszak, 1985). These readers slowly introduced both basal vocabulary and new words that built on the phonogram patterns of the basal words. The first page in the first buildup reader had only one word, *run*, which was repeated many times in different formats (e.g., "Run, _____, run. Run, run, run, _____."). In the blanks the child could tell the tutor, or could write on their own, what would "run." There was room to draw pictures. These pictures were often labeled by the children with words copied from the buildup pages. Each subsequent page in the buildup added another word.

A buildup reader was created for the core vocabulary included in the preprimers through the primer. There were a total of five buildup readers, ranging from about 25 to 100 pages. The buildup readers allowed the children to practice reading the vocabulary from the books that they would need to read in front of their peers in their classrooms. They gained speed, fluency, and self-confidence in reading these common words. The very gradual introduction of vocabulary words, as well as their repetition, ensured success in the buildups.

My Journal

Many of the first-grade children needed to develop "word consciousness" (Morris, 1981). They also needed to understand the communicative function of print, to see their own words written down. The children were encouraged by their tutors to tell them a special word each day. This word was written down by the tutor, copied by the child, and discussed while the child drew a picture involving it. Finally, the child dictated a short phrase, sentence, or passage for the tutor to write that involved the word. One day, for example, one girl's special word was *clouds*. She drew a picture of blue clouds. Her dictated reason was: "I like the clouds because they rain. I like the clouds because they are blue." So ingrained in my thinking were white clouds, that I stood in awe of that little girl as I left the tutoring room, headed outside, and looked up to see blue clouds.

Alphabet Book

Many of the children we tutored did not know the names of the letters of the alphabet. Alphabet books were generated by computer. Each page had one letter, a key picture, and a key word (e.g., D d, the word *dog*, and a picture of a dog). There was a lot of room for the child to write down other *d* words.

Sometimes these words were generated from a conversation between the tutor and the child and sometimes from using picture dictionaries. One boy's *d* words included: *doll, David, Donald, diamonds, duke, dog,* and *dare.* Some children used the page simply to write the letter. Later during the year, some children used their alphabet books to look up words for their own text writing. The second-grade children liked to use the books to write stories about the pictures (e.g., several used the *dog* page to write a new story about the dog from the *Clifford* storybooks).

Hearing Word Sounds

Like many other young children who have difficulty learning to read, many of the children we tutored had difficulty hearing the sounds in words; they lacked phonemic awareness (Clay, 1985; Griffith & Olson, 1992; Juel, 1988; Lundberg, Frost, & Petersen, 1988). One of the earliest phonemic insights about words is distinguishing the onset (i.e., the initial phoneme, like /k/) and rhyme (e.g., *at*) (Treiman, 1992). The child who can do this at its simplest level can distinguish which words rhyme among *cat, fat,* and *dog.* At more advanced levels, which probably require some print experience, the child can actually segment the rhyme and create new rhyming words with the phonogram.

To encourage this attention to the sounds in words, we had several activities. First, there were plenty of books with rhymes, such as Dr. Seuss books. The children were encouraged to predict the rhyme (e.g., *cat–hat*). Second, the tutors played many oral sound games with the children. They might have the children guess what word they were saying as they slowly said it. They might put on the *Daryl Dog* puppet, who likes only things that start, like his name, with a /d/, and decide what he might like. They might go on a "trip" to "Dallas" and be able to bring only things that start with a /d/. Third, a variation of the "Hearing the Sounds" activities described by Clay (1985, p. 65) was made. A sheet of paper was marked into a few columns. As the tutor slowly pronounced a short word like *up,* the child moved a penny into a column when a different sound was heard. *Up* required two pennies, *cup* needed three, and so forth.

Letter-Sound Activities

The major difference between most good and poor beginning readers is the good reader's ability to recognize words (Curtis, 1980; Juel, 1988; Perfetti, 1985; Stanovich, 1980). Poor decoding abilities can keep a child from reading much, contributing to the Matthew Effect (Juel, 1988; Stanovich, 1986).

Several activities were available for increasing letter-sound knowledge. First, after a child could complete the "Hearing the Sounds" activity just described, letters were substituted for the pennies. Second, letter-card boards were used to spell words. Third, books that contained words with repetitive phonograms were read and discussed (e.g., Wildsmith's, *Cat on the Mat*, 1982).

In each tutoring session the tutors were encouraged to spend the majority of the time with the child reading (e.g., predictable text, children's books, or *My Book*). Choral (i.e., tutor and child reading together, often after an initial reading of a text by the tutor) and echo reading (i.e., child reading a sentence or phrase immediately after the tutor) were demonstrated as ways to make text accessible to beginning readers. The tutors were shown that through these techniques they could induce children to read along with them (e.g., in predictable texts). In this way, the "reading to children" activity often became a shared reading event. The remaining tutoring time was spent on two or three other activities (e.g., hearing sounds in words, alphabet books, letter-sound activities, writing, *My Journal*).

Each tutor had a regular tutoring time. The tutoring times fit into the tutor's university schedule and did not conflict with the children's lunch or math periods. This meant that tutoring sessions started as early as 7:45 in the morning or as late as 2:00 in the afternoon. Although this schedule presented challenges to the university supervisors (e.g., some days I spent the whole day at the elementary school), the schedule had its advantages. There were seldom more than five tutors in the room at any given time. This allowed the supervisors (myself and a teaching assistant) to focus more fully on particular dyads. It also allowed more time for discussion with individual tutors, either before or after their tutoring.

Tutoring occurred in an empty first-grade classroom that was located off the same hall as the other first-grade classrooms. The accessibility of the tutoring room to the other classrooms (as well as the lengthy time periods when tutoring occurred) facilitated the visits of classroom teachers and other school personnel. These visitors both saw the tutoring and talked with the tutors and university supervisors. Teachers shared their ideas; they also borrowed ideas and books from the tutoring room (especially *My Book* and writing booklets from the themed writing centers).

SUMMARY OF INTERVENTION RESULTS

Children's Progress

During the 1990–1991 school year, 27 first-grade at-risk children were identified by their teachers and the principal as ones who most needed help. (The balance of the tutored children came from special education and second-grade classrooms.) The mean score of these 27 at-risk children in September on the Metropolitan Readiness Test (MRT) (Nurss & McGauvran, 1976) prereading composite was at the 26th percentile. Fifteen other first-grade (lower risk) children at the school were considered more likely to succeed at reading in first grade than the 27 at-risk children. The mean of these 15 lower risk children on the MRT was at the 46th percentile.

The 27 at-risk children were tutored twice a week for 45 minutes per session. The 15 lower risk children each had a student athlete mentor. At least once a week they met with the student athletes, who would talk to them and read stories to them. In April the school administered the Iowa Tests of Basic Skills (ITBS) (Hieronymous, Lindquist, & Hoover, 1983). The mean score of the 27 at-risk children on the reading comprehension subtest was at the 41st percentile. The mean score of the 15 lower risk children was at the 16th percentile.

Standardized tests were not meant to be the only measure of the program's success. Throughout the year I met with the teachers and the principal, frequently tape-recording their comments. The teachers and the principal were very enthusiastic about the program. They spoke about the increased reading ability of the tutored children, many of whom were moved from low reading groups to higher ones. They spoke about increased self-confidence in all the children. They reported that parents were also very enthusiastic about their children's increased reading ability and self-confidence (see comments in Juel, 1991).

Tutors' Progress

The effects of 4 hours of self-selected reading, interactive journal writing, writing children's books, and engaging in all the tutoring activities on the reading abilities of the 15 target student athletes was compared with the control group of 15 student athletes. The athletic department administered the Nelson-Denny Reading Test (Brown, Bennett, & Hanna, 1981). Form E was administered as a pretest to both groups immediately prior to the academic year in August. To get an indication of growth during the first semester in the tutoring class, a representative from the athletic department came to an evening class in December and readministered Form E. Finally, Form F was used as a post-test for both groups at the end of the academic year in May. We used the Vocabulary and Comprehension sections from the Nelson-Denny test. These two scores are combined to form a total score for the test. Raw scores were used in the data analysis but grade equivalents are given here for ease of interpretation. Although the tutors were initially poorer readers than the control group, they approached the reading level of the control group by December, and by May an Analysis of Covariance (using the August pretest as the covariate) indicated that the tutors had significantly surpassed the control group ($F[1,27] = 21.3, p < .001$). The grade equivalent for tutors' combined vocabulary and comprehension performances rose from 9.25 in August to 13.5 in May, whereas control students did not change much from their level of 11.5 in August to 12.5 in May. While growth occurred on both the vocabulary and comprehension subtests, the tutors made major growth in vocabulary (tutors: grade equivalent of 8.7 in August to 14.2 in May; controls: grade equivalent of 12.0 in August to 12.9 in May). This is in line with the proposal that after about third grade most new vocabulary is learned through reading (Nagy & Anderson, 1984). It seems likely that 4 hours of outside reading and reading to children contributed to the increase in vocabulary.

What Effective Tutors Taught Us About Effective Instruction

We learned a lot about effective instruction from watching the tutors. In order to determine what kinds of interactions were most effective, four volunteers (three graduate students and myself) viewed the videotapes and read transcripts of the tape-recorded sessions of the tutors who had the most success. We viewed the tapes and read the transcripts independently, and did not share our observations with one another. We each wrote comments and connected these to specific clips in the tapes or spots on the transcripts. There was considerable overlap in the comments, and the following briefly discusses those features upon which at least three of us commented.

1. *A warm, supportive, caring atmosphere.* All observers noted the supportive relationship that developed between tutor and child. One observer said, "You just look at the videos and you see love." Another observer commented, "It looks like family." One tutor described how she came to understand the type of relationship her child needed:

   > The thing that I have drawn upon from my own background and experiences that has helped me tutor is the fact that the memories that I have of learning to read are fun memories of one-on-one lessons. I learned to read at home with my mother, father, and sister each pulling me to the side at one point or another and trying to give me reading instruction. I guess the most fond of those memories are the ones with my sister, Cora. She was bound and determined, after she had become a very good reader, to teach her little sister the wonders of reading. I spent countless nights with my sister in our room with bedtime story books. After she had taught me the sounds to all the alphabet and that the vowels had a short and long sound, she would take a story and actually go through the entire piece marking short and long vowels. . . .
   >
   > When I first began tutoring Yvette, I could instantly see that she was a very rebellious little girl at times. I don't think that she's a bad person, but that she feels she must act in this rebellious way. I noticed that if she isn't talked to in a nurturing way, that rebellious side of her comes out. This was not immediately apparent to me. I began tutoring Yvette last semester, at that time

I was under a great deal of stress myself. . . . I would ask her questions in a mechanical voice and she would just sit there and refuse to answer. Many times the things that I asked her, I knew that she knew the answer. It didn't hit me until this semester that Yvette's problem could be that she wanted the same type of atmosphere and relationship that I had with my sister when I was learning to read. I think that in her classroom, she can sense that no one really expects her to know anything. What I try to do, when I tutor her, is turn this around and act like there is not a doubt in my mind that she knows the words or the answers. I also try to give her that one-on-one feeling that makes a person feel special. I think by tutoring Yvette with this mentality, I have been able to reach her. (Corinna, spring 1991)

The tutors made the children feel special. This was noted by their teachers and parents. One teacher commented: "The kids go to tutoring and come back with their chests all puffed out. They feel so special that someone cares enough about them to come and work with them. All of their reading has improved, their self-confidence has improved." This special attitude is reflected in the words of one tutor, words that were spoken to his child on the first tutoring day: "I'm going to come just to see you."

2. *Teaching the system.* Successful tutors frequently informed their children about how reading and writing work. They served as informants who were trying to explain how things work—they acted as if they were letting their children in on the secrets of how everything fits together. Some verbal examples follow:

"All you gotta do is put them together." (the sounds in words)

"Anytime you have words like 'ch,' 'ch,' 'ch,' 'ch,' . . . ."

"You gotta 'f,' you need something that will put the 'f' with the 'x' to say 'fox,' take off the 'f,' you have 'ox'." (spelling "fox" on letter-card board)

"This is how you are supposed to tell a story. . . ."

"You can't read a word without looking at it. Look at each word. Read 'em as you see 'em."

"Yvette, Yvette, stop. Listen to what I'm trying to tell you. When you just memorize, that isn't reading what you're doing, do you understand the difference? When you memorize a story then, that's good, too, 'cause you have it in your head, but then you look, when you read, you look at the word that you're reading and you remember the sounds that each letter makes and you put those sounds together and you make words out of them. So you can look here, and you can look there, and you know that that's an 'H' and an 'I.' The 'H' makes the 'huh' sound and that makes 'I' so you would know that's 'Hi.'" See, that's how you read. And you look at each word, you just, you don't look at the picture and guess what the words are, you just look here and look at each word and then you read it."

"Vowels are fancy letters. Now, what did I tell you what happens when I have a fancy letter, then I have a normal letter, then I have another fancy letter? What does that second letter do for the first one? It makes a long sound. It makes you hear it. Instead of a-a-h, it goes a-a-a. You don't even worry about the 'E' anymore. The 'E's' done it's purpose. So it will be. . . ."

"Sound it out. That's your little trick. That's how you figure out these words."

Or this dialogue after the child has misread a word:

Tutor: That doesn't make sense. Could "him" run?

Child: (laughs)

Tutor: Does that make sense?

Child: (laughs)

Tutor: Okay, what sounds better? The boy "him" run, or The boy "can" run?

Child: The boy can run.

Tutor: There you go. You see you gotta listen to yourself as you read and see if it sounds right.

3. *A "we're in this together and I know how you feel attitude"*. Tutors often shared stories of their own childhood struggles, likes, and dislikes. By doing so, they let the child know that they understood what it was like to be in the child's position, as in "When I was little like you . . ." or "Me and you, we gonna do it." Teasing and "tall tales" often contributed to the sharing, as in this discussion about the toy car that the child had drawn in *My Journal*:

Tutor: I used to have one of those a long, long, long, long time ago.

Child: When you was little?

Tutor: Yeah, when I was little. I'm not little anymore. I'm sitting in this big old chair because I can't sit in the chair you're sitting in.

Child: How you got big?

Tutor: Well, you know what happened? I was sleeping one night and I was your size, and I was sleeping, and I woke up the next morning and I was big and my Mama said, "Who are you?"

Child: (laughs)

Tutor: And I say, I'm Sammy, and she say, no you're not. My Sammy is not that big.

(The discussion changed, but later this topic was continued.)

Tutor: I sure enjoy visiting with you. One day when you get older you're gonna get hair on your chest and say, Ooooo, look at that, you're a big boy now.

Child: (laughs) Everybody gonna be looking.

Tutor: Yeah. And then you gonna go take a class like I'm taking and you gonna go and you gonna find you some kid like I'm talkin' to you, and you gonna say, you gonna say, hey little fella, I used to be your size a long time ago. . . .

Child: (laughs)

Tutor: And then you gonna tell him that story about waking up the next morning and being big you gonna tell him that story. You know that really didn't happen, don't you? I just kinda. . . .

Child: I'm gonna trick him.

Tutor: You gonna trick him? Yeah, that's good. But when you trick him, you do this, have fun with him, they like this.

Child: I'm gonna play with him, just like us.

Sometimes relating to being poor bound child and tutor together at the most unexpected times, such as during this dialogue as one tutor and child were spelling words on the letter-card board. The tutor had put up the word *bike*.

Tutor: And what does that say?

Child: Bike.

Tutor: But what if you have more than one bike? Then what would you put on there? What if you have three or four bikes? Rich kid.

Child: You'll put *S*.

Shared experiences could mean sharing vernacular language.

Tutor: This word is "don't," and "don't" is an abbreviation for the word do not. So instead of saying, "I do not have any money at all, you say, "Man, I don't have no money."

4. *Personalizing stories by playing and teasing each other while reading them.* (reading *Curious George*)

Tutor: Curious George (pointing to *George*). We're going to put Eddie right there. Curious Eddie. . . .

(Picture shows a bird eating a worm)

Tutor: He's eating a worm, do you like worms?

Child: NO!

Tutor: Yes you do.

Child: I don't either don't.

Tutor: You don't either?

Child: No.

(reading *John Henry*)

Tutor: So, what is that? Is that John Henry's house?

Child: Yep.

Tutor: Good. Okay. A hush settled over the hills, the sky swirled soundlessly around the moon, the river stopped murmuring, the wind stopped whispering, the frogs, owls, and crickets held silence. Sssshhh. All watching and waiting and listening. Then! The river roared. (growls) (laughs) Have you heard the sound of the river?

Child: Uh huh.

Tutor: The wind whispered, whistled, and sang. The crows croaked, the owls hooted, and all the crickets chirped. Welcome welcome, echoed through the hills. And John Henry was born. And just down the street Daryl was born.

Child: Hu uh. (laughs) I wasn't like that. I had a Pamper on when I was born.

Tutor: You had a what?

Child: I had a Pamper.

Tutor: Oh, they put a Pamper on you?

Child: Uh huh.

Tutor: John Henry came out smiling and laughing, but Daryl came out crying and crying and whining.

Child: (laughs) Hunh uh!

Tutor: You did!

Child: When I was a baby, I wasn't crying.

Tutor: You weren't crying? I was crying when I was a baby. I was mad because when I came I was tired. I was sleeping and they woke me up, and I didn't want to wake up and I was just mad.

Child: The doctor do that?

Tutor: Uh huh.

5. *Lots of visual and auditory support while child is reading.* All observers of the videotapes noted the frequent visual support given by the tutors, focusing on voice-print matches as children read. This included having child or

tutor or both point to words, using cards under text lines, pointing with the eraser end of a pencil, and slow, deliberate reading by the tutor while pointing to the words. Effective tutors often held and guided the child's hand, as the child pointed to words. Frequently the tutors employed support reading including choral or echo reading, or simple turn taking.

Tutors who engaged in role-reversals, pretending to be the child slowly sounding out words, modeled their thought processes as they read. In these role-reversals, the child, who became the teacher, was called on for assistance. The child's attention was easily focused on the printed words in these role-reversals. The children took particular delight in the role-reversals, perhaps because the pressure to read was lifted off them, and perhaps also because they felt more grown up. Role-reversals became one of the most effective techniques for helping children with word recognition.

6. *Breaking down word recognition and spelling into small steps.* Often the tutors modeled how to sound out words for the child by talking the child through the process step by step. As discussed in the preceding, role-reversals were common. Each observer remarked how often the tutor turned the tables: That is, the tutor pretended to be the child so the child would walk the tutor through the process. Here's an example of word recognition on the letter-card board.

Tutor: So whenever you see those two letters together, it sounds like aaaaattt, aaaaaatttt. So what is that?

Child: Aaaaattt.

Tutor: Right, so what word is that?

Child: At.

Tutor: Right. So you've got the "at." Let's put a sound on the front of it, okay? What's one of your favorite sounds? I know, it's "ssss."

Child: S.

Tutor: Right. (puts up the letter *s* in front of "at") So you go, "ssss—at," and put them together. What have you got? You see? You see how that works? "Ssss" plus "at" gives you "sat." What about *M* plus "at"? What does that give you? (replaces *S* with *M*)

Child: M.

Tutor: And what is the other part?

Child: At.

Tutor: Put them together. What do you get? You got the "at." You got the "mmmmm" sound. You put them together and what do you get? Mmmmmaaaaaaat.

Child: Mat.

Tutor: Good. (replace *M* with *F*) So you got *F* and *AT*. Gives you what?

Child: (laughs) Fat.

Tutor: Right. They come together. You have this word "fffffaaaat." Fat. What do you hear when you say that word "fat"?

Child: ffff.

Tutor: Right. And the last two?

Child: At.

Tutor: Right. All we did was change the letters, and you change the sound. (puts up appropriate letters) AT, then SssAT, then MmmAT, FAT. See? What about B plus the AT?

Child: Buh. Bat.

Tutor: Right. You got it.

The following dialogue depicts breaking down words while writing, which occurred as the child talked about, drew, and finally spelled his special words for the day for *My Journal*.

Child: . . . I'm gonna make me a bat.

Tutor: You gonna make a bat? Let me see that. Okay?

Child: Does a bat have ears?

Tutor: Uh huh. Do you know how they look?

Child: Does it have a neck?

Tutor: Yep.

Child: They got a nose?

Tutor: Whooee! They got some straight wings.

Child: How you like it?

Tutor: Here's some looong wings! Here's another picture in your book. Some day you can go back and say, "Hey, look at all this that I did. . . . Why don't you write it? Baaaat.

Child: (writes a *B*) Now what?

Tutor: Do you hear the "aaaa" sound?

Child: A.

Tutor: What about the "tuh, tuh," what is that?

Child: T.

7. *Routines*. The most successful tutors usually stuck to a similar schedule each session. A common opening was, "How do we always start?" Some

tutors had some kind of game at the beginning, such as the child and the tutor each writing their name as fast as they could, racing to see who would finish first. Some tutors always started with *My Journal*, moved on to *My Book*, and so forth.

8. *Verbal reinforcement.* The tutors pushed the children hard and encouraged them when they tried. They always let the children know that they believed in their abilities and that they had faith they would be successful. Typical comments were:

"You going to get better, better and better as the day goes. I want you to get better. I want you to concentrate on it. Do the best you can do."

"I'm proud of you."

"You smart."

"You're gonna be a famous writer someday, you got all the pages."

"Go for it."

"I think you're doing very good. Smack me."

"Thumbs up, dude!"

"You read a whole page. Way to go, dude!"

"That's a good try."

9. *Nonverbal reinforcement.* Each observer of the videotapes (or the actual tutoring sessions) was impressed by the physical closeness of the tutors and their children. They simply sat close together and frequently one saw hugs, hands held, and arms around shoulders.

Tutor: Did you like the session today?

Child: Yes.

Tutor: That's good. That's good. I'm glad you like it 'cause I like doing it too. Are you ready to go back to class?

Child: Could you take me in your lap?

Tutor: Yeah. (and he did)

I think we can be reminded of some fundamentals of teaching and learning by watching those who participate in it. These last nine features of what successful tutors do seem a good place to start. By sharing these insights with new tutors and those planning on becoming elementary school teachers, I have seen both improvements in teaching and more reflective teaching. One tutor, for example, began to hold her child's hand and help her child point to the words, after seeing examples of other tutors doing so. She told me what a great difference this simple interaction had made in keeping her child's attention. She further noted that she would never have thought of doing this on her own because it seemed too personal and intrusive. This tutor began to rethink her feelings about "personal space," as well as where they had originated. As another example, several students in my field-based language arts classes have successfully employed role-reversals in their group instruction.

ISSUES RELATED TO THE INTERVENTION

Longevity

The intervention was considered extremely successful and continued after I left the University of Texas. It also spread to other school districts. The superintendent of schools in San Marcos, Texas, visited the program in Austin. As a result of this visit, he requested Southwest Texas State University to establish such a program with the local schools. Ann Hall, at Southwest Texas State University, has a program with student athletes tutoring kindergarten children. The program spread to other states. Yvonne Wittreich, Chapter 1 coordinator in Fort Collins, Colorado, read about the program in *The Reading Teacher* (Juel, 1991). In coordination with Robert Williams at Colorado State University, student athletes are now tutoring in Chapter 1 classes at four elementary schools. Likewise, Michael DeRoss, a principal of an elementary school in Weed, California, established a tutoring program in conjunction with the College of the Siskiyous. Mary Raseye, at Clinch Valley College in Wise, Virginia, established a similar tutoring program with a local elementary school. In a further extension, Joanne Calhoun, a high school English teacher who was involved in the original program in Austin, established a tutoring program where at-risk high school students tutor first-grade children in Burlington, Vermont.

Although each of these programs had some original impetus from the Texas program, it is likely that each is unique. This is desirable because I am convinced that to be most effective, a tutoring program should evolve from the grass-roots level. It will be shaped by the interactions of the personalities of the particular children, tutors, school personnel, and communities involved. It will be most successful if the program truly belongs to and is molded by the local community.

When I came to the University of Virginia I wanted to invite students from various departments at the university to participate in a tutoring class. I believed that the course should be housed in the College of Arts and Sciences rather than in the College of Education. This is now a reality, and each semester the course attracts diverse and numerous students. While many of the tutoring methods described earlier in this chapter are incorporated in our tutoring of first-grade children, I have also benefited from the techniques used in the McGuffey Reading Clinic at the University of Virginia. The tutoring program is continually being revised.

Intentional Well-Designed Instruction Is Needed for Interventions to Succeed

It seems clear that both males and minority members who are able to role model reading and writing can have a powerful influence on children. The results of the tutoring study in Austin indicate that merely mentoring and reading to children, however, is not enough to help them improve. Children who were mentored, but did not receive the other academic tutoring activities, did not do as well as the tutored children. To be maximally effective, tutors need to know how to help children with specific skills such as word recognition and spelling. Encouragement and goodwill are excellent but, unfortunately, are not enough.

Tutors Do Not Need to Be Highly Trained Professional Teachers

At the invitation of the Charlottesville School District, my colleague, Marcia Invernizzi, and I recently undertook the training of community volunteers to serve as tutors to first-grade children in four elementary schools. One of the first questions we were asked by school district personnel was what should be the qualifications of tutors: Should they be college graduates? Should they have worked with children before? How much training would they need before they could start tutoring?

Our answers were that they needed no degrees, they did not need prior experience working with children, and that they would receive about 1 hour of training before beginning tutoring—although they would receive extensive ongoing supervision and advice. I do not want to underplay the necessity for training: It is vital that tutors receive well-designed instruction. Effective tutoring techniques can be learned, however, by those who are not experienced educators. The Texas experience has shown that with relatively little training, as compared with classroom teachers, many student athletes became excellent tutors. Our tutoring model is an inclusive one, rather than an exclusive model of highly credentialed and highly trained individuals: Privileged knowledge is not required to come aboard. (It might well be the case that the requirement of advanced credentialing would discourage the participation of those who could become effective tutors.)

The tutoring model we are now employing in Charlottesville uses community volunteers who have a wide diversity in backgrounds and employment history (e.g., members of the City Council, retired people, and those employed in various occupations). These volunteers are assigned to an elementary school and are under the direct supervision of a graduate student. One or two graduate students supervise at each elementary school (one graduate student per 12 community volunteers). The graduate students conduct the initial assessments of those children nominated for tutoring by their teachers. When a new tutoring volunteer joins the program, a graduate student spends about an hour with the volunteer, illustrating the tutoring techniques, the materials, and a typical daily plan. During the first tutoring session with a child, the graduate student tutors while the volunteer watches. Until the volunteer feels comfortable creating the tutoring plan, the graduate student supplies the tutor with a plan for each session. (On average the graduate students require about 10 minutes to write each tutoring plan.) We have periodic open meetings for the community volunteers to get together to socialize as well as observe tutoring sessions. Since we are still in our first year of the program, we have not yet had an opportunity to analyze its success. It looks promising.

We are currently supervising 72 community volunteers and are considering training either instructional aides or other paraprofessionals at the schools to take over the on-site jobs that our graduate students currently hold. This would allow us to increase the number of children we tutor. In some cases, current community volunteers will take over these supervisory jobs.

One Year of Intervention Might Not Be Enough

Ideally, we would like to have the same community volunteer follow a child along into the upper grades, as well as begin the tutoring in kindergarten. The reason for this is that 1 year of intervention is often not sufficient for long-term results (see chapters 5 and 9, this volume). In the Texas study reported in this chapter, the tutored group did significantly better than the nontutored group. Yet, at the end of first grade the mean performance of the tutored children was only at the 41st percentile on the ITBS reading comprehension subtest. Relative to other first-grade children at the school (whose mean was at the 16th percentile) the tutored children are doing exceptionally well; but compared with a normative group, they have a way to go. It is in comparison to the wider population of first-grade children that interventions need to judge their results and consider if enough has actually been done. We also need to be concerned that *all* the children at a school are reading at the appropriate level, and not just those in the intervention (see chapter 5, this volume).

Successful intervention in first grade may be enough to ensure word recognition skill, or at least to have this skill under way so that a follow-up in second grade could cement it. Without such a follow-up, those children who do not read during the summer are in danger of losing some of their skill in word recognition. Until word recognition becomes automatic, it requires practice to prevent it from eroding.

Word recognition is not all that is required for reading comprehension, however. As the children shift into more challenging narrative and expository texts after first grade, their reading will require greater vocabulary knowledge, world knowledge, and strategic reading skills. Some children are likely to require continued intervention—only now the focus will be on these higher-order skills rather than on word recognition.

SUMMARY

This chapter illustrates one tutoring intervention that made a difference. The tutors were not highly trained professionals; they were student athletes. A program using trained tutors (who both care and can identify with the children they tutor) can be implemented at almost any school. The tutors can be student athletes or other university students, community volunteers, or older elementary or high school students. The experience described in this chapter suggests that the best tutors will not necessarily be (or have been) the best students themselves.

The chapter also illustrates that much can be learned about instruction by watching effective tutors at work. Training is necessary, along with the tutor's demonstrated motivation to help the tutored child. It is clearly the interaction between the academic activities and the social context of the tutoring situation, that yields the positive results.

REFERENCES

Brown, J.I., Bennett, J.M., & Hanna, G. (1981). *The Nelson-Denny Reading Tests, Forms E and F.* Chicago, IL: Riverside.

Calhoun, J.S., & Juel, C. (1991, April). *Effects of cross-age tutoring on at-risk college student-athlete tutors and their at-risk first grade tutees.* Paper presented at the meeting of the American Educational Research Association, Chicago, IL.

Clay, M.M. (1985). *The early detection of reading difficulties* (3rd ed.). Portsmouth, NH: Heinemann.

Cohen, P., Kulik, J.A., & Kulik, C. (1982). Educational outcomes of tutoring: A meta-analysis of findings. *American Educational Research Journal, 19,* 237–248.

Curtis, M.E. (1980). Development of components of reading skill. *Journal of Educational Psychology, 72,* 656–669.

Downing, J. (1979). *Reading and reasoning.* New York: Springer-Verlag.

Elley, W.B. (1989). Vocabulary acquisition from listening to stories. *Reading Research Quarterly, 24,* 174–214.

Feitelson, D., Kita, B., & Goldstein, Z. (1986). Effects of listening to series stories on first graders' comprehension and use of language. *Research in the Teaching of English, 20,* 339–356.

Gardiner, J.R. (1980). *Stone fox.* New York: Harper & Row.

Glass, G., Cahen, L., Smith, M.L., & Filby, N. (1982). *School class size.* Beverly Hills, CA: Sage.

Gordon, F.J., & Braun, C. (1982). Schemata: Meta-textual aid to reading and writing. In J.A. Niles & L.A. Harris (Eds.), *New inquiries in reading research and instruction* (pp. 262–268). Thirty-First Yearbook of the National Reading Conference. Rochester, NY: NRC.

Gregory, D. (1964). *Nigger.* New York: Washington Square Press.

Griffith, P.L., & Olson, M.W. (1992). Phonemic awareness helps beginning readers break the code. *Reading Teacher, 45,* 516–523.

Guszak, F.J. (1985). *Diagnostic reading instruction in the elementary school* (3rd ed.). New York: Harper & Row.

Hieronymous, A.N., Lindquist, E.F., & Hoover, H.D. (1983). *Iowa Tests of Basic Skills, Levels 7 & 8.* New York: Houghton Mifflin.

Johnston, P., & Allington, R. (1991). Remediation. In R. Barr, M.L. Kamil, P.B. Mosenthal, & P.D. Pearson (Eds.), *Handbook of reading research* (Vol. 2, pp. 984–1012). New York: Longman.

Juel, C. (1988). Learning to read and write: A longitudinal study of fifty-four children from first through fourth grade. *Journal of Educational Psychology, 80,* 437–447.

Juel, C. (1990). The role of decoding in early literacy instruction and assessment. In L.M. Morrow & J.K. Smith (Eds.), *Assessment for instruction in early literacy* (pp. 135–154). Englewood Cliffs, NJ: Prentice Hall.

Juel, C. (1991). Cross-age tutoring between student athletes and at-risk children. *Reading Teacher, 45,* 178–186.

Labbo, L.D., & Teale, W.H. (1990). Cross-age reading: A strategy for helping poor readers. *Reading Teacher, 43,* 362–369.

Lundberg, I., Frost, J., & Petersen, O. (1988). Effects of an extensive program for stimulating phonological awareness in preschool children. *Reading Research Quarterly, 23,* 263–284.

Morris, D. (1981). Concept of word: A developmental phenomenon in the beginning reading and writing processes. *Language Arts, 58,* 659–668.

Nagy, W.E., & Anderson, R.C. (1984). How many words are there in printed school English? *Reading Research Quarterly, 19,* 304–330.

Nurss, J.R., & McGauvran, M. (1976). *Metropolitan Readiness Tests, Level II.* New York: Harcourt Brace Jovanovich.

Perfetti, C.A. (1985). *Reading ability.* New York: Oxford University Press.

Petrosky, A. (1982). From story to essay: Reading and writing. *College Composition and Communication, 33*(1), 19–35.

Stanovich, K.E. (1980). Toward an interactive compensatory model of individual differences in the development of reading fluency. *Reading Research Quarterly, 16,* 32–71.

Stanovich, K.E. (1986). Matthew effects in reading: Some consequences of individual differences in the acquisition of literacy. *Reading Research Quarterly, 21,* 360–406.

Terry, W. (1984). *Bloods.* New York: Ballantine Books.

Treiman, R. (1992). The role of intrasyllabic units in learning to read and spell. In P.B. Gough, L.C. Ehri, & R. Treiman, (Eds.), *Reading acquisition* (pp. 65–106). Hillsdale, NJ: Erlbaum.

Wildsmith, B. (1982). *Cat on the mat.* New York: Oxford University Press.

▶ 4

Implementing Reading Recovery® in New York
Insights from the First Two Years

M. TRIKA SMITH-BURKE   ANGELA M. JAGGAR

*Smith-Burke and Jaggar discuss the first 2 years of imple-
mentation of Reading Recovery in 57 public schools from
inner city, urban, suburban and rural areas in New York.
Since the Reading Recovery Program was not yet fully
implemented in most schools, a total of 457 children were
served by the Reading Recovery program in 1990/1991. By
the end of the year, 78% of the program children, children
who received at least 60 lessons and/or who were successfully
discontinued (n = 328), were successfully discontinued from
the program; 86% of them scored at or above grade level at
the end of the year. In June, 211 children remained on the
waiting list; 71% of these children were reading below grade
level, even though many received some type of supplementary instruction. The authors conclude with a discussion of
the importance of the unique staff development program in
Reading Recovery, the problems of absenteeism that they
encountered across their training sites, and the need for good
literacy instruction within first-grade classrooms to
complement Reading Recovery.*

In the summer of 1988, the authors attended a presentation by Gay Su Pinnell of the Ohio State University on Reading Recovery at a New York State Department of Education meeting. After much excitement and discussion, an assistant commissioner asked the group: "Who is interested in bringing Reading Recovery to New York State?" Only two hands shot up, *ours*, because we had been working for several years on a joint comprehensive, early literacy proposal with colleagues at the Ohio State University. Similar to Clay (1987b), who wondered if Reading Recovery could transplant cross-culturally from New Zealand to the United States, Australia, and England, we also questioned whether Reading Recovery could be implemented successfully and sustained in New York public schools. Further, could Reading Recovery be a catalyst for change in classroom teaching? We also viewed Reading Recovery as a way to redefine inservice education through a new type of university-public school collaboration. The first challenge was to find support in our university and the public schools in order to implement the program.

With vague promises of support from the New York State Department of Education, we proposed a 3-year plan to the Dean of the School of Education, Health, Nursing, and Arts Professions. Assuming a leadership role, the Dean accepted the proposal in August and within a month Trika, one of the coauthors, was on her way to Ohio to spend a year learning about Reading Recovery at the Ohio State University.

In this chapter, we present a description of the key features of Reading Recovery, a brief overview of the New York University (NYU) pilot project, and describe the first year of program implementation. Following a summary of the major findings (see Jaggar & Smith-Burke, 1990; Jaggar & Smith-Burke, 1991b), we discuss some concerns and insights gained from 2 years of implementation of Reading Recovery in the metropolitan New York City area.

READING RECOVERY: A CLARIFICATION

Clay (1990) maintains that there are two problems an education system must solve: (1) how to provide excellent instruction in literacy, and (2) how, after 1 year of instruction, to deliver intensive opportunities to individuals who have difficulty with the established program. To intervene early in a positive, short-term manner, gives these children a second chance. Reading Recovery was designed specifically to provide this second chance. Clay refers to these opportunities as the first and second waves of instructional service. The third wave is long-term, specialized instruction for a small percentage of students.

Clay argues that a plan for systemic change requires an instructional component for children, an in-depth staff development component, and continual evaluation. Reading Recovery is often mistaken as an instructional program for just children. Many fail to see the importance of year long staff development and rigorous program evaluation. Clay stated that "Reading Recovery was not designed to be something a teacher does with individual children. It was designed to be used by an education system to reduce reading difficulties in its schools" (Pinnell, 1991). These three components are interconnected and essential. *No* specific part can stand alone and be called Reading Recovery.

The Instructional Component

Since first-graders' problems are only "confusions" (Clay, 1979), early intervention provides a greater chance of success and the instructional period in Reading Recovery is brief—usually 12 to 20 weeks. The target population is the lowest 20% of first grade children in reading (achievement) as determined by the Diagnostic Survey (Clay, 1979).

Reading Recovery instruction is theoretically based, not a collection of atheoretical teaching techniques found in other reading programs. The instructional framework

> *was developed from an interactionist view of reading continuous text, based on information theory which emphasizes how knowledge, strategies, and processes at each level of language organization expand and become interrelated. (Clay & Tuck, in preparation, p. 2)*

Unlike other programs, which stress item learning (e.g. letter-sound correspondences and words), the focus is on teaching for strategies (e.g., monitoring, searching for information, and self-correction), which can accelerate learning. Teachers support their students as they learn how to learn; they never do for the children what they can do for themselves. This leads to independent problem solving in new texts.

Children are successfully discontinued from the program only if: (1) they can read at the average (or above) class-level, and (2) they have a self-extending system (Clay, 1991). A self-extending system means that a child functions like a good reader who approaches texts strategically and continues to learn to read by reading.

The framework of the lesson consists of four major components: (1) the rereading of familiar books, (2) observing the child's independent reading, (3) writing, and (4) introducing and reading a new book (see Pinnell, Fried, & Estice, 1990). Optional components include fluent writing of words, letter identification and word analysis. The four components allow for several important instructional concepts, which facilitate reading acquisition.

Clay (1991) insists that reading and writing must emphasize meaning and use whole texts. As a result, hundreds of "little books" from different publishers have been assigned a level of difficulty and then field-tested. The procedure for assigning difficulty levels is based on Clay's theory of reading acquisition (see Peterson, 1991).

First, Clay argues that it is a disservice to children to limit their access to textual information by emphasizing one particular cueing system (e.g., sound-symbol regularity). Natural language texts provide the full array of information (i.e., meaning, language structure, and visual-sound cues) and allow the child to integrate the use of all cueing systems.

Second, Clay (1979, 1991) argues that children need two kinds of reading: (1) they need to read fluently to practice and orchestrate what they know, and (2) they need to read challenging material to extend learning. Each lesson begins with familiar rereading of previously read books. The focus is on fluent reading or "sounding like a good reader." During the latter part of the lesson, a challenging new book (i.e., a book at the instructional level) is introduced. This provides opportunities for the child to problem solve with the support of the teacher, who selects teaching points to move the child's learning forward. These challenges change as the child's skill progresses. For example, format changes initially provide new learning opportunities for a child who is learning one-to-one matching. Later in the program, text style or words with more complex spelling patterns offer the challenges.

Third, Clay argues that during literacy acquisition children need both reading and writing experiences. Using a global strategy, children initially rely on meaning and language structure to read: writing slows the processing, forcing them to focus on the details of print in relation to meaning (Clay, 1975, 1987a). Consequently, there is a writing component built into the lesson before reading a new book. The child creates a message and writes it with the help of the teacher. As they work together, the teacher helps the child learn how to hear the sounds in words and how to fluently write high frequency words. It is the teacher's responsibility to help the child use the knowledge derived from writing in their reading and vice versa.

Fourth, in order to teach effectively and accelerate learning efficiently, the teacher must know what the child knows about reading. Observation is the basis for tailoring each lesson to each child. No two lessons are the same. After the familiar rereading, the teacher takes a running record of the child independently reading the new book that was introduced the preceding day. Since the child has read this book once or twice with instructional support, the running record allows the teacher to see if the child has taken on new behaviors (i.e., evidence of new, cognitive strategies) and whether the teaching has been effective. The analysis of the running record, as well as observations from other parts of the lesson, provide the basis of instruction for the next day.

Teachers must be well trained professionals, to carry out this moment-to-moment decision making and careful observation of children. Through observation, they begin to understand Clay's grounded theory of reading and writing acquisition. They also learn the menu of possible teaching techniques and how to relate them to the strategic thinking of young readers.

The Staff Development Component

Three important roles in Reading Recovery are: (1) the university-based trainer of teacher leaders, (2) the field-based teacher leader (i.e., teacher trainer), and (3) the Reading Recovery teacher. The "three-tiered system" of staff development is essentially an old tradition—teachers teaching teachers—cast in a new form (i.e., teacher leader trainers, teacher leaders, and Reading Recovery teachers). The participants must be volunteers because to learn and carry out Reading Recovery, at every level, requires a major commitment of time and energy as well as a shift in thinking.

Everyone involved in the program is required to teach children. Learning is a continuous process and teachers must continually observe in order to test their own theories about children's learning (Clay, 1991). Consequently, the staff development program includes continuing education sessions for both teacher leaders and teachers, beyond the first year of training. Affiliation with a university further assures that new theory and research will continue to influence practice.

The primary goal of staff development is the growth of professionals who are skilled observers and can articulate the teaching decisions they have made and the rationale for making them. Clay recognized that the shifts in thinking required to implement Reading Recovery would take more interactive sessions in the United States, a country where classroom instruction tends to be based on instructional packages (i.e., basal programs) and not the observation of children. Consequently, she designed the inservice course to last 1 full year with weekly meetings as compared with meetings every 2 weeks in New Zealand (see Clay, 1987b).

Program Implementation and Evaluation

Clay realized that to be effective and bring about systemic change, a district must train enough teachers to service the lowest 20% to 25% of first-grade children. She refers to this as "full implementation" of the program.

Implementing a Reading Recovery program requires a major commitment from districts to educate concerned parties on the benefits of prevention, which minimizes the need for remediation. Unlike other programs, Reading Recovery requires the support of parents, teachers, support staff, and administrators in order to create a successful program. Long-range planning, as well as year-to-year planning, is essential in order to reach full implementation.

Consistent and continuous evaluation that provides information on how to improve implementation is critical to the success of the program. The

Reading Recovery teacher takes a daily Running Record for each child and records what the child is able to write during that specific portion of the lesson. A weekly book graph with the child's text reading level and a record of writing vocabulary are also maintained. In addition, data are collected on each child in the fall on entry to instruction, on exit from the program, and at year end; sometimes the collection dates coincide. For comparison, data are collected from a random sample of the remaining first-grade children in the classrooms from which Reading Recovery children are selected.

With full implementation and the support and collaboration of school personnel, Reading Recovery can be very successful. As Clay (1987b) states:

> . . . *my personal orientation in developing Reading Recovery was to take ac-count of the complex interdependence among parts of the system. . . . A new attack on this problem was needed, and it called for more than an analysis of the counterforces that could be operating when a new programme is tried.*
>
> *The origins of progress would lie in the child-teacher interactions but the success of the programme would also depend on many other variables. Support at several levels of the education system would be necessary for an effective program. . . . In an effective system intervention the interdependence of variables demands a systemic plan, for an innovation cannot move into an education system merely on the merits of what it can do for children. (p. 38)*

In order to be successful with the lowest 20%, Reading Recovery must be fully implemented in a district. In addition, the school district must work to ensure there is good classroom literacy instruction. Particularly in inner city settings where many children are not learning to read and write successfully, a comprehensive approach is necessary. This includes good classroom instruction and Reading Recovery for the children who are most at-risk.

NYU PILOT PROJECT AND FIRST YEAR OF IMPLEMENTATION: 1989–1991

In 1989, (NYU) became the first Reading Recovery Teacher Leader Training site in the Northeast. NYU prepares teacher leaders who, following a year of intensive training, are qualified to train Reading Recovery teachers at sites in their local school districts or regions. The project is a cooperative venture between the university and a school district or a consortium of districts that have made the required long-term commitment to implement Reading Recovery.

During the pilot year, 1989/1990, NYU trained six teacher leaders for five teacher training sites in New York State and a class of 12 Reading Recovery teachers: four from Community School District #2 (CSD #2) in New York City, seven from public schools in Westchester County, and one from an independent school in New York City. The teacher training class also served as a laboratory for the teacher leaders in-training.

A total of 106 first-grade children, representing inner city, urban, and suburban school districts, were served by the teachers and leaders in-training in 1989/1990. By the end of the year, 57% of the children who received a full program of instruction had been successfully discontinued, that is, released because they had achieved the goals of the program. A large proportion of the children who were successful in the pilot project scored within or above the average band for their grade level on the three dependent measures: Writing Vocabulary (82%), Dictation (100%), and Text Reading (97%). Furthermore, these Reading Recovery children exceeded the mean score of the average band for their grade level on all three measures. Based on the encouraging pilot year results (see Jaggar and Smith-Burke, 1990), the program was expanded in the second year.

During 1990/1991, the six previously trained teacher leaders implemented the program and trained 56 new Reading Recovery teachers at five sites in New York State: Community School District #2 in New York City, Glens Falls, Newburgh City, Putnam/Northern Westchester Board of Cooperative Educational Services (BOCES), and the Suffolk #2 BOCES at Shoreham Wading River. Fifty-seven public schools in 26 school districts were involved in the project. The districts represented a wide geographic distribution and included inner city, urban, suburban, and rural schools. During this first year of program implementation, NYU provided technical assistance and continuing education to the teacher leaders at the five training sites and trained an additional nine teacher leaders for sites located in New York, New Jersey, and Maine.

The children selected for Reading Recovery instruction at the five sites were in the lowest 20% of the first-grade classes in their respective schools in reading, as determined by teacher judgment and the Diagnostic Survey (Clay, 1979). A total of 457 children (54% boys, 46% girls) at the sites in New York received individualized Reading Recovery tutoring during 1990/1991. The children represented different ethnic and racial groups: Black (26%), Hispanic (18%), White–Non-Hispanic (47%), Asian (6%), and Native American (2%). Forty-nine percent were in a free or reduced-price lunch program. For many children, particularly in urban areas, English was not their native language.

The following section reports the results for 1990/1991. It is followed by a discussion of the insights gained from our first 2 years of involvement in Reading Recovery.

First Year Results: 1990/1991

The goal of the 1990/1991 evaluation was to gather data and identify specific strengths of the program and areas for improvement. Comparisons were made among several groups of children, using four tasks from the Diagnostic Survey (Clay, 1979): The tasks were: (1) the Ohio Word Test, Forms A and B, each consisting of 20 high frequency words; (2) writing vocabulary (all the words a child can write with some prompting in 10 minutes); (3) a dictation task where children are read a sentence and asked to write the words; and (4) text reading of passages in graded levels of difficulty where the score represents the highest level passage read at 90% accuracy or above.

Fall and spring data were used to compare the progress of Reading Recovery children to: (1) a *random sample* selected from the population of other first graders who were not eligible for Reading Recovery (this group provided a basis for determining a site average band), and (2) *waiting list* children who were diagnosed in the fall as being in need of Reading Recovery but who did not receive the specialized tutoring and remained on the waiting list at the end of the year.

Further comparisons were made of the progress of three groups of Reading Recovery children. These groups were: (1) program children who were successfully discontinued, (2) program children who were not successfully discontinued, and (3) nonprogram children. Previous research in Ohio (conducted by the Ohio State University and the Columbus Public Schools) indicates that successful completion of the program usually requires a minimum of 10 to 12 weeks, including 2 weeks of Roaming Around the Known (a diagnostic period) and 8 to 10 weeks of daily lessons. Some children will take longer than that period to achieve success, particularly those with limited English proficiency. Others will be discontinued in less time. However, 60 lessons represents a good estimate of the minimum time needed to complete a full program. Reading Recovery *program children* are defined as all children who received 60 or more lessons or were successfully discontinued. *Nonprogram children* are defined as those children who received less than 60 lessons during the year.

Number Served and Successfully Discontinued

We were interested in knowing how many children received a full program of instruction and what percentage of these children were successfully discontinued. Reading Recovery children are successfully discontinued (i.e., released) from the program when, and only when, they are reading at or above the average of their class and demonstrate a self-extending system (see Clay, 1979; 1991).

Table 4-1 shows that, of the 457 children who received Reading Recovery instruction in 1990/1991, 328 (72%) were program children while 129 (28%) were nonprogram children. Of the 328 program children, 257 (78%) successfully completed the program during the school year. The percent of discontinued program children ranged from 64% in CSD #2 in New York City to 90% at the Putnam/Northern Westchester BOCES site.

TABLE 4-1 End of Year Status of Children Served and Percent Successfully Discontinued Year Two, 1990–1991

Site	Number Served	Non Program Children	Program Children	Discontinued	Discontinuing Rate
		End of School Year Status			
CSD #2, New York City	139	42 (30%)	97 (70%)	62	64%
Glens Falls	70	25 (36%)	45 (64%)	35	78%
Newburgh City	72	21 (14%)	51 (71%)	45	88%
Putnam/Northern Westchester BOCES	130	30 (2%)	100 (77%)	90	90%
Suffolk 2 BOCES at Shoreham-Wading River	38	10 (2%)	28 (74%)	19	68%
Little Red Schoolhouse	8	1 (1%)	7 (88%)	6	86%
TOTAL	**457**	**129 (28%)**	**328 (72%)**	**257**	**78%**
		End of Summer Status			
CSD #2, New York City	457*	129 (28%) **	328 (72%) ***	10	74%
GRAND TOTAL	**457***	**129 (28%) ****	**328 (72%) *****	**267 ******	**81%**

* Includes all children served regardless of time spent in the program.
** Students who received less than 60 lessons, including 26 (6%) who moved (16) or were withdrawn to special education (10).
*** Students with at least 60 lessons or successfully discontinued; figure represents 72% of all children served.
**** Students who successfully completed the program and were discontinued. This figure represents 81.4% of the program children and 58.4% of all children served.

Furthermore, 10 children in CSD #2, who were program children in June but had not been discontinued, received additional Reading Recovery instruction during the summer. These were children who had demonstrated accelerated learning but did not have time to complete the program. All 10 successfully completed the program, making the final discontinuing rate in New York City 74%. This raised the total number of children who were successfully discontinued in New York State to 267, or 81% of the program population. This represents 58% of the total served.

The results of the summer program in CSD #2 are noteworthy. This may be the first successful attempt in the United States at using a summer program to extend instructional time. These efforts should be replicated and studied further to see if the children maintain their gains, since they did not have additional time in the classroom to consolidate their learning after discontinuation from the program.

When released, the 267 children who were successfully discontinued from Reading Recovery during the first year of program implementation were reading at or above the average of their first-grade class and functioning as independent learners. Most important, they are expected to continue to make progress in the classroom and need no additional special help or remediation.

Among the Reading Recovery children were a substantial number whose first language is not English. We eventually plan to systematically document the effects of language background on length of instruction. Informal observations by teachers suggest that children who are less proficient in English can successfully participate in Reading Recovery but may take somewhat longer than native English speakers. Clay (personal communication, May 1991) reports that this is also true in New Zealand.

The overall discontinuing rate of 78% was substantially higher than that attained in the pilot study (57%). This is excellent for the first year of implementation, considering that most of the teachers (56 of 74) who provided Reading Recovery instruction to children in 1990/1991 were in their training year. As trained teachers gain more skill and districts provide the support required for program success, improvement is expected at these program sites in the future.

For the purposes of this chapter, results presented in the following sections are based on end-of-school-year data for the 1990/1991 school year.

Progress of the Discontinued Children

Clay (1979, 1991) argues that when children are discontinued from the program they should continue to make progress through independent reading and classroom instruction; they should need no additional help. Our findings support this position.

We compared the entry, exit, and end-of-year scores of 96 children who

TABLE 4-2   Progress of Children Successfully Discontinued Prior to April 15

Measure	Entry	Exit	End-of-Year
Word Test (Max = 20)	0.78	14.98	18.94
Writing Vocabulary (10 Mins)	7.22	42.91	53.48
Dictation (Max = 37)	11.15	34.55	35.80
Text Reading (Max = 30)	1.00	13.75	23.01

N = 96

were discontinued 2 months prior to the final testing on the four measures of the Diagnostic Survey. As Table 4-2 shows, these first graders continued to make progress after returning to the classroom. These children illustrate the concept of a self-extending system (Clay, 1991), having made an average gain of 9.26 levels in text reading from the time they exited the program to year end with no further special intervention.

The progress of the successfully discontinued program children, as well as that of the total program group, was assessed by comparing their end-of-year performance to a random sample of first graders at the five sites. The scores of the random sample children were used to calculate an average band, defined as .5 standard deviation above and below the mean. In computing the average band, children who received any Reading Recovery lessons or were on the waiting list were deleted from the sample. Thus, the performance of Reading Recovery children was measured against that of children who began the school year at substantially higher levels of achievement.

The first comparison showed that a large proportion of the successfully discontinued children scored within or above the average band for their grade level on Word Recognition (86%), Writing Vocabulary (84%), Dictation (96%), and Text Reading (93%). Results indicated that a substantial percent of the total Reading Recovery Program group, including those who were and were not discontinued, also scored within or above the average band on the four measures: 77%, 76%, 90%, and 77%, respectively.

Another comparison indicated that both groups, the successfully discontinued children and the total program group, attained end-of-year mean scores that fell within the average band on all four measures: the Word Test, Writing Vocabulary, Dictation, and Text Reading. In addition, the discontinued group attained a higher mean score than the random sample on all four dependent measures.

Figure 4-1 illustrates the impressive gains made in reading by Reading Recovery program children. The progress of the successfully discontinued children and the total program group is compared to the progress of waiting list children. The waiting list sample comprises those children diagnosed in

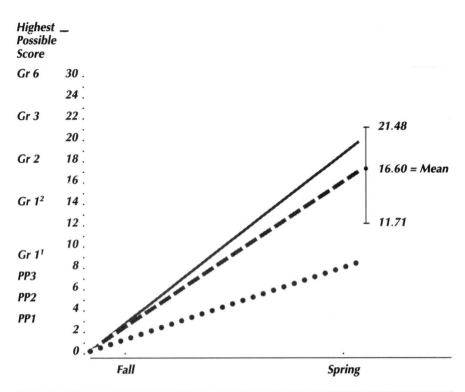

FIGURE 4-1 Comparison of Successfully Discontinued Children, Total Program Group and Waiting List Children to First Grade Average Band on Text Reading

September as students who could benefit from the individualized tutoring but who did not receive Reading Recovery instruction during the year. Two hundred thirty children remained on the waiting lists at the six program sites. Two hundred eleven to 216 children were tested again in June on the four dependent measures.

At the start of the school year, the Reading Recovery program children (discontinued and not discontinued) and the waiting list children were all in the lowest 20% of their first-grade cohort. On average, both groups recognized less than 1 out of 20 high frequency words, could write no more than 4 to 6 words and, as Figure 4-1 shows, scored less than 1 on text reading, beginning readiness material, at the start of first grade. (Reading Recovery text reading level passages are correlated with basal levels for comparison purposes.) By the end of the year, however, the discontinued children, on average, were able to read with 90% accuracy at level 19, second grade material; whereas the waiting list children were only able to read passages at level 8, which is roughly equivalent to the third preprimer. In fact, none of the mean scores of the waiting list group fell within the average band for their grade level on the four measures.

These results are even more striking when data from a follow-up survey revealed that while 49% of the waiting list children received classroom reading instruction only, 51% received compensatory reading or other services in addition to classroom instruction during the year. These compensatory and other services included: small group Chapter 1 or PSEN reading instruction, individualized reading instruction by an aide, resource room instruction, early intervention programs other than Reading Recovery, English as a Second Language (ESL) instruction, speech and language instruction, and, at a few sites, small-group reading instruction specifically for waiting list children as provided by a Reading Recovery teacher. Some waiting list children received more than one compensatory service.

Table 4-3 provides another view of the progress of the successfully discontinued children. The table shows the percent of discontinued children who scored at each text reading level at the end of the year, compared to two other Reading Recovery groups—program children who had received 60 or more lessons but were not discontinued by year end and nonprogram children who received less than 60 lessons, and to the comparison groups made up of random sample and waiting list children. The end-of-year means, standard deviations, and mean gains are presented for all groups as well as the mean number of lessons and weeks of instruction for the three Reading Recovery groups.

If one assumes that by the end of first grade children can be expected to score at a 1^2 level, then the data reveals that 86% of the successfully discontinued children were reading at or above grade level, compared to 62% of the random sample and only 29% of the waiting list children. Note that after a year of first-grade classroom reading instruction or classroom instruction plus compensatory services, 28% of the waiting list children were able to read passages only roughly equivalent to materials generally thought to be at the readiness level.

The results show that the discontinued Reading Recovery children made strikingly greater gains in text reading than both the not discontinued program children and the nonprogram group. Comparisons of the progress of the program children who were not discontinued and nonprogram children

TABLE 4-3 Percentage of Reading Recovery, Random Sample, and Waiting List Children Scoring at Each Text Reading Level At End of School Year

Sample Size	Random Sample (397)	Reading Recovery Children		Non Program Group (103)*	Waiting List Children (211)
		Not Discontinued (68)	Discontinued Children (245)		
0–2 Readiness	18 (5%)	2 (3%)	0	3 (3%)	58 (28%)
3–4 Preprimer 1	18 (5%)	5 (7%)	0	16 (16%)	32 (15%)
5–6 Preprimer 2	35 (9%)	11 (16%)	0	30 (29%)	22 (10%)
7–8 Preprimer 3	31 (8%)	15 (22%)	3 (1%)	20 (19%)	15 (7%)
9–12 Primer 1[1]	45 (11%)	29 (43%)	34 (13%)	25 (24%)	23 (11%)
SUBTOTAL	**147 (38%)**	**62 (91%)**	**37 (14%)**	**91 (91%)**	**150 (71%)**
On or Above Grade Level					
14–16 Grade 1[2]	39 (10%)	4 (6%)	60 (24%)	8 (8%)	15 (7%)
18–20 Grade 2	49 (12%)	2 (3%)	70 (28%)	1 (1%)	16 (8%)
22–24 Grade 3	57 (14%)	0	52 (20%)	0	20 (9%)
26–30 Grade 4–6	105 (26%)	0	35 (14%)	0	10 (5%)
SUBTOTAL	**250 (62%)**	**6 (9%)**	**217 (86%)**	**9 (9%)**	**61 (29%)**
N	444	71	254	103	215
Mean	**16.60**	**8.65**	**18.96**	**7.47**	**8.81**
SD	9.61	3.76	5.60	3.65	8.52
Range	0–30	0–20	8–30	0–18	0–30
MEAN GAIN	**12.45**	**8.24**	**18.13**	**6.83**	**8.30**
Lessons					
Mean #	*	95.85	59.80	21.64	
Range	*	60–132	3–127	0–57	
Weeks					
Mean #	*	29.46	21.31	8.56	
Range	*	16–36	3–34	1–19	

*Excludes the 26 nonprogram children who moved or were withdrawn to special education during the year.

76

revealed some interesting findings. The nonprogram children received an average of 22 lessons (range from 0 to 57) over an average of 9 weeks. Data revealed that 70% did not have enough time to complete 60 lessons because they entered the program in April or later in the school year. However, preliminary analysis indicates that the nonprogram children made almost as much progress as the program children who were not discontinued, even though the former group was in the program a shorter time. We are conducting further analysis that should provide insights on other variables (e.g., attendance, teaching effectiveness) that had an impact on the progress of these two groups of Reading Recovery children.

DISCUSSION

The overall end-of-year discontinuing rate of 78% and end-of-summer discontinuing rate of 81% in the first year of program implementation is excellent, considering that 73% of the teachers who provided Reading Recovery instruction were in their training year. The results corroborate earlier research on Reading Recovery that shows that good teaching, which is theory-based and responsive to individual needs, can have a significant impact on children's literacy development.

Impact of Program on Teachers

The success of Reading Recovery is due to its unique staff development program which is based on a model of collaborative learning. It provides teachers with demonstrations and time to practice what they are learning. It asks teachers to observe children closely, discuss what they see, problem solve with colleagues, critically analyze their assumptions, and consider instructional alternatives. It also requires that they talk and reflect on their teaching decisions and their knowledge of children, learning, and the reading process. (See Pinnell [1985] for a detailed description of the rationale and components of the staff development program).

One measure of the success of the staff development program is reflected in the children's reading progress. Another measure is the level of satisfaction expressed by the teachers in their comments about the impact of the program on their own development. The following comments are drawn from an analysis of teacher responses to a questionnaire that asked teachers about their views on Reading Recovery (reported in Jaggar & Smith-Burke, 1991a).

Reading Recovery is based on the assumption that teachers have a sound knowledge of the reading process. When asked how their views of that process and of the teaching of reading had changed, some responded that their views had shifted dramatically away from a skills approach to a more holistic orientation. For example:

I used to be a skills oriented teacher. Phonics in isolation was a big part of my teaching of reading and working for accuracy in reading was important to me also. I went from a skills oriented approach to a meaning approach. I now see reading as an active process whereby the child uses strategies to learn how to become an independent reader. (Jaggar & Smith-Burke, 1991a, p. 14)

Others stated that their concepts of reading had not changed radically. Instead they found a deeper understanding of the process itself:

I think I understand the process of learning reading and language a lot better. My ideas on teaching reading had already been changing or had changed. I understand why now! I have a better idea of how it [learning to read] happens and where we have gone astray with past instruction. (Jaggar & Smith-Burke, 1991a, p. 15)

Other comments focused on new insights about the reading-writing connection and the importance of teaching strategies:

I had not understood until this year the importance of writing in the reading process. I had thought it played a secondary role. (Jaggar & Smith-Burke, 1991a, p. 15)

I see the . . .learning of strategies, which are actually problem-solving techniques, as vital and related to all learning. (Teacher leader in-training, NYU) (Jaggar & Smith-Burke, 1991a, p. 15)

Reading Recovery is based on the assumption that teachers need detailed knowledge of the child to make effective moment-to-moment instructional decisions. This knowledge can be acquired only through close observation. As one teacher in CSD #2 said, "I have learned the importance of observing children and building on their strengths." Another wrote:

The concept of observing children, while not entirely new to me, proved to be fascinating when I went about it in a systematic way. I will never teach the same way again. (Jaggar & Smith-Burke, 1991a, p. 17)

Furthermore, the program is based on the view that all children can learn. When asked to describe how their views of children changed, several reported that they now view children as active rather than passive learners, and recognize that all children, including those who are having difficulty learning to read and write, bring knowledge to their learning experiences. They also grew to understand the importance of building on a child's strengths, having high expectations, and holding children responsible for their own learning.

The following statements (Jaggar & Smith-Burke, 1991a) reflect these changes in teachers' views:

I now focus on children's strengths . . .rather than their weaknesses. (p. 16)

[My view] continues to evolve and I have more confidence in each child's ability to learn. (p. 16)

I now realize how much even the weakest child knows and [I] think in terms of strategic learning rather than items of knowledge. If I were to go into the classroom tomorrow, I would approach other subjects from a strategic view rather than a skills approach. (p. 16)

I have always believed that all children can learn to read. However, while I believed this, I did not hold individual children responsible for [learning]. I accepted much that I should not have and realize now that I wasn't doing these children any favors. I now have not only the expectation that a child will become a reader, I'm holding the child responsible to become one. (p. 16)

Finally, when asked to comment on the ways Reading Recovery contributed to their growth as a teacher, many commented that they felt more confident and were more reflective about their teaching. The following statements (Jaggar & Smith-Burke, 1991a) illustrate this:

In my 16 years of teaching, I never felt better able to help children learn to read. (p. 17)

I have become more reflective, much less apt to generalize about kids, much more accountable to myself and to the kids on a daily basis. (p. 17)

I find myself examining and reexamining what I'm trying as a teacher. . . . I'm also writing things down more to go back to read and think about. (p. 17)

Most importantly, teachers reported that they were treated like and, therefore, felt like professionals.

Reading Recovery has helped me to be more flexible, more sensitive to the children's needs, and to become a more reflective person. I feel like a professional. I feel like I am constantly growing and learning. (p. 17)

Some Issues and Concerns

There are issues that need to be addressed in order to increase program effectiveness. Though successful with 78% of the program children who participated in the first year, we need to find ways to increase the success rate, which is the number of children successfully discontinued as well as the total number served. Here, we focus on two critical issues: (1) loss of instructional time, and (2) classroom instruction. Combined with other issues they create synergistic forces that positively support or negatively impede program effectiveness. First, we present the issues and, second, we follow with specific recommendations for dealing with the problems.

Loss of Instructional Time

We found that loss of instructional time was a key factor in program effectiveness. Absenteeism was, and still is, a major problem in both urban and suburban schools. Reading Recovery is designed to be a short-term program. Children need five lessons per week for accelerated learning to occur, however, many children were frequently absent. Table 4-3 shows that the children who successfully completed the program did so in an average of 60 lessons that took place over an average of 19 weeks of instruction. In Reading Recovery, 19 weeks of instruction usually includes 2 weeks of Roaming Around the Known (a diagnostic period) and 17 weeks of daily lessons or a total of 85 lessons. Even allowing for shorter school weeks because of holidays, it is clear that many children were frequently absent. This was particularly true for the program children who were *not* successfully discontinued. They received an average of 96 lessons that took place over an average of 30 weeks, which usually consists of 135 lessons. The data indicate that, for many children, the instruction was spread out over the entire year, diluting its effectiveness.

The reasons for missing instruction differed in urban and suburban contexts. Most children in urban schools missed Reading Recovery instruction because they simply did not come to school. Although school absence was not as extensive in the suburban schools, children missed Reading Recovery lessons because they attended numerous special events—such as class trips, school entertainment programs, or other specialized instruction. Often sessions could not be made up due to the inflexibility in most schedules.

Teacher absences from Reading Recovery were also a problem. In urban and suburban schools, teachers were frequently pulled out to cover other classes, take lunch duty, or attend meetings. This problem stems from the fact that many schools are understaffed or the administration does not fully understand the importance of consistent, short-term instruction in the Reading Recovery program. Often, the immediate pressing issue (e.g., lunch or bus duty) takes precedence over other services.

The attendance problem must be addressed if Reading Recovery is to have the impact it is designed to have. Successful school districts have established policies to deal with children's unexcused absences through a system designed to monitor attendance. Reading Recovery teachers are encouraged to proactively contact parents because they realize that *not* reporting absences and *not* doing something about them has a negative impact on the child's progress. In situations where parent-teacher communication was proactive and consistent, parents would bring children in for their Reading Recovery lessons, even if they kept them home for the rest of the day.

A comprehensive team effort is needed, particularly in urban schools, to support Reading Recovery and classroom teachers. The guidance counselor, the social or community worker, the principal, the school psychologist, the school nurse, the classroom teacher, the Reading Recovery teacher, and the parents need to work as a team *with parents* to solve problems and prevent absenteeism. Absenteeism might be viewed as an indicator that parents may need more support to help their children succeed (see Richardson, Casanova, Placier, & Guilfoyle, 1989, for an interesting model).

Schools wrestle with priorities such as how children and teachers spend their time. If Reading Recovery is to be effective, special events need to be limited during the brief period of Reading Recovery instruction. Reading Recovery instruction that occurs daily for all children is a necessity if the program is going to have its intended impact.

Classroom Instruction

A second instructional issue returns to Clay's (1990) suggestion about good literacy instruction—namely, that there must be good literacy instruction in classrooms as well as a second chance (i.e., a program like Reading Recovery) for children having the most difficulty after 1 year of school, which is the kindergarten year in the United States. In schools in which Reading Recovery teachers and the classroom teachers share a common theoretical perspective on literacy development, work as a team, and discuss the progress of their Reading Recovery children, accelerated learning is supported and enhanced. However, our informal observations in classrooms raised serious questions about the literacy instruction provided in many of the schools that participated in the Reading Recovery project.

What should good literacy instruction look like in a supportive first-grade classroom? Clay (1979, 1991) and others (Goodman et al., 1987; Holdaway, 1979; McKenzie, 1986; Smith, 1988) argue that beginning reading instruction must be meaning-centered, use whole texts, and facilitate strategic processing, not the teaching of item knowledge (i.e., sound-symbol correspondences and words). As Clay (1979) states:

> *The child cannot afford to spend much time practicing detail, and he may become addicted to it and find it difficult later to take a wider approach to the reading act. [The teacher must realize] that knowledge of the detail is of very limited value on its own. It must in the end be used in the service of reading continuous text. Details must receive attention but always in a subsidiary status to message getting. (p. 53)*

Clay (1979, 1991) also argues that to carry out effective instruction, teachers must closely observe children's reading and writing behavior and *base their instructional decisions on these observations*. This is almost impossible if teachers depend on materials and predetermined instructional sequences in commercial programs (i.e., basals) because there is no way that such programs can take individual differences into account.

To summarize, effective teachers observe children closely and make instructional decisions based on these observations—adjusting the curriculum as they teach to fit the children—not just carrying out a program based on a manual. They have a command of a wide variety of books, both easy and challenging, that they want children to read. Literacy instruction is meaningful and purposeful. It helps children learn about print in the context of authentic reading and writing and focuses on both the process and the product. These teachers do so because they understand the psycholinguistic nature of the reading process (Clay, 1991; Goodman, 1975; Smith, 1988).

What did we observe? In many classrooms—whether basal or more holistic—we observed prepared environments, telling, or children left on their own. There was minimal teaching. Teachers were unfamiliar with ways to observe children and how to use this information as the basis for planning or modifying their instruction.

In basal/skills-oriented classrooms, there was little emphasis on reading as meaningful; children rarely read continuous text or wrote for communicative purposes. Much of the reading instruction we observed consisted of having children complete workbook pages or skill sheets, confirming Osborn's (1984) findings. We encountered teachers who believed firmly that children should not skip a single page in the basal reader and related workbook materials, even when they are able to read and write. These teachers failed to recognize the success of the Reading Recovery children and often would not promote them to a higher reading group. In other situations, the discontinued children were not permitted to shift to a higher level reading group because of their work habits or behavior.

In more holistic classrooms, teachers frequently read aloud to children and provided opportunities for them to read easy books and to write. However, an active instructional role on the part of the teacher was often missing. There were few opportunities for students to learn problem solving and interact with challenging texts. Children who invent text and are not helped to negotiate the print system (i.e., understand how speech relates to print), sometimes develop the misconception that reading is simply inventing the text—a belief that can be counterproductive if allowed to go unchallenged for too long.

Some teachers, new to holistic instruction, were aware of their lack of knowledge and experience in helping children figure out how the print system works. They commented that workshops never seemed to go beyond a superficial level. These teachers knew that they needed to assist children in learning about print, but were not sure how to do it in ways that remain consistent with holistic theory and practice.

To bring about needed changes in teaching, a school district must have a plan for on-going staff development that includes demonstrations, collaboration, opportunities for practice, and time for reflection. In our experience, staff development is most effective when it is school-based and teachers have the opportunity to interact with their peers and with their mentors who work with teachers and children in the classrooms. As Tharp and Gallimore (1988) insist, in *Rousing Minds to Life*, teachers need support to change and become better at what they do.

One Reading Recovery staffing model has great potential for bringing about change in literacy teaching. A Reading Recovery teacher who has a broad knowledge base—familiarity with writing process, shared reading and writing, response to literature, integrating language across the curriculum—and has experience in staff development may serve as a mentor, supporting classroom teachers in their quest to improve literacy instruction. (For an example, see *Transitions*, Routman, 1988.)

Although the evidence shows that a large proportion of children who receive Reading Recovery instruction will become successful readers, it is abundantly clear that Reading Recovery alone is not sufficient enough to address the critical issues facing schools today, particularly our urban schools. What is needed is a comprehensive approach to early literacy instruction, which includes good classroom literacy instruction for all children and effective short-term, early intervention, namely Reading Recovery, for those children who are having the most difficulty learning to read and write.

REFERENCES

Clay, M.M. (1975). *What did I write?* Portsmouth, NH: Heinemann Educational Books.

Clay, M.M. (1979). *Early detection of reading difficulties* (3rd ed.). Portsmouth, NH: Heinemann Educational Books.

Clay, M.M. (1987a). *Writing begins at home*. Portsmouth, NH: Heinemann Educational Books.

Clay, M.M. (1987b). Implementing Reading Recovery: Systemic adaptations to an educational innovation. *New Zealand Journal of Educational Studies, 22*(1), 35–58.

Clay, M.M. (1990). The Reading Recovery Programme, 1984–1988: Coverage, outcomes and education board district figures. *New Zealand Journal of Educational Studies, 25*(1), 61–70.

Clay, M.M. (1991). *Becoming literate: The construction of inner control*. Portsmouth, NH: Heinemann Educational Books.

Clay, M.M. & Tuck, B. (in preparation). *A study of Reading Recovery subgroups: Including outcomes for children who did not satisfy discontinuing criteria*. Technical Report prepared for the Ministry of Education, Wellington, New Zealand.

Goodman, K.S. (1975). Reading: A psycholinguistic guessing game. In H. Singer & R. Ruddell (Eds.), *Theoretical models and processes of reading* (2nd ed.) pp. 259–272. Newark, DE: International Reading Association.

Goodman, K.S., Smith, E.B., Meredith, R. & Goodman, Y.M. (1987). *Language and thinking in school* (3rd ed.). New York: Richard C. Owen.

Holdaway, D. (1979). *The foundations of literacy*. New York: Ashton Scholastic.

Jaggar, A.M. & Smith-Burke, M.T. (1990). *Reading Recovery™ project, technical report no. 1: Pilot year, 1989–1990*. New York: New York University.

Jaggar, A.M. & Smith-Burke, M.T. (1991a). *Reading Recovery™ voices: Teachers, administrators and parents, 1990–1991*. New York: New York University.

Jaggar, A.M. & Smith-Burke, M.T. (1991b). *Reading Recovery™ project, technical report no. 3, year 2, 1990–1991*. New York: New York University.

McKenzie, M. (1986). *Journeys into literacy*. Hudderson, England: Schofield & Sims, Ltd.

Osborn, J. (1984). The purposes, uses, and contents of workbooks and some guidelines for publishers. In R.C. Anderson, J. Osborn, & R.J. Tierney (Eds.), *Learning to read in American schools* (pp. 45–111). Hillsdale, NJ: Lawrence Erlbaum.

Peterson, B. (1991). Selecting books for beginning readers children's literature suitable for young readers: A bibliography. In D. DeFord, C. Lyons, & G.S. Pinnell (Eds.), *Bridges to Literacy: Learning from Reading Recovery* (pp. 119–147). Portsmouth, NH: Heinemann Educational Books.

Pinnell, G.S. (1985). Helping teachers help children at risk: Insights from the Reading Recovery Program. *Peabody Journal of Education, 62*(3), 70–85.

Pinnell, G.S. (1991, October). *Reading Recovery: A success-oriented system for the future.* Paper presented at the second New England Reading Recovery Conference, Nashua, NH.

Pinnell, G.S., Fried, M.D., & Estice, R.M. (1990). Reading Recovery: Learning how to make a difference. In D. DeFord, C.A. Lyons, & G.S. Pinnell (Eds.), *Bridges to Literacy: Learning from Reading Recovery* (pp. 11–35). Portsmouth, NH: Heinemann Educational Books.

Richardson, V., Casanova, U., Placier, P., and Guildfoyle, K. (1989). *School children at-risk*. New York: Falmer Press.

Routman, R. (1988). *Transitions*. Portsmouth, NH: Heinemann Educational Books.

Smith, F. (1988). *Understanding reading* (4th ed.). Hillsdale, NJ: Lawrence Erlbaum.

Tharp, R.G. & Gallimore, R. (1988). *Rousing minds to life: Teaching, learning and schooling in social context.* New York: Cambridge University Press.

▶ 5

A Small-Group Literacy Intervention With Chapter 1 Students

ELFRIEDA H. HIEBERT

Hiebert describes an intervention program that was developed with Chapter 1 teachers in which the teachers worked with three children in half-hour sessions on repetitive reading, writing, and guidance on the words in texts that emphasized phonemic awareness and word patterns. The Chapter 1 students had text-level reading scores at the end of the year that were slightly higher than those of children designated as the middle group in their classrooms at the beginning of the year. Hiebert discusses critical features of this intervention, such as teachers setting high expectations for children and increasing the amount of time spent on reading and writing by the children in the project. The chapter concludes with the important observation that a variety of different intervention models, ranging from one-on-one tutoring to small-group Chapter 1 and small-group classroom intervention, be coordinated within a school to provide extra help in reading to all children who need it.

By fourth grade, most American students can function at basic levels (Educational Testing Service, 1991), contrary to the popular conceptions of illiteracy. Many students, however, come to a level of basic reading proficiency too late to become proficient at critically reading text, especially informational text (Applebee, Langer, & Mullis, 1988). The students who are most likely to get off to a poor start in literacy, and remain in the bottom half, are often those who come from low-income homes.

Chapter 1, the program designed to give poor children a chance to catch up with their higher-income peers, has not been doing the job. Funded since 1965 to give poor children supplementary support in reading and mathematics, reading levels of this group have not changed appreciably since the early 1970s (Educational Testing Service, 1991). Participation in Chapter 1 results in a slight increase in standardized test performance (Kennedy, Birman, & Demaline, 1986) that usually disappears after the supplementary instruction stops. This pattern means that students have not gained the levels of literacy proficiency that will allow them to function in classroom contexts. Critics go so far as to lay part of the blame for continuing failure of poor children on Chapter 1 itself. Allington (1991), foremost among those critics in the literacy community, has identified factors that contribute to Chapter 1 children's receiving even poorer instruction than their initially more advantaged peers. For example, instructional time is wasted as children travel to and from a Chapter 1 classroom. Even more problematic, Chapter 1 instruction often emphasizes disjointed skills that are difficult for children to transfer to classroom tasks. These factors, and others, have prompted Allington and others to advocate in-class Chapter 1 guidance. Evidence is quite compelling, however, that the issue is not *where* the instruction occurs (Bean, Cooley, Eichelberger, Lazar, & Zigmond, 1991) but *what* instruction is provided. Until the arrival of Reading Recovery from New Zealand in the mid-1980s, little attention was paid to the kind of instruction that might be appropriate as the preventative instruction that Chapter 1 was originally conceived to be.

Reading Recovery has directed attention to early literacy in a manner that has not been the case for at least the past 20 years. The finding that initially low-performing students can be taught to read is by no means unique (Durkin, 1974–1975). However, at a time when the number of children who depend on schools is increasing, the ability of Reading Recovery instruction to bring from 75% to 90% of children who receive an entire program to at least the average level of their class in about 30 hours has been understandably met with enthusiasm (see Chapters 4 and 8, this volume). As Reading Recovery has swept the country, however, little thought has been given to the contexts of many American school districts that differ in appreciable ways from the school system of New Zealand where Reading Recovery was initiated and has been implemented nationwide (Goldenberg, 1991; Guthrie, 1981). In California, for example, tutoring cannot be the entire solution for the approximately 40% of a cohort that is eligible for Chapter 1.

It is not clear what percentage of at-risk students can become effective readers in formats other than individualized tutoring. The stance of Reading Recovery was surprisingly so unprecedented in American literacy instruction that the original review that identified individual tutoring as the best form of intervention involved only a handful of studies (Madden & Slavin, 1989). There are many studies of beginning reading (see Stahl & Miller, 1989), but few of those studies have focused on the lowest-performing students. It may be, for example, that some contexts besides individual tutoring could be effective for teaching the children in the lowest quarter. There clearly is a need for a research literature that extends the models of early literacy instruction to small-group contexts.

Another reason for examining a small-group model stems from the confusion of classroom teachers about whole language (Hiebert, Potts, Katz, & Rahm, 1989). Reviews that criticized long-term ability grouping have been misinterpreted by teachers as meaning that all small-group instruction should be abandoned in favor of individual conferencing or whole class lessons. The issue, as has been argued elsewhere (Hiebert, 1987), is not whether teachers should work with small groups but rather the longevity and the intentions of the grouping practices. Models of literature-based reading instruction are few, and existing ones such as reader's workshop have been generalized to all grade levels and contexts (Reyes, 1992). Alternative models of early literacy instruction that use holistic strategies and small-group contexts have not been described and examined. The project that is described in this chapter was designed to examine the efficacy of whole literacy events like repeated reading of books and writing in small groups for children with initially low levels of literacy.

A full description of results from the first-year implementation with first-grade Chapter 1 students is presented in Hiebert, Colt, Catto, and Gury (1992). This chapter details curriculum and instructional choices that were made in this implementation and attends to issues related to these decisions in beginning literacy programs. The presentation of this intervention would be better seen as a case study from which others could glean *principles* that underlie the success of the children who learned to read and write through this project, than as a prescription for a particular set of choices. To this point, the more global rationale for the project has been presented. The remainder of this chapter outlines the particular decisions that were made about components of the project and the theoretical and empirical bases for these decisions. The final section addresses issues that require consideration in future implementations of interventions such as this one.

MAJOR COMPONENTS OF THE PROJECT

The project represented a comprehensive restructuring of experiences for grade 1 students in Chapter 1. It was a joint venture between Chapter 1 teachers from a school district, master teachers from the district who were part of a district-university partnership, and a professor and several doctoral students from the local university. As is the case of Chapter 1 programs nationally, the district had no designated curriculum or common expectations for Chapter 1 (Rowan & Guthrie, 1989). Although the curriculum of Chapter 1 was unclear, the district's curriculum was not. The district had an integrated whole-language curriculum-assessment framework that had been developed over a several-year period by the district's teachers. Chapter 1 had been advocated as a context particularly appropriate for whole-language instruction in regional workshops and professional meetings (Shanklin & Rhodes, 1989).

The application of whole language with grade 1 students, whether in the classroom or in Chapter 1, exemplified the "one size fits all" assumption that Reyes (1992) has described. Adaptations for students with unique learning needs were not part of the accepted view of whole language for either Chapter 1 or classroom contexts. This project examined adjustments to Chapter 1 that would maintain the authentic tasks of whole-language instruction but would address the needs of children who entered grade 1 with low levels of emergent literacy. Adams' (1990) review and a growing body of studies on shared book reading and writing in kindergartens and first-grade classrooms gave direction for curriculum and instruction. Once discussions began between university faculty and district teachers, it became apparent that a restructuring effort in Chapter 1 needed to attend to components like organization, assessment, and teacher support, in addition to instructional activities that were in tune with a whole-language philosophy.

Organization

As Goldenberg (see chapter 9, this volume) has argued, decisions about organization and time allocation in a restructuring effort should reflect the local context. Decisions about the composition and number of students in a group were made in response to the particular context of the project. All three of the Chapter 1 teachers who agreed to implement the instruction during the first year of the project had aides assigned to them. Although Chapter 1 guidelines state that the maximum number of children assigned to a Chapter 1 teacher and an aide should be 37, this figure was interpreted to mean a mandated figure. Teachers usually took more than this figure, usually about six to eight during a half-hour time block. Prior to the project, aides either worked with students individually, or they prepared materials. Observations of the groups during a pilot year had indicated that it was difficult for teachers to ensure all students' participation when there were six to eight children in a group. Conversations began with the teachers to look at ways in which the teacher-student ratio could be decreased.

Chapter 1 teachers were sensitive to the expectations of classroom teachers who were concerned that services would be provided for the maximum number of students. Consequently, the team began discussions as to how the same number of students could be served but in ways that increased student learning. A model was proposed in which aides assumed more of an instructional role. One of the aides had been trained as a teacher but in secondary business methods, while the other two had high school diplomas. At no point was the intention to transfer entire responsibility for instruction to aides. However, the two activities of repeated reading and of writing in journals and on acetate slates are similar to ones that parents might do with their children and seemed to be a reasonable expectation of teachers' aides.

The model that evolved from discussions was to divide in half the group of six assigned to a time slot. Teachers' aides worked with three children for the first semester, while the teachers worked with the other half. Since a focus of Chapter 1 previously had not been on bringing first-grade students to proficient reading, the Chapter 1 teachers were initially skeptical that most of the children could become proficient readers by the end of grade 1. Consequently, the more able students were assigned to the teachers for the first semester so that they could see substantial progress early on. Students' entry levels in these groups were not high but these levels were higher than those of students who worked with the aides during the first semester. This decision about group placement had the intended effect in that the teachers soon saw that children could engage in reading and writing tasks and could progress toward the goal of proficient grade-level reading. Throughout the project, aides were guided in their lesson plans and selection of books by the teachers and university associates.

Curriculum and Instruction

The goal was for children to attain grade-level proficiency in reading interesting texts and in writing messages. Three activities were seen as the source for gaining that proficiency: (1) reading, (2) writing, and (3) guidance on the words in the texts, emphasizing phonemic awareness and word patterns.

Reading

Dahl and Samuels (1979) provided substantiation that the reading of the same text numerous times supports fluency and automaticity. However, numerous questions remain about the nature of the text that should be used at these initial stages. While studies of low-performing students indicate that their exposure to text is considerably less than that of high-performing students

(Allington, 1984), a substantial literature also exists on the need for students to be reading material that is at appropriate difficulty levels. Finding material sufficiently easy for children at a point where they are not reading, while at the same time exposing them to substantial amounts of text is a dilemma. Repeated reading of predictable text has been suggested as a means of overcoming this apparent dilemma (Bridge, 1986) and was the route chosen for this project. From the first session, there was an abundance of repetitive reading (reading one review book and several readings of a new book), and children were taught to track or follow along in their books.

The development of a home reading pattern was a goal that was shared by teachers and project staff. Each session included a time when children could choose books to take home. The book bags in which children transported books back and forth from school to home contained a form for parents to verify children's reading at home. When children had completed a card that indicated they had read 10 books at home, they could choose a trade book from a set donated by a trade book publisher. This component provided a means for children to establish a home library.

Writing
Development of proficiency in writing was seen as an integral part of children's literacy development. Early on, many young children express themselves more readily in writing than in reading. Writing permits children to participate in meaningful functions of literacy (Sulzby, 1992), and it also provides a means of concretely applying their hypotheses about sound-letter correspondences. Clarke (1988) found that first graders who had opportunities regularly to use invented spelling made strides in word recognition, as well as spelling, relative to children in instruction where conventional spelling was stressed. However, many classroom teachers have interpreted research on invented spelling to mean that instruction should not be given and that sound-letter knowledge will become more sophisticated naturally.

This project provided children with many opportunities to write and also substantial guidance on the sound-letter system. At least two or three times a week, children wrote about topics of choice in individual notebooks or journals. Children were encouraged to write about personal experiences such as "My brother and I made a snowman yesterday." As children's proficiency increased, their entries were longer. While teachers assisted children in this journal writing to some degree, the primary guidance from teachers on sound-letter correspondences came in the context of another writing experience that occurred daily. The reading of predictable books was followed by writing activities that involved words of designated patterns from predictable books. For example, after reading *Have You Seen My Cat?*, (Carle, 1991), the writing activity might revolve around *cat, hat,* and *bat.* Initially, children created words with magnetic letters. As students developed fluency in recognizing letters, they wrote on acetate sheets with felt-tip markers. A consistent part of writing activities was for children to read what they had written, whether the activity involved the journal or the acetate slate.

Instruction in Word-Level Strategies

Proficiencies in phonemic awareness and in the use of word patterns in identifying unknown words were viewed as central processes to reading and writing (Cunningham, 1975-1976; Gaskins, Gaskins, & Gaskins, 1991). Within the multifaceted construct of phonemic awareness, some aspects seem to appear after some literacy proficiency has been gained, others appear more integral to literacy acquisition (Juel, 1991). From a series of studies that examined relationships of numerous phonemic awareness measures (Perfetti, Beck, Bell, & Hughes, 1987; Stanovich, Cunningham, & Cramer 1984), Cunningham (1989) selected three tasks that predicted reading acquisition best—phonemic segmentation, blending, and oddity—and designed an intervention that fostered these proficiencies in kindergarten children. Based on Cunningham's success in that project, these three tasks were included in the assessments of this project. Further, phonemic awareness activities became part of the intervention.

Phonemic awareness was supported through two different activities. First, the target word or words from a book were presented so that children needed to listen for the words that rhymed with the target word and for those that did not. After reading *Have You Seen My Cat?*, for example, the list might consist of *cat, that, pig, back,* and *fat*. Second, an activity modeled after Elkonin's (1963) suggestions was used. Children had cards that were divided up into blocks of four or five, and chips that they moved for every sound they heard as the teacher stretched out a word like /hat/. As children's proficiency increased, they wrote the letters for the sounds on the laminated cards with felt pens. This activity was used while children were writing in their journals. When a child was struggling with the spelling of a word, he or she was encouraged to write down letters for sounds that he or she heard. The child was then encouraged to make a check for every sound as the teacher and child stretched out the word. Teacher and student worked on figuring out the letters for places where there was a check representing a sound but no letter.

The rationale for the use of word patterns in reading and writing is extensive. Adams (1990) has reviewed this literature, and it is supported in projects like Gaskins et al.'s (1991) Benchmark program as well as by other studies (Cunningham, 1975–1976). Guidance in word patterns was supported in several ways, some of which should be apparent from the preceding descriptions of reading and writing.

One way was to integrate instruction in word patterns as part of predictable books. A feature of many predictable books is rhyme (Bridge, 1986). However, companies that produce sets of predictable books have not ordered these books according to the features of words. High-frequency words have been taught through these books, and predictability of text patterns is highly encouraged. However, children are apparently left to discover these patterns themselves. As Juel and Roper-Schneider (1985) established, children can benefit from text that contains words of high-regularity that have been highlighted previously by the teacher. Studies have not been conducted to determine if low-performing children intuitively pick up the patterns in predictable books without this guidance, or if their teachers, without the prompting of manuals or workshops, emphasize these patterns. It is doubtful that low-performing students pick up on these patterns at the point where this information would be most helpful to them. One aim of this project was to support teachers and children in making these connections, and not leave to chance this opportunity afforded by predictable books.

One of the mechanisms for providing this support was the development of a book list. Teachers and project staff collaborated in creating this list. All of the predictable books that were available to Chapter 1 teachers were ordered according to difficulty level and salient word patterns. For example, the word *cat* is a critical one in the book *Have You Seen My Cat?* (Carle, 1991). On the book list, that title would be designated as appropriate for teaching words that rhyme with *at*. The shortage of books complemented the goal of rereading books. Consequently, books frequently were listed for more than one pattern. Project staff did not designate the length of time that Chapter 1 teachers should spend on any particular pattern. Teachers were encouraged to observe their students' progress (especially through Running Records) to establish the patterns that needed to be covered. A consistent message in the meetings with participating teachers was the need to pick and choose the length of time devoted to any one pattern, as well as the patterns that were instructed. The aim was to develop generalizability among children in their knowledge of patterns, not to teach each and every pattern of the English sound-letter system.

Second, once books had been read, students wrote the words in the manner that was indicated in the description of writing activities. As soon as children had learned several patterns, they were asked to transform words from one pattern to another. For example, children might be asked to change *can* to *cat*.

Third, occasions for application of word pattern knowledge were provided through very easy booklets that children could read by themselves (see chapters 3 and 9, this volume; McCormick & Mason, 1989). During the first part of the year, little books were developed for various patterns. One little book, for example, had eight pages, with phrases like "a log" on one page, "a frog" on the next, and so forth. The last two pages of the book, which were blank, encouraged children to write words and phrases. In the second semester of the project, pictureless forms of some predictable books were provided. The impetus for this activity was the overreliance of some children on using the context of pictures for figuring out unknown words. These booklets were read only after repeated reading of the illustrated version. Children were encouraged to illustrate the booklets and to share their reading with family members.

A Typical Session. The best sense of the instruction comes from an overview of a typical session. As soon as the three children enter the room, Mary Ann (pseudonym), the teacher, checks who brought books back and with whom they read their books at home the previous evening. A book that was read the previous day—*Stop!* (Cowley, 1982)—is reread together and then children read several pages individually. Children have remembered the book well, and when Mary Ann asks children to frame the word that they talked about the day before—*stop*—they pipe up with words that rhyme like *top, shop,* and *hop.*

Next, Mary Ann introduces children to a new book, *Who's Coming for a Ride?* (Butler, 1989). Mary Ann has selected this book (like the book *Stop!*) from the list of predictable books that have been ordered according to difficulty and presence of words with common patterns—in this case patterns like "op" in *stop* and "ot" in *not.* Mary Ann begins by asking children what they anticipate the book will be about from the title. Children then read the book aloud, assisted by Mary Ann, talk about what happened in the book, and take turns reading individual pages. After several readings of the book, Mary Ann asks the children to find the word *not,* a key word in the book, asking them how it is alike and different from words that they have learned during the past several weeks. Acetate boards are distributed and children write on the boards. The word *not* is written and then changed to *hot, dot,* and *got,* with children and teacher using the words in phrases and sentences as they are written, talking about what is the same and different about the words, and reading the words after they have been written. Children read *Who's Coming for a Ride?* again and then write a sentence or two describing a personal experience in their notebooks. Writing these sentences about mutant ninja turtles (a popular topic) or favorite weekend activities gives children an excellent opportunity to apply their knowledge about written language. If there is time, children read another predictable book. Meanwhile, three children are working with the teacher's aide. They are also reading predictable books and writing on acetate boards and in notebooks but with less word-level guidance.

Assessment

A system for classroom-based assessment in which teachers gathered information on students' progress toward the critical district goals was part of the district's curriculum. However, Chapter 1 teachers had not become part of the district curriculum-assessment system, and Chapter 1 continued to be highly influenced by the demands of the state and national Chapter 1 program for standardized test results. Chapter 1 teachers did not believe particularly that the tests represented critical dimensions of literacy, especially with beginning readers. However, tests were seen as inevitable. Ostensibly, standardized test results were not required of kindergarten or first-grade students in Chapter 1. However, spring-to-spring standardized test results needed to be reported to the state for grade 2 students, so grade 1 students in Chapter 1 and those in the classroom deemed eligible for Chapter 1 were given standardized tests in spring. The emphasis on standardized tests in Chapter 1 was so pervasive that all placements into Chapter 1, even at the kindergarten level, were based on standardized tests.

In order to maintain a realistic perspective on students' progress toward the goal of proficient text-level reading and writing, better representations of reading and writing were needed on a more regular basis. Teachers were guided in sampling students' performances in an ongoing manner. A daily lesson plan form included space to record relevant comments about student performance on the various tasks of book reading, journal writing, and writing of rhyming words.

In addition, a performance assessment was also initiated. This assessment consisted of the critical goals of the program—text-level reading and writing—and was instituted at the beginning of the year and at the end of each quarter. Word-level assessments of reading and writing were used as windows into students' knowledge of graphophonic relationships. The assessments at the end of the first and third quarters were shorter versions, while those at the beginning of the year and at the end of the second and fourth quarters were considerably more extensive.

The text-level reading task consisted of reading and answering questions about passages on an informal reading inventory (IRI) (Woods & Moe, 1989), which consists of a graded series of passages. The IRI was supplemented by a preprimer passage with pictures, and a predictable book for those who were not fluent on the preprimer passage. For the text-level reading task, children were assigned a fluent reading level—the last text that they read fluently at 90%, the same criterion as used in Reading Recovery assessments (Clay, 1985).

For the text-level writing task, children wrote a message. The task began with a discussion about what children might write. When children were uncertain about what they might write, they were shown a picture from a trade book. Children were asked to read what they had written, the content of which was written down by the interviewer. The quality of the message and its communicativeness were assessed according to a six-stage category scheme (see Hiebert et al., 1992).

The reading and writing word-level tasks used a set of four lists of 15 words. The lists had been developed after consulting frequently used graded reading and spelling lists. Each set of lists contained new word patterns not on previous lists. Consequently, judgments could be made that placed the lists at primer, first-grade, second-grade, and third-grade difficulty levels. The lists for reading and writing had the same word patterns but used different initial consonants. For example, the primer list for reading contained words like *cat* and *red*, while the primer list for writing included *hat* and *bed*. The two tasks were given on different days, with reading preceding writing. Since there was an interest in establishing students' responses to exemplars of word patterns about which they had not been instructed, children continued on the word tasks until they got fewer than 60% of a list right.

Standardized tests continued to be given at the beginning and end of the year. In the fall, the Gates-MacGinitie (GM) Readiness test (Form PRE) was given by the Chapter 1 teachers and, in the spring, the California Test of Basic Skills (CTBS) Reading and Language Arts subtests were given by Chapter 1 teachers to students in small groups. Since performances on more authentic literacy tasks were of primary interest, standardized tests were not administered for research comparisons if children did not typically take these tests. Consequently, as will become evident in the discussion of findings, the comparison with classroom peers does not include standardized test results because these students did not take the standardized test at the end of the year.

Support for Teachers

Support structures within schools are erratic at best. For example, typical faculty meetings seldom focus on instruction or even on students. Support structures are needed especially for Chapter 1 teachers whose entire school day is spent instructing students who are not already proficient readers and writers. District Chapter 1 programs usually involve meetings but, at least in the case of this district, focus on administrative issues rather than on student progress and on ways of sustaining or enhancing this progress. Establishment of a support system that would focus teachers' discussions on student progress toward the goals of proficient reading and writing meaningful text and on the ways in which instruction could maintain or reinforce that progress was viewed as a priority.

A structure that was intended as an ongoing one in the district was a monthly meeting of all project participants. The aim of these meetings was to provide a context where teachers could share their students' accomplishments and to discuss activities that would foster progress to the goals of proficient reading and writing for all students. An assiduous effort was made by the project participants to guard against use of these sessions as a time for complaints. Consequently, sessions always began with a time of sharing the processes that were evident in students' reading and writing. Teachers were encouraged to bring examples of student work (e.g., Running Records). The quarterly assessments also provided a focus for the discussion of student accomplishments. Problems were not ignored but the stance was to look for solutions to shared problems. When aspects of instruction needed to be modified for all of the children or for particular children, a brainstorming approach was taken. The systematic home reading program resulted from this brainstorming of problems, as did the creation of the little books and the pictureless forms of the predictable books. During the spring semester, an added feature of these meetings was the viewing of videotaped lessons.

The second dimension of support for teachers—visits by project staff to teachers' small-group sessions—was regarded as necessary for the first year of implementation in this district but was not seen as an ongoing support structure. Interestingly, however, the district has worked hard to maintain continued guidance for teachers through peer coaching. During this implementation of the project, a project staff member (graduate student, professor, or district mentor teacher) visited each Chapter 1 teacher or aide weekly. The staff member took notes on small-group sessions. After the session, a copy of the notes was given to the teacher or aide and the content of the session was discussed. During the fall semester, the associates took the small groups biweekly so that the teacher could visit the aide's groups. These efforts were substituted by monthly videotaping of teachers and aides during the spring semester.

FINDINGS OF THE PROJECT

Since the naturalistic context of the project precluded a tightly controlled experiment, the stance was to take multiple perspectives of children's performances. The first perspective was to examine participating students' performances against an absolute level of achievement (proficient grade-level reading). Second, end-of-the-year performances of participating Chapter 1 students were compared with those of students in other Chapter 1 programs in the district that were not part of the project. The third perspective was a comparison of end-of-the-year performances of Chapter 1 students with those of classmates who had begun the year with higher levels of literacy.

In regard to these comparisons, especially the one with Chapter 1 students who did not receive the intervention, it should be stressed that this project was not considered an experiment. All components were not evenly matched. For one, random assignment was not possible. Consequently, the comparisons should be viewed as general indications of the effectiveness of the intervention and should remain in the background to the central question of the project, which was whether children had accomplished the goal of proficient grade-level reading and writing.

How Well Did the Participating Children Learn to Read?

All of the 45 children who participated in the project were at very early stages of emergent literacy in the fall of their first-grade year. Their responses to text modeled those of Sulzby's (1985) initial stages, such as labeling pictures or telling a story. Compositions consisted of drawings, an idiosyncratic word or two, or a production of invented spelling that was difficult to match to children's reading of the composition. One or two children knew a word such as *red*, and most showed a willingness to attempt to write words on the word-writing tasks, although the best productions consisted of the initial consonant of the word. According to a conventional measure of reading readiness—the GM Reading Readiness test, the children did not have high levels of reading readiness.

At the end of first grade, over half of the children could read a first-grade text at 90% fluency or higher, and another 25% could read a primer text (the third-quarter of first grade) fluently. The literacy proficiency of these children was also evident on a standardized test. Eighty percent of the group had moved out of the bottom quartile on the CTBS Reading test (a composite of comprehension and vocabulary), with 20% in the top half. Twenty-three percent (11 children) of the group were not able to read the primer text fluently. Of this group, three were clearly struggling, unable to give even a good rendition of the predictable text. While all had moved beyond the initial stages of emergent literacy with which they had begun the year, these children had not attained the fluency that would enable them to function with their peers in a second-grade classroom and were expected to return to Chapter 1 the following year.

How Well Did the Participating Children Read and Write in Relation to Students in the District's Regular Chapter 1 Program?

As stated earlier, the district's curriculum emphasized content and strategies that drew on a whole-language philosophy. The intervention emanated from a similar research base. Half the district's Chapter 1 teachers, however, interpreted whole language as meaning little systematic attention to words. Because of this perception, they declined to participate in the intervention. They agreed, however, to have a sample of their students assessed on the same set of reading and writing tasks as were given to the students in the restructured Chapter 1 program at the end of the year. Students in the regular Chapter 1 program also took the CTBS Reading and Language Arts tests at the end of the year and these results were available as well.

At the beginning of the year, both groups of students had scored well below the 33 National Curve Equivalent (NCE) level on the reading readiness test (the NCE level corresponding to 20 percentile, which the district used as the cutoff point this particular year for Chapter 1 participation). Since the mean of 12.9 NCE for the students in the regular Chapter 1 program was lower than the mean of 16.4 NCE for the students in the restructured Chapter 1 program, an analysis with the reading readiness measure as a covariate was used to compare the performances of the two groups on all reading and writing measures (including the standardized test results). Comparisons showed significant differences in the performances of the two groups on all measures, whether text-level or word-level, reading or writing, standardized or alternative. In all cases, the mean for the restructured Chapter 1 group was significantly larger than that for the regular Chapter 1 group.

As was suggested in the overview of the findings, the project does not represent a pure experiment. For one, assignment into the restructured and regular Chapter 1 programs did not occur on a randomized basis. However, the presence of differences on all measures supports the notion that the restructured program did have an impact. Comparing the number of children who attained grade-level proficiency according to the informal reading inventory and the standardized test underscores this conclusion. The difference in the percentage of each sample that reached primer-level fluency or higher was substantial: 77% of the restructured Chapter 1 group as compared with 18% of the regular Chapter 1 group. Whereas 56% of the restructured group could read the first-grade text fluently, 6% of the regular Chapter 1 group attained that level. A similar pattern was found on the results of the CTBS Reading test. When a cutoff of 25 NCE was used, 22% of the regular group would no longer be eligible for Chapter 1, as compared with 80% of the restructured group. Many of the children in the regular Chapter 1 group had not moved very far during their first-grade year. Most of them would return to Chapter 1 the following year.

How Well Did Participating Students Read and Write Relative to Their Classmates Who Began at Higher Levels but Remained in the Classroom?

There have been suggestions that pulling children out of classrooms to participate in a Chapter 1 classroom might be detrimental to children. Time is taken away from instruction, Chapter 1 instruction and materials are often incompatible with those in the classroom; and children are stigmatized as poor readers (Allington, 1991). To date, there has been no evidence that placing Chapter 1 programs in classrooms works more effectively than pull-out programs (Bean, Codey, Eichelberger, Lazar, & Zigmand, 1991), and this project was not designed to address that question. However, one question that could be addressed is the comparable growth that Chapter 1 students made relevant to that of their classmates. All their classmates began with higher levels of literacy. Data were available to address the question of whether Chapter 1 students made comparable growth to their classmates, even though they were pulled out of the classroom for a half hour a day.

This question was answered by looking at the performances of students across the seven classrooms in which Chapter 1 students spent the majority of their school day. Based on the rankings of teachers, four groups were formed from the non–Chapter 1 students in each class, and the middle two students in each group were given the same set of text- and word-level reading and writing tasks. A sampling of these students had been given the GM Reading Test at the beginning of first grade. The comparison of GM scores across the five groups (four classroom groups and Chapter 1) indicated that all of the classroom groups had had significantly higher reading readiness scores than Chapter 1 students at the beginning of the year.

Most of the classroom teachers did not group their students, and so these grouping designations are for this research discussion only. In a traditional achievement grouping format, the designations of the five groups at the beginning of the year might have been: high, high–middle, middle, middle–low, and low, with the Chapter 1 students being the latter. At the end of the year, the rankings had been reshuffled considerably. On the most critical measure—text-level reading—Chapter 1 students had scores that were just a little higher than the middle group, and substantially higher than the middle–low group.

ISSUES RELATED TO THIS EARLY INTERVENTION

Results of a 1-year effort in schools should be interpreted cautiously in that projects come and go. However, results of this project were sufficiently encouraging to justify its continuation and extension. The patterns of results also led to several extensions of the project. A particular question that arose from this project was the nature of support for students who are eligible for Chapter 1 but cannot be served by Chapter 1 because of limited services, as was the case with many of the children in the low classroom group. An intervention cannot do the job if, while some children are learning to read in the intervention, another group of low readers is being created in classrooms. In the year subsequent to the project described here, classroom teachers implemented a similar form of instruction with this group of students (Hiebert & Almanza, 1993). The hypothesis that underlies that effort—that this group of students would benefit from focused, although not necessarily as intensive, instruction (most of the teachers' groups had three to six students)—appears to have been true in that a new group of candidates for Chapter 1 was not produced in the first-grade classrooms. The initial findings of the classroom extension suggest that a modified form of the intervention can provide the nudge that this group of students needs and that classroom teachers can provide this instruction. Some classroom teachers, however, provide this instruction reluctantly (Hiebert & Almanza, 1993), believing that Chapter 1 has the responsibility for teaching children to read.

Another finding—the failure of about a quarter of the sample to become fluent readers—along with the finding that some children in the regular classroom had failed to become fluent readers led to the creation of another project: an extension of the intervention to second grade. When a quarter of the group of first graders who had become successful readers in Chapter 1 did not show up on the attendance rosters in the fall of their second-grade year but were replaced by an equal number of transfer children who had not learned to read, the need for a second-grade extension became even more apparent. An intervention like Reading Recovery stops abruptly at the end of first grade, even with the children who have started but not completed the programs in first grade. In this project, some children had begun with very low levels of emergent literacy, and they made progress as first graders. The second-grade extension addressed the issue of whether these children could become completely successful with continued support. Initial analyses of the second-grade extension indicate that such an extension was most appropriate for all groups (transfer children, children who had not learned to read in first-grade classrooms, and children who were not entirely fluent at the end of the first-grade intervention) (Catto, 1993).

In some schools, the majority of students are given a poor prognosis for becoming literate. Many teachers are anxious for guidelines, solutions, and support to change these patterns and bring more students to higher levels of literacy. This project was intended as a research effort to address questions that have not been examined in previous interventions. It was not intended as the initiation of a dissemination effort. However, given the interest and questions of teachers, what insights might be gained from this project?

With the other interventions described in this volume, this project shares several critical features that seem necessary for children in the lowest quarter to be brought to grade-level literacy. It also has a unique feature or two. The research design of this project makes it impossible to establish precisely whether these unique features are necessary and sufficient to bring initially low-performing students to literacy. However, features that are shared by the various projects can be identified and the unique features discussed.

The most critical ingredient of this and other interventions could easily be overlooked. A core group of teachers set high expectations for children. This is not to say that there were not many conversations where goals had to be repeated and where questions were raised about them. However, a conscious commitment was made by a group of teachers to bring initially low-performing students to grade-level literacy. In contexts where classroom teachers and other Chapter 1 teachers applied what they regarded to be a whole-language philosophy, initially low-performing children did not attain literacy levels as high as those children in the intervention. The intervention shares many characteristics with the manifestation of whole-language philosophy in this district. In both whole-language and intervention contexts, students read from books other than textbooks, and they wrote extensively. However, one element on which the intervention differed from the Chapter 1 comparison instruction was the consistency of instructional experiences. The Chapter 1 teachers in the remainder of the district's program were interested in providing a range of activities, including extension activities like creating artwork and making puppets.

Within the field of literacy, fierce debates have raged as to the appropriate methodology for early literacy instruction. The source of these great debates, as Chall (1967, 1982) characterized it, has been a very specific dimension of literacy—the degree to which early instruction should focus on the patterns of English words. Too much effort in the field of literacy might have been taken up with arguing the specifics of reading techniques such as too much or too little phonics, and not enough attention given to some general features of effective schools and classrooms. For example, one principle from the literature on effective schools is that schools where poor children are brought to high levels of accomplishment have high expectations (Purkey & Smith, 1983). The intervention described in this chapter shares with the other efforts in this volume high expectations for children who typically have been failed by schools.

A second principle—from the effective instruction literature—also applies to this intervention, and the other interventions described in this volume: Time spent on reading or writing results in higher achievement in reading or writing (Fisher et al., 1978). Children in this intervention read approximately 50,000 during the sessions over the year. This figure is about four times more than the amount that low-performing students typically read in classrooms (Allington, 1984). This feature appears to distinguish the intervention from instructional experiences in the classroom and in other Chapter 1 settings. From the first day of instruction in the intervention, all children followed along in several books, including children who could not recognize a majority of letters.

Another characteristic of this intervention that is shared with other interventions is a support system for teachers. The support for teachers is by no means as extensive or fine-tuned as that of Reading Recovery. However, a system was in place so that teachers received guidance about their instruction through weekly or biweekly visits. Monthly meetings gave teachers a forum in which to voice successes and problems, and to talk with others who shared their vision of high literacy accomplishments for initially low-performing students. The quarterly assessments gave teachers an opportunity to assess student progress relative to goals. The typical load of the Chapter 1 teacher—six to seven groups of youngsters, most of whom do not become literate over-night—makes it difficult to maintain high expectations without sharing goals, successes, and problems. National and state Chapter 1 organizations would do well to develop local and regional networks among teachers.

This project shared with other projects described in this volume high expectations, assessments that kept track of students' progress toward those high goals, and high levels of time spent on productive reading and writing tasks. While all of the projects share the three elements that are described next—instruction in word-level strategies, instruction in contexts other than whole class groups, and home liaisons—each of these elements was manifest somewhat uniquely in this intervention and deserves further attention.

The first was the focus on word patterns. This intervention is somewhere in between Success for All, which apparently provides an even greater emphasis on decoding instruction and practice, and Reading Recovery, which includes guidance in word patterns as part of an array of word-level strategies. Neither Reading Recovery nor Taylor et al.'s project (see chapter 6, this volume) emphasizes word patterns in the same way that this project does, such as organizing books around patterns. The degree to which the guidance in word patterns assists students and the degree to which this guidance takes away from other word-level strategies is an issue that needs to be considered in future work.

Although instruction in small groups is by no means unique, the placement of children in groups of three was unique. Slavin (1989) has concluded that, until the group decreases to one, group size is not a factor. From Slavin's review, it could be surmised that six, the number that teachers had served initially and the typical size for groups in the regular Chapter 1 program, should work as well as three. Could the intervention with first-grade Chapter 1 students proceed as effectively by doubling the number of children in a group? Questions such as this one have not been addressed but should be the focus of future study. This particular group of teachers found that three was workable. When there were more than three children with low-entry literacy levels, it was difficult to maintain appropriate levels of feedback and involvement.

There was no intention, however, of establishing that three in a group is a necessary feature of an intervention. Those designing projects in their schools should be flexible to the composition and size of groups, selecting plans that fit the conditions of their local context. In the original proposals to this school district, one plan was to have six children in a group, with three collaborating on activities independent of the teacher while the other three worked with the teacher. The original pilot study began with mixed-performing groups (as mixed as Chapter 1 can be). This plan was quickly nixed by other Chapter 1 teachers in the district who insisted that only the very lowest students be part of the intervention. Our experiences suggested that, for the very lowest students who were oblivious to print initially, a mixed-performing group might be difficult since students had a hard time tuning in to peers (not just print). However, this experience is tied to a particular context and should not be the guiding factor for the design of instructional groups in another school or district.

Like other interventions, a home reading component was emphasized. Unlike other interventions, a part of this home reading component was to assist children who were reading at home with the creation of home libraries. What role did these books have in children's accomplishments? A subsequent analysis has shown that home reading accounted for a very insignificant amount of variation in children's end-of-the-year performances (Hiebert, 1992). The only variable that accounted for a substantial amount of variation, once prior knowledge (in the form of the reading readiness measure) had been entered into the regression analysis, was regular class assignment. The nature of instruction that children received in their classrooms made a substantial difference in their development as readers and writers. In particular, all the children in one teacher's class learned to read while, in another class, many of the children did not (not just children in Chapter 1). It may well be that some students only begin extended reading at home after they have had some success at reading and that at-home reading habits are most influential at third grade and beyond (Anderson, Wilson, & Fielding, 1988). Establishing these patterns early, however, can be important to ensure that students are reading extensively at third-grade level and above. The sustenance and effects of home reading patterns for this particular group of children are being examined as students move to third grade and above.

One issue that needs to be resolved is the relationship between text difficulty and extensive exposure to text for novices. Work on text difficulty has developed into somewhat of a science. The use of readability formulas appears to have waned but difficulty level continues to be an issue that arises in conversations with teachers. As crucial an issue, however, may be amount of text that children see. Poor readers typically don't get to see much text. In this project, children were involved with many texts. Initially, at least, much of the exposure was in the context of following along, without the expectation that children could read the texts themselves. Future studies need to attend to the many questions that remain about this technique of following along, such as the rapidity with which high-frequency words are learned.

There are other pressing issues related to this intervention such as the nature of restructuring when an entire class of students requires support in becoming literate. Questions such as that will be addressed in the final chapter of this volume since issues like that one need to be addressed by most of the projects described in this volume.

SUMMARY

This project, and the others reported in this volume, indicate that expectations for Chapter 1 can be much higher than they currently are. After an intervention in Chapter 1, the majority of children who began in the bottom quartile performed at levels comparable with the average students in their classes. This progress was made by most children in the context of small groups. Further, teachers provided this instruction by focusing on activities that they had used in the past—repeated reading and extensive writing.

Some children did not become proficient readers and might well have benefited from a one-to-one tutorial. In schools like the ones in this project where more than 20% of the population was eligible for Chapter 1 services, an intervention like this small-group effort can support a portion of the population that might not be served in a tutorial design. Further, the performances of students in the classroom indicate that this Chapter 1 effort was not sufficient. Another group of students became eligible for Chapter 1. An effort like the one described by Taylor et al. (see chapter 6, this volume) would have been an appropriate addition in the classrooms. The entire profile of a school requires consideration when designing interventions.

REFERENCES

Adams, M. (1990). *Beginning to read: Thinking and learning about print.* Cambridge, MA: MIT Press.

Allington, R.L. (1984). Content coverage and contextual reading in reading groups. *Journal of Reading Behavior, 16,* 85–96.

Allington, R.L. (1991). Children who find learning to read difficult: School responses to diversity. In E.H. Hiebert (Ed.), *Literacy for a diverse society: Perspectives, practices, and policies* (pp. 237–252). New York: Teachers College Press.

Anderson, R.C., Wilson, P.T., & Fielding, L.G. (1988). Growth in reading and how children spend their time outside of school. *Reading Research Quarterly, 23,* 285–303.

Applebee, A.N., Langer, J., & Mullis, I.V.S. (1988). *Who reads best? Factors related to reading achievement in grades 3, 7, and 11.* Princeton, NJ: Educational Testing Service.

Bean, R.M., Cooley, W.W., Eichelberger, R.T., Lazar, M.K., & Zigmond, N. (1991). Inclass or pullout: Effects of setting on the remedial reading program. *Journal of Reading Behavior, 23,* 445–464.

Bridge, C.A. (1986). Predictable books for beginning readers and writers. In M.R.

Sampson (Ed.), *The pursuit of literacy: Early reading and writing* (pp. 81–96). Dubuque, IA: Kendall/Hunt.

Butler, A. (1989). *Who's coming for a ride?* Crystal, IL: Rigby.

Carle, E. (1991). *Have you seen my cat?* Saxonville, MA: Picturebook Studio.

Catto, S. (1993). *An examination of a second-grade literacy intervention: Patterns of student performance and the relationship of selected factors.* Unpublished doctoral dissertation, University of Colorado-Boulder.

Chall, J.S. (1967, 1982). *Learning to read: The great debate* (2nd ed., with a new introduction). New York: McGraw-Hill.

Clarke, L. (1988). Invented versus traditional spelling in first graders' writings: Effects on learning to spell and read. *Research in the Teaching of English, 22,* 281–309.

Clay, M.M. (1985). *Early detection of reading difficulty* (3rd ed.). Portsmouth, NH: Heinemann.

Cowley, J. (1982). *Stop!* San Diego, CA: The Wright Group.

Cunningham, A. (1989). Phonemic awareness: The development of early reading competency. *Reading Research Quarterly, 24,* 471–472.

Cunningham, P.M. (1975/76). Investigating a synthesized theory of mediated word identification. *Reading Research Quarterly, 11,* 127–143.

Dahl, P.R., & Samuels, S.J. (1979). An experimental program for teaching high speed word recognition and comprehension skills. In J.E. Button, T.C. Lovitt, & T.D. Rowland (Eds.), *Communications research in learning disabilities and mental retardation* (pp. 33–65). Baltimore: University Park Press.

Durkin, D. (1974–1975). A six year study of children who learned to read in school at the age of four. *Reading Research Quarterly, 10,* 9–61.

Educational Testing Service (1991). *Trends in academic progress.* Washington, DC: Office of Educational Research and Improvement, U.S. Department of Education.

Elkonin, D.B. (1963). The psychology of mastering the elements of reading. In B. Simon & J. Simon (Eds.), *Educational psychology in the U.S.S.R.* (pp. 165–179). London: Routledge & Kegan Paul.

Fisher, C.W., Filby, N.N., Marliave, R., Cahen, L.S., Dishaw, M.M., Moore, J.E., & Berliner, D.C. (1978). *Teaching behaviors, academic learning time, and student achievement* (Technical Report V-1). San Francisco: Far West Regional Educational Laboratory.

Gaskins, R.W., Gaskins, J.C., & Gaskins, I.W. (1991). A decoding program for poor readers—and the rest of the class, too! *Language Arts, 68,* 213–225.

Goldenberg, C. (1991). Learning to read in New Zealand: The balance of skills and meaning. *Language Arts, 68,* 555–562.

Guthrie, J. (1981). Reading in New Zealand: Achievement and volume. *Reading Research Quarterly, 17,* 6–27.

Hiebert, E.H. (1987). The context of instruction and student learning: An examination of Slavin's assumptions. *Review of Educational Research, 57,* 337–340.

Hiebert, E.H. (1992, May). *Impact of home, classroom, and prior knowledge factors on the reading performances of intervention students.* Paper presented at the CORR preconvention of the International Reading Association, Orlando, FL.

Hiebert, E.H., & Almanza, E. (1993, April). *Extending an early literacy intervention across Chapter 1 and classroom contexts.* Paper presented at the annual meeting of the International Reading Association, San Antonio, TX.

Hiebert, E.H., Colt, J.M., Catto, S.L., & Gury, E.M. (1992). Reading and writing of Grade 1 students in a restructured Chapter 1 program. *American Educational Research Journal, 29*, 545–572.

Hiebert, E.H., Potts, T., Katz, H., & Rahm, D. (1989, December). *Characteristics of reading and writing instruction in whole language classrooms.* Paper presented at the annual conference of the National Reading Conference, Austin, TX.

Juel, C. (1991). Beginning reading. In R. Barr, M.L. Kamil, P.B. Mosenthal, & P.D. Pearson (Eds.), *Handbook of reading research* (Vol. 2, pp. 759–788). New York: Longman.

Juel, C., & Roper-Schneider, D. (1985). The influence of basal readers on first grade reading. *Reading Research Quarterly, 20*, 134–152.

Kennedy, M.M., Birman, B.F., & Demaline, R.E. (1986). *The effectiveness of Chapter 1 services.* Washington, DC: Office of Educational Research and Improvement, U.S. Department of Education.

McCormick, C.E., & Mason, J.M. (1989). Fostering reading for Head Start children with little books. In J. Allen & J.M. Mason (Eds.), *Risk makers, risk takers, risk breakers: Reducing the risks for young literacy learners* (pp. 125–153). Portsmouth, NH: Heinemann.

Madden, N.A., & Slavin, R.E. (1989). Effective pullout programs for students at risk. In R.E. Slavin, N.L. Karweit, & N.A. Madden (Eds.), *Effective programs for students at risk* (pp. 52–72). Boston: Allyn & Bacon.

Perfetti, C.A., Beck, I., Bell, L.C., & Hughes, C. (1987). Phonemic knowledge and learning to read are reciprocal: A longitudinal study of first-grade children. *Merrill-Palmer Quarterly, 33*, 283–319.

Purkey, S.C., & Smith, M.S. (1983). Effective schools: A review. *Elementary School Journal, 83*, 427–452.

Reyes, M. de la Luz (1992). Challenging venerable assumptions: Literacy instruction for linguistically different students. *Harvard Educational Review, 62*, 427–446.

Rowan, B., & Guthrie, L.F. (1989). The quality of Chapter 1 instruction: Results from a study of twenty-four schools. In R.E. Slavin, N.L. Karweit, & N.A. Madden (Eds.), *Effective programs for students at risk* (pp. 195–219). Boston: Allyn & Bacon.

Shanklin, N.L., & Rhodes, L.K. (1989). Transforming literacy instruction. *Educational Leadership, 46*, 59–63.

Slavin, R.E. (1989). Class size and student achievement: Small effects of small classes. *Educational Psychologist, 24*, 99–110.

Stahl, S.A., & Miller, P.D. (1989). Whole language and language experience approaches for beginning reading: A quantitative research synthesis. *Review of Educational Research, 59*, 87–116.

Stanovich, K.E., Cunningham, A.E., & Cramer, B. (1984). Assessing phonological awareness in kindergarten children: Issues of task comparability. *Journal of Experimental Child Psychology, 38*, 175–190.

Sulzby, E. (1985). Children's emergent reading of favorite storybooks: A developmental study. *Reading Research Quarterly, 20*, 458–481.

Sulzby, E. (1992). Research Directions: Transitions from emergent to conventional writing. *Language Arts, 69*, 290–297.

Woods, M.L., & Moe, A.J. (1989). *Analytical reading inventory* (4th ed.). Columbus, OH: Merrill.

Early Intervention in Reading

Supplemental Instruction for Groups of Low-Achieving Students Provided by First-Grade Teachers

BARBARA M. TAYLOR   **JEAN STRAIT**

MARY ANNE MEDO

The authors describe a program that they have been using with first-grade teachers in one urban, one suburban, one rural, and one inner city school in the Twin Cities during the past 4 years. The program involves first-grade teachers taking 20 minutes a day to provide supplemental reading instruction to a group of from five to seven of their lowest level readers. The program has been effective in improving the end-of-year reading performance of these lowest readers. In addition to describing the program, the authors discuss issues related to program maintenance over time. Most teachers have continued to use the Early Intervention in Reading (EIR) program after the pilot year and have continued to have good results with the program. The chapter concludes with a discussion of the important role that first-grade teachers involved with EIR have played in helping their lowest level readers learn to read by the end of the year.

Exciting work in early reading intervention in which young children are engaged in extensive authentic reading and writing experiences is occurring in many elementary schools around the country today. Children at risk of failing to learn to read in first grade are receiving supplemental reading instruction beginning early in the school year through specially designed programs emphasizing the reading of and writing about books. It is encouraging that such efforts are making a real difference in terms of low-achieving students' reading ability by the end of first grade.

Several notable programs, such as Reading Recovery (Pinnell, Fried, & Estice, 1990; see also chapter 4, this volume) and Success for All (chapter 7, this volume), provide daily one-on-one tutoring to first-grade children at the greatest risk of failing to learn to read in first grade. Results from these programs have been impressive. In another noteworthy program, Chapter 1 teachers and aides work with first-grade children in groups of three, using extensive book reading and writing activities (see chapter 5, this volume). Strategic instruction in word attack is emphasized. This program also has been highly successful. The preceding programs, however, are all pull-out programs in which the instruction is provided by special reading teachers away from the regular classroom. One-on-one tutoring and small-group Chapter 1 instruction are important but will not be sufficient to meet all children's needs. It is crucial that classroom teachers be providers of special reading instruction for low-achieving readers as well, in any schoolwide attempt to teach all first-grade children to read.

A number of researchers who have investigated the reading instruction provided to low-achieving students through special education, Chapter 1, and regular classroom programs have concluded that increased access to quality instruction for low-achieving readers is needed in regular classrooms (Allington & McGill-Franzen, 1989; O'Sullivan, Ysseldyke, Christenson, & Thurlow, 1990). Classroom teachers should spend extra time working with their lowest readers, and this instruction should maximize active teaching, academic responding, and academic engaged time on the part of the students, and minimize time spent on seat work.

This chapter describes a first-grade intervention program that involves the classroom teacher. Beginning in the fall, first-grade teachers provide daily supplemental reading instruction to a group of from five to seven lowest emergent readers in their classrooms. For 15 to 20 minutes a day, children receive extra help from their teacher as they read and write about stories supplemental to the regular reading program. Strategic instruction in word attack is emphasized as is the development of students' phonemic awareness and phonics knowledge.

A high correlation has been found between low phonemic awareness at the beginning of first grade and poor reading progress by the end of first grade (Juel, Griffith, & Gough, 1986; Liberman, 1973; Share, Jorm, Maclean, & Matthews, 1984; Stanovich, Cunningham, & Feeman, 1984; Tunmer & Nesdale, 1985). Experts have stressed the importance of phonemic awareness training for low-achieving beginning readers (Juel, 1988; Stanovich, 1986), and such training has been found to be beneficial (Ball & Blachman, 1991; Bradley & Bryant, 1983; Cunningham, 1990; Lundberg, Frost, & Peterson, 1988). In the program described in this chapter, phonemic awareness is specifically developed through teacher modeling of the sounding and blending of words in stories and through the children's writing of words and sentences.

A large body of research indicates that phonics instruction is important in beginning reading (Adams, 1990; Bond & Dykstra, 1967; Chall, 1983; Pflaum, Walberg, Karegianes, & Rasher, 1980). Authorities have argued for the teaching of phonic skills to children in conjunction with the reading of actual stories (Adams, 1990; Anderson, Hiebert, Scott, & Wilkenson, 1985). In our EIR program, teachers talk about the common sounds for particular letters as story summaries are read from charts. They also frequently refer to a short vowel chart when children have difficulty decoding words in stories with short vowel sounds.

Teachers help children learn strategies for word attack. They remind children to use their sounding and blending skills and to use the vowel chart if necessary to help them remember the short vowel sounds. Additionally, children are encouraged to use context clues by thinking about what would make sense in the story as they are attempting to decode unknown words. They are reminded to monitor their word recognition by asking themselves if the words they are reading make sense.

Writing is also an important aspect of the program. On two of three days devoted to one story, children write a sentence related to the story with teacher assistance. The importance of writing by beginning readers has frequently been observed (Adams, 1990; Clay, 1985). Typically, children begin to write letters and words at about the same time they begin to recognize printed words (Clay, 1975; Mason, 1980). Furthermore, the writing of words and sentences helps children learn about phonemic segmentation, blending, and symbol sound correspondences (Chomsky, 1979; Ehri & Wilce, 1987).

Repeated reading is an important component of the EIR program. Repeated reading of stories has been found to improve students' reading rate, phrasing, and word recognition accuracy (Carver & Hoffman, 1981; Dowhower, 1987; Herman, 1985; Samuels, 1979). Children in our program read stories repeatedly with the teacher or the aide, to one another, and to parents. They are often asked to reread old stories as well as the ones they are currently working on with the teacher.

The EIR program has been studied in four different districts with varied populations and approaches to reading instruction: District A, a middle-class suburban school using a literature-based reading program; District B, a middle-class suburban school using an intensive systematic phonics program and basal in first grade; District C, a rural school using a basal reader program; and District D, a large urban school using an intensive systematic phonics program and basal in first grade. As the program has continued in each of these districts beyond the pilot year, minor changes have been made to meet different teachers' and schools' needs. The results of a survey to investigate teachers' continued use of the program will be described later in this chapter.

Importantly, the program has been integrated into a variety of schools. What is particularly exciting about the EIR program is that classroom teachers are demonstrating that they can make a substantial difference in the reading attainment of their lowest readers by providing daily, quality supplemental instruction based on repeated reading of and writing about stories, rather than word drill.

EARLY INTERVENTION IN READING PROGRAM

By the end of September, the teacher selects from five to seven children who at this point appear to be the lowest in the class in emergent reading behaviors. These children have low phonemic awareness as demonstrated by their difficulty producing the individual sounds in words and in blending sounds together to make words (Taylor, 1990). They also know fewer consonant sounds than their peers.

Children's feelings of success in reading are important from the start of the program. For this reason, reading materials are kept extremely short at first so that the children can successfully read them by the end of 3 days. Books that appeal to 6- and 7-year-olds and that also can be easily retold have been selected for the first half of the program. These books are listed in Figure 6-1. Children not only feel good about being able to read the books, but also genuinely enjoy the stories. Many of the books selected contain a repetitive episode, and in the retelling a number of the episodes have been eliminated. For example, in *Ask Mr. Bear* (Marjorie Flack), the little boy (in the retelling) asks the hen, the goat, and the bear for advice on what to get his mother, but not the goose, the sheep, and the cow. In other instances, the story line was simply condensed to produce a retelling. For example, in *Imogene's Antlers* (David Small), instead of the repeated references in the text to the parent's reactions to Imogene's antlers, the retelling simply said, "Her mom and dad weren't too happy, but Imogene had fun."

The teacher begins a 3-day cycle by reading a picture book to the entire class. A 40- to 60-word retelling of this story (Level A) becomes the instructional reading material for the EIR group for the next 3 days. Actual books could be used for the instructional reading material instead of story retellings, but we strongly believe that the short length of the reading material (e.g., 40 to

Group A—40–60 word summaries (October–December)

Five Little Monkeys Jumping on the Bed—Eileen Christelow

Ask Mr. Bear—Marjorie Flack

You'll Soon Grow into Them, Titch—Pat Hutchins

Herman the Helper—Robert Kraus

Milton the Early Riser—Robert Kraus

I Wish I Could Fly—Ron Maris

All by Myself—Mercer Mayer

Just for You—Mercer Mayer

Who Took the Farmer's Hat?—Joan Nodset

Imogene's Antlers—David Small

The Carrot Seed—Ruth Krauss

Group B—60–90 word summaries (December–February)

Charlie Needs a Cloak—Tomie dePaola

Across the Stream—Mirra Ginsburg

Three Kittens—Mirra Ginsburg

Good Night, Owl—Pat Hutchins

Geraldine's Blanket—Holly Keller

Round Robin—Jack Kent

Owliver—Robert Kraus

Stone Soup—Ann McGovern

If You Give a Mouse a Cookie—Laura Nemeroff

The Farmer and the Noisy Hut—folk tale

Rosie's Walk—Pat Hutchins (actual book used)

Big Brother—Charlotte Zolotow

Group C—90–120 word summaries, 100–150 word books (February–March)

A Dark, Dark Tale—Ruth Brown (actual book read by students)

Freight Train—Donald Crews (actual book read by students)

School Bus—Donald Crews (actual book read by students)

Hattie and the Fox—Mem Fox

The Monkey and the Crocodile—folk tale

The Three Billy Goats Gruff—folk tale

The Chick and the Duckling—Mirra Ginsburg (actual book read by students)

The Doorbell Rang—Pat Hutchins

The Very Worst Monster—Pat Hutchins

Group D—120–200 word books, actual books read by students (April–May)

You'll Soon Grow into Them, Titch—Pat Hutchins

Herman the Helper—Robert Kraus

All by Myself—Mercer Mayer

Just for You—Mercer Mayer

The Bear's Toothache—David McPhail

There's a Nightmare in My Closet—Mercer Mayer

Planes—Anne Rockwell

If You Look Around You—Fulvio Testa

If You Take a Paintbrush—Fulvio Testa

Noisy Nora—Rosemary Wells

FIGURE 6-1.   Stories Used in the Early Intervention in Reading (EIR) Program

60 words from October to December) is crucial in this particular program so that the children can feel successful.

The story retelling is printed on a chart spread across three or four pages. If books are used instead of retellings for the actual reading material, they need to be in a big book format or the typeface needs to be large enough so that children can follow as the teacher points to the words and provides instruction in word recognition while he or she reads the story. Also, if books are used, multiple copies of the book will be needed so that children, working in pairs, can practice rereading the story. If retellings are used, children receive two personal copies, one to illustrate and take home to read to a family member, and one to keep at school for future rereadings.

The teacher and children read and reread the story together from the chart or from the book over the 3 days. The teacher provides as much help as needed and stops at appropriate words to talk about the strategies of using context clues and of sounding and blending the phonemes in words to decode words not instantly recognized. By the second or third day the teacher is no longer the leading voice as the story is reread. Children, taking turns or chorally, initiate the reading. The teacher continues to provide help with decoding as needed, encouraging the children to use context and phonic clues.

On day 1 for Level A stories the teacher selects three short, phonetically regular words from the story to look at more closely, and asks the children what sound they hear first, second, and third in each word and how they might spell each sound. The children write the words in a series of boxes (on paper or small chalk boards), putting one phoneme per box (i.e., [ch] [i] [ck]). This activity develops the children's phonemic awareness and their knowledge of consonant sounds.

On days 2 and 3, the children write a different sentence each day about the story. For *Stone Soup* (Ann McGovern), the children might come up with the sentence, "The young man could make soup from a stone," on day 2, and "The little old lady and the young man had soup fit for a king," on day 3. Once the group agrees on a common sentence to write, they basically stay together, with teacher guidance, as they write. The teacher provides help as needed but also encourages the children to do as much on their own as possible of the spelling for these sentences. For example, the teacher might ask children what letter they hear first in *young* and then show them how to spell the rest of the word. However, the teacher would ask them to come up with the letters for the beginning, middle, and end sounds in *man* because this is a phonetically regular word. Children write the sentence at the back of one of their personal copies of the story retelling or on a blank sheet of paper. The purpose of this activity is to develop students' phonemic awareness as well as their phonics knowledge.

In addition to the 15 to 20 minutes with the teacher, an aide or volunteer spends an additional 5 minutes a day with each child individually as the child practices rereading the story. If an aide or volunteer (or perhaps an older student) is not available, children can reread their stories with a partner in the program or another student in the class.

By December or January, retellings of picture books or actual books first read aloud are increased to 60 to 90 words in length (Level B stories). By mid-February, retellings or books to be used for group instruction are from 90 to 120 words long (Level C stories). Also, actual books from 100 to 150 words long that are not first read aloud to the group are also used in the program at this time to help the children make the transition to independent reading. By April, only actual trade books that are 120 to 200 words long are used (Level D stories). These books are not read aloud prior to being read by the children. The teacher does not work with all of the children at once in a group at this stage. Instead she reads with pairs of students over a 3-day period. As children practice reading material that has not first been read aloud to them, they are encouraged by the teacher to use the strategies they have learned in the program to decode words not instantly recognized. The primary strategies are phonemic segmentation and blending and using context clues to unlock the meaning of words.

After the third day on a story, a running record is taken as a child reads the story just finished. Running Records provide useful information about children's ongoing success rate as well as about their abilities to self-correct word recognition errors.

RESULTS

The EIR program has been used in four districts in which data have been collected. It is currently being continued in these four districts as well as eight others.

In addition to the EIR program, children in this program in all four districts received from 70 to 90 minutes of reading instruction during the regular reading period. In District A, children in the EIR program did not receive any other supplemental reading instruction. In District B, about 40% of the children also received Chapter 1 help. In District C, about two thirds of the children in EIR were also in Chapter 1. (However, any child under the 45th percentile qualifies for Chapter 1 in this rural district.) In District D, two thirds of the children in EIR also received Chapter 1 help. Chapter 1 help in Districts B, C, and D was not connected to EIR in any way.

District A is a suburban district that uses a literature-based reading program in which children are not ability-grouped for their basic reading instruction. In District A, the 30 children in the program in Year 1 (from the bottom 25% of their class in emergent reading abilities in the fall) were at the 29th percentile on a standardized reading readiness test in September and at the 37th percentile on the first-grade level of this standardized reading test in May. The 28 comparison children were at the 34th percentile on the standardized test in September and at the 27th percentile in May. Perhaps more importantly, 67% of the EIR children were reading on at least a preprimer level in May (with 93% accuracy or better, in word recognition on the Burns-Roe Informal Reading Inventory [IRI]) and 40% were reading on an end-of-first-grade level or better. In contrast, 36% of the comparison children were reading on at least a preprimer level in May, with only 11% reading on an end-of-first-grade level or better.

District B, another suburban district, uses a systematic phonics program for reading instruction from September through February in first grade and a basal reader program from March through May. Children are not ability-grouped in this program. In May of Year 1, 83% of the 24 children in the EIR program (from the bottom 25% of their class in the fall) were reading on at least a preprimer level, and 54% were reading on an end-of-first-grade level or better. Of the 21 comparison children, 38% were reading on at least a preprimer level in May; 10% on an end-of-first-grade level or better.

District C, a rural district, uses a basal reader program for reading instruction. In May, 93% of the 15 EIR children in this district were reading on at least a preprimer level and 73% reading on grade level or better. Of the 5 control children, 60% were reading on at least a preprimer level; 20% on an end-of-first-grade level or better.

In District D, a large urban school with many lower socioeconomic status students and a high minority population, the school uses the same systematic phonics program as District B from September through February and a basal reader program for the remainder of the school year. In May, 53% of the 32 children in the EIR program were reading on at least a preprimer level and 28% on an end-of-first-grade level or better.

As children progressed through the EIR program, running records were taken after 3 days had been spent on a story. In District A, children averaged 94% correct on these running records. In District B, the EIR children averaged 96% correct on the running records, in District C, 98% correct, and in District D, 88% correct. This data indicates that children, for the most part, were successfully reading the stories or story summaries in the EIR program by the end of the third day.

Clearly, results have varied across districts. The finding that fewer EIR children were reading on grade level in May in District A, than in Districts B or C might have been related, in part, to the differences in the basic reading programs used in the three schools. Also, EIR children from District A were somewhat lower than EIR children in District C on emergent literacy measures obtained in September.

Children made the slowest progress in District D, but the EIR children from this district were performing at a lower level in emergent literacy at the beginning of the school year than were the EIR children from each of the other three districts as evidenced by their performance on the phonemic awareness test and their knowledge of consonant sounds. Also, children from District D were from a lower socioeconomic level than children in the other three districts. Unfortunately, we know that children of poverty traditionally have performed less well in reading than middle-class children.

There were a number of instructional factors that might have contributed to the poorer performance of the EIR children in District D. The program got off to a late start, beginning in the middle of November instead of the beginning of October. An aide was not available to listen to children read independently, so the one-on-one reading took place only 2 days a week when university project assistants were present instead of the intended 5 days a week. This may have been a major reason that children in District D were averaging only 88% correct on running records as opposed to 94% to 98% correct in the three other districts. Because of copying costs, booklets were not available to send home with the children; booklets were kept at school for rereading practice instead. In other sites, children have had a copy of each story retelling at school and at home. In spite of these difficulties the teachers in District D who used EIR in their classrooms were generally pleased with the program because they could see great improvement in their very lowest readers. Problems that arose in the pilot year will be corrected as teachers continue with the program in the second year.

Follow-up testing has been conducted in Districts A and B to investigate the second-grade reading performance of children who were in the EIR program in first grade. By mid-March, 72% of the second-grade children in District A who had been in EIR the previous year were reading on a second-grade level. By mid-May, 98% of the second-grade children in District B who had received EIR help in first grade were reading on a second-grade level. These data indicate that although a number of the EIR children were not reading on grade level by the end of grade 1, most were reading independently on at least a preprimer level (on an IRI) at the end of first grade and continued to make good progress in reading in second grade.

In addition to the student performance data across four districts indicating that the program has been quite successful, teacher comments also attest to the success of the program. On a questionnaire, teachers have reported that their low readers made excellent progress, felt good about the program and the extra time spent with the teacher, and had good self-concepts about themselves as readers.

Comments on the questionnaires have indicated that most of the teachers who used the program were quite enthusiastic, and many planned to continue with it. Of the 18 teachers in Districts A, B, C, and D using the program for the first year, 12 continued to use the program on their own the following year. Three other teachers continued using the program, but had a reading resource teacher provide the instruction because they felt they didn't have the time and someone else was available to provide the instruction. Three others did not continue with the program because they felt they did not have the time.

ISSUES RELATED TO A CLASSROOM INTERVENTION MODEL

Although the EIR program has been effective as a classroom reading intervention program, questions pertaining to the program in particular and to supplemental classroom reading intervention in general remain to be answered. One frequently raised question pertains to program effectiveness over time. Do teachers who choose to continue with the EIR program on their own without university support maintain good results in subsequent years? Innovative programs might not be implemented as rigorously as in the university-sponsored pilot year and consequently can lose some of their effectiveness in enhancing student performance. Year 2 results from Districts A and B, however, are encouraging along these lines. In District A, the EIR program was expanded from 6 to 13 first-grade classrooms under the leadership of two part-time coordinators (one for each building) funded by the district. During Year 2, teachers were operating without the assistance from the university that they had had the year before. By May, 78% of the EIR children were reading on at least a preprimer level; 36% were reading on a first-grade level or better.

In District B (Year 2), the program was continued by the three teachers who had used it in Year 1. In Year 2, in which the program continued without university involvement, 100% of the children in the EIR program were reading on at least a preprimer level and 45% were reading on grade level.

Another frequently raised question pertains to voluntary, continued use of a program over time. Will classroom teachers who received the year-long university support as they implemented EIR for the first time actually choose to continue using EIR or some modification of it in subsequent years? Quite frankly, the model of systematic, supplemental reading instruction for low-achieving readers being provided by the classroom teacher has not been popular or widespread (Allington & McGill-Franzen, 1989; Johnston & Allington, 1991). Supplemental instruction for low-achieving readers typically has been the domain of Chapter 1 and learning disabilities teachers or district-supported reading specialists. Classroom teachers might feel they either do not have the time or expertise, or both, to adequately help their lowest readers. Consequently the answer to the preceding question remains unknown. However, the fact that 67% of the teachers in four districts said they planned to continue using the EIR program on their own and, in fact, did so is encouraging. The fact that in District A, the EIR program has been used for a fourth consecutive year and in Districts B and C for a third year is also encouraging.

A survey was conducted of teachers who had been using the EIR program for several years. Teachers who used the EIR program in Districts A and B past Year 1 were interviewed to determine what types of support have been helpful to facilitate their continued implementation of the program, or modifications of it, over time. Also, teachers were asked what kinds of modifications they have made to the program and why.

In District A, five teachers in Year 3 were interviewed. In Building 1, one classroom teacher was continuing to provide the small-group instruction. She liked the opportunity that the EIR program gave her to really know her lowest readers. Also, during the regular reading instruction she could reinforce for these children things taught during EIR time. In the other first-grade classrooms in this building, a reading resource teacher was coming into the class to provide the intervention. This was at a time other than during the reading-writing block. Classroom teachers who chose not to do the teaching themselves felt they did not have time to fit it into their days. Furthermore, two special reading teachers hired by the district were available to provide the EIR instruction. Instructional aides were available to listen to children read one on one each day.

The program procedures had not been modified in Building 1 (District A). However, the special reading teachers did not get started with the EIR program until November because they were working in kindergartens in September and October. They said they saw the need for and hoped to get started with the EIR program in first-grade classrooms by the end of September the following year.

In Building 2 (District A), the classroom teachers were providing the EIR instruction themselves. The teachers had written their own retellings of literature used in the regular reading program. They did this because they believed that the EIR program would blend in better with their regular program than when the original EIR materials were used.

Other than this change with materials the two teachers interviewed did not report making many changes in procedures. One teacher had had two groups in the fall for several months and thought that children who were of average ability but not yet reading would benefit from the EIR program. The other teacher had had two groups all year because she believed her slightly below average children as well as her very below average children were benefiting from the program. A reading resource teacher came into the class to work with the slightly below average group, and the classroom teacher worked with the lowest group.

Teachers in Building 2 (District A) did not seem to require or expect much assistance with the program. An aide got materials ready for teachers as they requested them. The aide also listened to children read independently each day.

Unlike classroom teachers in Building 1 (District A), the classroom teachers who were interviewed in Building 2 had strong feelings about the importance of providing the EIR instruction themselves. One teacher said that the program gave her a better understanding of the children's abilities. Also she felt that the program provided almost instant results in the fall.

In District B, three classroom teachers and one resource teacher who were interviewed in Year 2 indicated that they were still very enthusiastic about the program. The one modification they had made was covering one story a week, and consequently spending only 3 days a week instead of 5 days on the program. The teachers chose to do this to give themselves flexibility in terms of deciding whether to implement the program on a particular day. In this way the teachers said they had reduced the feelings of pressure they had experienced previously to fit the program into their busy schedules every day. By mid-February, the teachers were beginning Level C books, which was not far behind their location in the program the year before.

The classroom teachers in District B believed that a support person was important to help keep the program running. The reading resource teacher functioning as this support person was spending about 30% of her time assisting the three classroom teachers with the program. She was listening to all 24 children read one on one for about 5 minutes 3 days a week in their classrooms. She was providing the small-group instruction to a group of five children while one classroom teacher was providing instruction to another group of six in the same room. The reading resource person also was overseeing materials, making sure the classroom teachers always had the books, charts, and retellings they needed to implement the program. Although the classroom teachers highly valued the expertise of their reading resource teacher, they believed that a well-trained instructional aide could serve as the support person in the program if a reading resource teacher were not available.

The interviews with teachers who have been using the EIR program for 2 or 3 years showed interesting similarities and differences. We had expected more modifications in procedures than teachers reported. Most indicated they were following the 3-day cycle of activities fairly closely. Also, all teachers interviewed reported having an instructional aide or reading resource teacher listen to children read one on one each day the program was implemented.

Teachers in different buildings had nevertheless made different adjustments in the program. In one building, reading resource teachers instead of classroom teachers, for the most part, were providing the EIR instruction. In another building, teachers had written their own story retellings. In another, teachers were using the program 3 days a week instead of 5 days. What is encouraging is that most classrooms teachers who piloted the EIR program have continued to use the program with or without modifications and feel it is worth the extra effort.

CONCLUSIONS

A number of conclusions warrant highlighting. First, the EIR program has been effective in helping many low-achieving readers in first grade get off to a better start in reading than would have been the case without their participation in the program. Second, the children have been successful throughout the program, reading their stories at the end of 3 days with at least 92% accuracy, on the average, from the start of the program in October. Third, classroom teachers have demonstrated that they can make an important difference in the end-of-first-grade reading ability of many of their lowest readers by providing quality supplemental reading instruction on a daily basis. Fourth, classroom teachers involved with the EIR program are positive about it and most have continued to use it in subsequent years.

A classroom intervention program like the EIR should not be the only source of supplemental reading instruction for low-achieving readers in first grade. While we have found that a majority of children receiving help through this program are at least reading by the end of the year, in most instances we have found that only one third to one half of these lowest readers are reading on an end-of-first-grade level by May. Obviously, we would like to see even more reading on grade level by the end of the year. An individual tutoring program like Reading Recovery would be particularly beneficial for some of the very lowest readers.

However, many first-grade readers who appear in September to be potentially at risk of failing to learn to read during the year or making very slow progress in reading can be helped substantially through a supplemental program like the EIR provided by classroom teachers. The classroom teachers who have contributed to the EIR studies have shown that they can make a significant difference in the reading performance of their lowest readers by providing high quality, daily, supplemental reading instruction. Furthermore, they have made an important contribution to the field of literacy education. They have demonstrated that special help for low-achieving readers does not have to be provided by specialists alone.

REFERENCES

Adams, M. (1990). *Beginning to read: Thinking and learning about print.* Cambridge, MA: MIT Press.

Allington, R., & McGill-Franzen, A. (1989). School response to reading failure: Instruction for Chapter 1 and special education students in grades two, four, and eight. *Elementary School Journal, 89*, 529–542.

Anderson, R.C., Hiebert, E.H., Scott, J. A., & Wilkinson, I.G.A. (1985). *Becoming a nation of readers*. Champaign, IL: University of Illinois, Center for the Study of Reading.

Ball, E.W., & Blachman, B.A. (1991). Does phoneme awareness training in kindergarten make a difference in early word recognition and developmental spelling? *Reading Research Quarterly, 26*, 49–66.

Bond, G.L., & Dykstra, R. (1967). The cooperative research program in first-grade reading instruction. *Reading Research Quarterly, 2*, 5–142.

Bradley, I., & Bryant, P. (1983). Categorizing sounds and learning to read. A causal connection. *Nature, 301*, 419–421.

Carver, R.P., & Hoffman, J.V. (1981). The effect of practice through repeated reading on gain in reading ability using a computer-based instructional system. *Reading Research Quarterly, 16*, 374–390.

Chall, J.S. (1983). *Learning to read: The great debate* (2nd ed.). New York: McGraw-Hill.

Chomsky, C. (1979). Approaching early reading through invented spelling. In L.B. Resnick & P.A. Weaver (Eds.), *Theory and practice of early reading* (Vol. 2, pp. 43–65). Hillsdale, NJ: Erlbaum.

Clay, M. (1985). *What did I write?* Portsmouth, NH: Heinemann Education Books.

Clay, M. (1985). *The early detection of reading difficulties* (3rd ed.). Portsmouth, NH: Heinemann.

Cunningham, A.E. (1990). Explicit versus implicit instruction in phonemic awareness. *Journal of Experimental Child Psychology, 50*, 429–444.

Dowhower, S.L. (1987). Effects of repeated reading on second-grade transitional readers' fluency and comprehension. *Reading Research Quarterly, 22*, 389–406.

Ehri, L., & Wilce, L. (1987). Does learning to spell help beginners learn to read words? *Reading Research Quarterly, 12*, 47–65.

Herman, P.A. (1985). The effect of repeated readings on reading rate, speech pauses, and word recognition accuracy. *Reading Research Quarterly, 20*, 553–564.

Johnston, P., & Allington, R. (1991). Remediation. In R. Barr, M. Kamil, P. Mosenthal, & P.D. Pearson (Eds.), *Handbook of reading research* (Vol. 2). New York: Longman.

Juel, C. (1988). Learning to read and write: A longitudinal study of fifty-four children from first through fourth grade. *Journal of Educational Psychology, 80*, 437–447.

Juel, C., Griffith, P.L., & Gough, P.B. (1986). Acquisition of literacy: A longitudinal study of children in first and second grade. *Journal of Educational Psychology, 78*, 243–255.

Liberman, I. (1973). Segmentation of the spoken word and reading acquisition. *Bulletin of the Orton Society, 23*, 65–77.

Lundberg, I., Frost, J., & Petersen, O. (1988). Effects of an extensive program for stimulating phonological awareness in preschool children. *Reading Research Quarterly, 23*, 263–284.

Mason, J. (1980). When do children begin to read: An exploration of four-year-old children's letter and word recognition competencies. *Reading Research Quarterly, 15*, 203–227.

O'Sullivan, P.J., Ysseldyke, J.E., Christenson, S.L., & Thurlow, M.L. (1990). Mildly handicapped elementary students' opportunity to learn during reading instruction in mainstream and special education settings. *Reading Research Quarterly, 25,* 131–146.

Pflaum, S.W., Walberg, H.J., Karegianes, M.L., & Rasher, S.P. (1980). Reading instruction: A quantitative analysis. *Educational Researcher, 9,* 12–18.

Pinnell, G., Fried, M., & Estice, R. (1990). Reading Recovery: Learning how to make a difference. *Reading Teacher, 43,* 282–295.

Samuels, S.J. (1979). The method of repeated readings. *Reading Teacher, 32,* 403–408.

Share, D.L., Jorm, A.F., Maclean, R., & Matthews, R. (1984). Sources of individual differences in reading achievement. *Journal of Educational Psychology, 76,* 1309–1324.

Stanovich, K. (1986). Matthew effects in reading. Some consequences of individual differences in the acquisition of literacy. *Reading Research Quarterly, 21,* 360–406.

Stanovich, K.E., Cunningham, A.E., & Feeman, D.J. (1984). Intelligence, cognitive skills, and early reading progress. *Reading Research Quarterly, 19,* 278–303.

Taylor, B. (1990). *A test of phonemic awareness for classroom use.* Unpublished paper, University of Minnesota.

Taylor, B., Short, R., Frye, B., & Shearer, B. (1992). Classroom teachers prevent reading failure among low-achieving first grade students. *Reading Teacher, 45,* 595–597.

Tunmer, W.E., & Nesdale, A.R. (1985). Phonemic segmentation skill and beginning reading. *Journal of Educational Psychology, 77,* 417–427.

 # Part III

Extending Interventions Across Schools

Success for All: Getting Reading Right the First Time

ROBERT E. SLAVIN NANCY A. MADDEN

NANCY L. KARWEIT LAWRENCE J. DOLAN

BARBARA A. WASIK

The authors developed Success for All, a program involving a comprehensive reorganization of the urban elementary school, based on the conviction that reading failure in the primary grades is preventable. Success for All provides excellent instruction in preschool, kindergarten, and primary grades as well as intensive one-on-one intervention if reading problems begin to emerge. Parent support is another important component of the program. Only 4% of Success for All third graders from five schools who were in the program since first grade were found to be performing 2 years below grade level in reading. Also, special education placement were reduced by about half and retentions in grade reduced to near zero. After describing the program the authors conclude by making the bold point that the problems of education in the inner city can be solved and that as educators we have the moral obligation to see that this happens.

Portions of this chapter were adapted from Slavin, Madden, Karweit, Dolan, and Wasik (1992).

Every child who enters elementary school expects to learn to read. Yet we can predict with depressing accuracy that in every generation of bright, enthusiastic kindergartners, a certain proportion will either end up as poor readers, be retained, be assigned to special education, or need long-term remedial services. According to the National Assessment of Education Progress (NAEP), 38% of all 9-year-olds cannot read at the basic level, considered a minimum requirement for success in school. Among African-American 9-year-olds, 61% fall below the basic level (Mullis & Jenkins, 1990). Students who do not read in the early grades often end up in remedial programs (e.g., Chapter 1) or special education; many are retained in grade. Remediation, special education, and retention are all very expensive. In purely economic terms, preventing reading failure pays off quickly in reduced need for these interventions. More importantly, early reading failure causes major damage to children. Disadvantaged third graders who are reading a year or more below grade level have little chance of ultimately graduating from high school (Lloyd, 1978).

As other projects in this volume demonstrate, there is a growing body of evidence from several sources to indicate that reading failure in the early grades is fundamentally preventable. There is some evidence that these improvements can be maintained into the later elementary grades. What would happen if we decided to provide children with the programs and resources necessary to ensure that every child in every school would reach the third grade on time with adequate reading skills, no matter what? If we decided that no child would need to be assigned to special education for a learning problem unless they were seriously disabled? If we decided that no child would need to be retained in grade or relegated to long-term remedial services? How could we design an urban elementary school that simply refuses to accept the idea that even a single child will fail to learn to read?

These questions led to the development of Success for All, a comprehensive reorganization of the urban elementary school designed to use existing and additional resources in a coherent way to ensure the success of every child. Our basic approach to designing a program to ensure success for all children begins with two essential principles: (1) prevention and (2) immediate, intensive intervention. That is, learning problems must first be prevented by providing children with the best available preschool, kindergarten, and elementary classroom programs and by engaging their parents in support of their school success. When learning problems do appear, corrective interventions must be immediate, intensive, and minimally disruptive to students' progress in the regular program. That is, students receive help early, when their problems are small. This help is intensive and effective enough to catch students up with their classmates so that they can profit from their regular classroom instruction. Instead of letting students fall further and further behind until they need special or remedial education or are retained in grade, students in Success for All are given whatever help they need to keep up in reading and other basic skills. This chapter describes the Success for All program and its outcomes, and discusses the policy implications of a demonstration that reading failure can be prevented.

COMPONENTS OF SUCCESS FOR ALL

Reading Program

While the program has many components, three fundamental building blocks are (1) innovative curriculum and instruction in reading, (2) tutorial support, and (3) regrouping for reading instruction so that students are receiving reading material that is appropriate for them. Based on our conclusions that one-to-one tutoring is the most effective form of instruction known (see Slavin, Karweit, & Madden, 1989; Wasik & Slavin, 1990), a priority in designing the program was to provide tutorial support for students who need it. The tutors are certified teachers with experience teaching Chapter 1, special education, and primary reading. Tutors work one-on-one with students who are having difficulties keeping up with their reading groups. The tutoring occurs in 20-minute sessions usually taken from an hour-long social studies period. In general, tutors support students' success in the regular reading curriculum, rather than teaching different objectives. However, tutors seek to identify learning problems and use different strategies to ensure progress. For example, tutors teach such metacognitive skills as comprehension monitoring, self-questioning, rereading, and use of context cues.

During daily 90-minute reading periods, tutors serve as additional reading teachers to reduce class size for reading. Information on students' specific deficits and needs pass between reading teachers and tutors on brief forms, and reading teachers and tutors are given regular times to meet for purposes of coordinating their approaches with individual children.

Initial decisions about reading group placement and need for tutoring are made based on informal reading inventories given to each child by the tutors. After this, reading group placements and tutoring assignments are made based on 8-week assessments, which include teacher judgments as well as more formal assessments. First graders receive first priority for tutoring, on the assumption that the primary function of the tutors is to help all students be successful in reading the first time, before they become remedial readers.

While only a few students receive tutorial support at any given time, all first- through third-grade students participate in a daily instructional program that has been restructured substantially from the organization and content that characterizes most elementary schools. A basic change was to regroup students for reading periods so that they move from their heterogeneous, age-grouped classes of 25 students to a reading class of 15 to 20 students who are all reading at the same level for a daily 90-minute period. A 2-1 reading class might contain first-, second-, and third-grade students all reading at the same level. Regrouping allows teachers to teach the whole reading class without having to break the class into reading groups. This greatly reduces the time spent in seat work and increases direct instruction time, eliminating workbooks, dittos, or other follow-up activities that are needed in classes that have multiple reading groups. The regrouping is a form of the Joplin Plan, which has been found to increase reading achievement in the elementary grades (Slavin, 1987).

Beginning Reading

The Beginning Reading program used in Success for All (Madden & Livermon, 1990) is based on research that points to the need to have students learn to read in meaningful contexts and at the same time to have a systematic presentation of word attack skills (see Adams, 1990). Three basic components—(1) reading of children's literature by the teacher, (2) "shared story" beginning reading lessons, and (3) systematic language development—combine to address the learning needs of first graders in a variety of ways.

A major principle of Beginning Reading is that students need to learn comprehension strategies at their level of receptive language, not only their reading level. What this means is that the teacher reads children's literature to students and engages students in discussions, retelling of the stories, and writing. The idea is to build reading comprehension skill with material more difficult than that which students could read on their own. This process begins in preschool and kindergarten with the Story Telling and Retelling (STaR) program, which continues through part of the first grade, and continues through fifth grade with a "Listening Comprehension" program.

The shared story beginning reading lessons emphasize immediate application of skills to real reading. For example, by the fifth lesson (usually a lesson takes about two class periods), when students have learned only three letter sounds, they read an entire book. This book is part of a series of shared stories, which contain some material written in small type to be read by the teacher and other material in large type to be read by students. The adult text adds background and richness to the story that would not be possible with the limited vocabulary of an early reader. This scaffolding approach, gradually turning responsibility over to the students, is adapted from Beck et al. (1989). In addition, pictures are used to represent certain words so that students can read interesting stories long before they even know the entire alphabet. For example, a shared story that might be used in November or December of first grade is *The Duck in the Pond* (from Madden & Livermon, 1990). The story is about two children, Jenny and Tom, who want to try out for the football team on Monday. On Saturday before the try-out, they go to the park to practice. Their favorite place in the park is right beside the pond.

They've forgotten that it has rained the night before. As the first page of the text indicates, the mud causes a problem for Jenny and Tom:

Jenny and Tom are at the pond. Jenny kicks the football to Tom. O, no! The football is stuck in the mud! Tom grabs the football. Tom says, "Yuck! Mud is on the football."

The teacher provides additional context by reading, "The football stuck in the mud, so Tom grabbed it. Now the football was muddy, and so were Tom's hands." Questions to ask children are also provided, such as the one that follows this text for children and teachers: "What do you think Tom would do about the mud on the football and on his hands?" Throughout the story, which involves an increasing problem as the football and Tom slide into the pond, the text that children read is augmented by teacher reading and questions.

While the stories are designed to be meaningful and interesting, the students' portions of the shared stories use a phonetically regular vocabulary, so that the skills students are learning will work in cracking the reading code. At Lesson 56, students begin to use the Walker Learn to Read Series, an engaging set of stories that uses some phonetically controlled vocabulary. Of course, students learn many sight words along the way, but the intention of Beginning Reading is to empower students by giving them decoding strategies that will work and then to give them interesting, worthwhile material that they can successfully read using their new skills.

Beginning Reading makes extensive use of partner learning. Students take turns reading to each other and helping each other with difficult words, and they help each other with "share sheets," reinforcing skills the teacher has taught. While students read to each other, the teacher circulates among the students to listen in on them, and occasionally asks a student to read. This gives students substantial practice in oral reading and rereading. When a pair of students feels that both have mastered the story, they read it to the class in a "reading celebration" followed by comments and applause.

Beginning Reading lessons emphasize a rapid pace of instruction, a variety of activities, and many opportunities for students to actively participate. Each day following STaR or Listening Comprehension, the shared story lesson begins with rereading a familiar shared story in a group or with partners and a quick writing review of some of the words and sounds from that story. Then, students sing an alphabet song to coax Alphie (a puppet) to come out of his box. Alphie brings the students the letter of the day, including a silly tongue twister. For example, Alphie might say: "A lot of words start with the sound /s/. Listen to this: 'Sam said he was sorry he put salt in Sally's sandwich.'" The teacher then works with the tongue twister to emphasize the /s/ sound. Alphie shows the students objects and pictures that do or do not start with the sound, and students use whole-class responding (choral responses, pointing, or signing) to discriminate between them. Students learn the shapes of letters by tracing them in the air and on each others' backs, and by learning a little couplet: "Curve left, curve right, around and stop. The sound for s is /s/."

The lesson goes on to help students identify letter sounds within words, to come up with words of their own using the sound, to match the written letter with pictures, to use sound blending skills to stretch and then compress words, to spell words from their sounds, and so on. The idea here is to teach the same discriminations many ways, to involve many sensory modalities, and to maintain students' active engagement, enthusiasm, and interest. The words and sounds practiced are immediately used in a new shared story that is read and discussed and then read again for fluency.

Beyond the Basics

Beyond the Basics (Madden, Slavin, Stevens, & Farnish, 1987) is the reading approach used in Success for All from the first-reader level (usually spring of first grade) to the end of elementary school. It is an adaptation of Cooperative Integrated Reading and Composition (CIRC), a cooperative learning program that encompasses both reading and writing, and language arts. Studies of CIRC have shown it to be effective in increasing students' reading, writing, and language achievement (Stevens, Madden, Slavin, & Farnish, 1987).

The curricular focus of Beyond the Basics is primarily on building comprehension, thinking skills, fluency, and pleasure in reading. Beyond the Basics assumes that students coming out of Beginning Reading have solid word attack skills, but need to build on this foundation to learn to understand and enjoy increasingly complex material.

Students in Beyond the Basics are assigned to four- or five-member learning teams that are heterogeneous in performance level, sex, and age. These teams choose team names and sit together at most times. The teams have a responsibility to see that all team members are learning the material being taught in class. Each week, students take a set of quizzes. These contribute to a team score, and the teams can earn certificates and other recognition based on the team's average quiz scores. Students also contribute points to their teams by completing book reports and writing assignments, and by returning completed parent forms indicating that they have been reading at home each evening.

The main activities of Beyond the Basics are described in the following sections (adapted from Slavin, Madden, & Stevens, 1989–1990).

Basal-Related Activities.   Students use their regular basal readers, novels, anthologies, or whatever materials are available in the school. Stories are introduced and discussed by teachers. During these lessons, teachers set a purpose for reading, introduce new vocabulary, review old vocabulary, discuss the story after students have read it, and so on. Story discussions are structured to emphasize such skills as making and supporting predictions about the story and understanding major structural components of the story.

After stories are introduced, students are given a series of activities to do in their teams when they are not working with the teacher in a reading group. The sequence of activities is as follows:

- *Partner reading.* Students read the story silently first and then take turns reading the story aloud with their partners, alternating readers after each paragraph. As their partner reads, the listener follows along and corrects any errors the reader makes.
- *Story structure and story-related writing.* Students are given questions related to each narrative story emphasizing the story structure (characters, setting, problem, and solution). Halfway through the story, they are instructed to stop reading and to identify the characters, the setting, and the problem in the story, and to predict how the problem will be resolved. At the end of the story, students respond to the story as a whole and write a few paragraphs on a topic related to the story (for example, they might be asked to write a different ending to the story).
- *Words out loud.* Students are given a list of new or difficult words used in the story, which they must be able to read correctly in any order without hesitating or stumbling. These words are presented by the teacher in the reading group, and then students practice their lists with their partners or other teammates until they can read them smoothly.
- *Word meaning.* Students are given a list of story words that are new in their speaking vocabularies and asked to write a sentence for each that shows the meaning of the word ("An octopus grabbed the swimmer with its eight long legs," not "I have an octopus").
- *Story retell.* After reading the story and discussing it in their reading groups, students summarize the main points of the story to their partners. The partners have a list of essential story elements that they use to check the completeness of the story summaries.
- *Spelling.* Students pretest one another on a list of spelling words each week, and then work over the course of the week to help one another master the list.
- *Partner checking.* After students complete each of the preceding activities, their partners initial a student assignment record form indicating that they have completed or achieved criterion on that task. Students are given daily expectations as to the number of activities to be completed, but they can go at their own rate and complete the activities earlier if they wish, creating additional time for independent reading.
- *Tests.* At the end of three class periods, students are given a comprehension test on the story, are asked to write meaningful sentences for certain

vocabulary words, and are asked to read the word list aloud to the teacher. Students are not permitted to help one another on these tests. The test scores and evaluations of the story-related writing are major components of student's weekly team scores.

Direct Instruction in Reading Comprehension.   Students receive direct instruction from the teacher in reading comprehension skills such as identifying main ideas, drawing conclusions, and comparing and contrasting ideas. A special curriculum was designed for this purpose. After each lesson, students work on reading comprehension worksheets or games as a whole team, first gaining consensus on one set of worksheet items, then practicing independently, assessing one another's work, and discussing any remaining problems on a second set of items.

Independent Reading.   Every evening, students are asked to read a trade book of their choice for at least 20 minutes. In most schools, classroom libraries of paperback books are established for this purpose. Parents initial forms indicating that students have read for the required time, and students contribute points to their teams if they submit a completed form each week. In a twice weekly "book club," students discuss the books they have been reading and present more formal book reports, trying to entice others to take home the same book. If students complete their basal-related activities or other activities early, they may also read their independent reading books in class.

Listening Comprehension.   Each day, the teacher presents a lesson focusing on comprehension of stories at students' interest level but above their current reading level. This lesson uses readings from children's literature to teach such skills as visualization of story characters and settings, identification of problems and attempts to solve problems, story mapping, and sequence of events in narratives.

Writing and Language Arts

Writing and language arts instruction in Success for All is provided to students in their heterogeneous homerooms, not in their reading groups. The basic philosophy behind the writing and language arts programs is that writing should be given the main emphasis and that language arts, especially mechanics and usage, should be taught in the context of writing, not as a separate topic.

There are two levels in the Success for All writing and language arts approach. Both are based on a writing process approach, which emphasizes writing for a real audience, writing for revision, and gradually building spelling and mechanics in the context of writing (Calkins, 1983; Graves, 1983). Writing

From the Heart, used in grades 1 and 2, uses an informal version of writing process, while CIRC Writing, used in grades 3 through 6, uses a more formal writing process model with regular four-member peer response groups and students working compositions through from plan to draft to revision to editing to publication. These programs are described in the following.

Writing From the Heart

The goal of Writing From the Heart (Madden, Wasik, & Petza, 1989), the writing and language arts program used in grades 1 and 2 in Success for All, is to tap students' innate desire, energy, and enthusiasm for communication and to move them to the next step of sharing their ideas with others through writing. Students need to see writing as a personal expression, not an ordinary school task. They must put their hearts into their writing, not just their minds.

Writing From the Heart is a writing process model, which means that students write for a real audience and learn to revise their writing until it is ready for "publication." Students do not work in formal writing teams (that will come in third grade), but they do work informally with partners while they are writing. The main elements of Writing From the Heart are as follows:

- *Modeling and motivating writing.* At the beginning of each lesson, the teacher provides a model or motivator for writing. For example, the teacher might read a story similar to what students will be writing, or ask students to describe experiences that relate to a particular kind of writing. The teacher may introduce formats to help students plan their writing. For example, in writing about myself, students are given a set of questions to answer, which they then use to create a story.
- *Writing a "sloppy copy."* Students are encouraged to write a sloppy copy, a first draft of their composition. They are taught to use "sound spelling" (invented spelling) if they cannot spell a word. For example, *dnsr* is a way a student might write dinosaur.
- *Partner sharing.* At several points in the writing process students share their writing with partners and receive feedback and ideas from them.
- *Revision.* Beginning after several weeks of the program, students learn to revise their compositions using feedback from partners and from the teacher. Specific revision skills are taught and modeled in the lessons.
- *Editing.* In preparation for publication, the teacher helps each child prepare a perfect draft of his or her composition, complete with pictures.
- *Publication.* Final drafts of students' writings are published in a class book, read to the class, and recognized in as many ways as possible.
- *Sharing and celebration.* At many points in the writing process students have opportunities to share their writing with the class. The teacher sets up a special "author's chair" from which the authors present their latest works.

Writing From the Heart shows students that they are authors and have something to say; teaches them that writing is a process of thinking, drafting, revising, and polishing ideas; and lets them know that writing is fun. They are then ready to learn more about the craft of writing with more formal instruction in style, mechanics, and usage.

CIRC Writing and Language Arts

The writing and language arts program used in the upper elementary grades is one developed earlier as part of CIRC for grades 3 and up (Madden, Wasik, & Petza, 1989). In this program, students are assigned to four- or five-member heterogeneous writing teams. CIRC Writing and Language Arts has two major instructional formats. About 3 days each week are used for writing process activities, and 2 days are used for language arts instruction.

Writing Process Activities.   Each writing process day begins with a brief lesson on a writing concept. For example, the first lesson is on "mind movies," visualization of events in a narrative to see where additional detail or description is needed. Other lessons include organizing imaginative narratives, using observation to add life to descriptions, writing personal narratives, using persuasive arguments, exploring explanatory writing, and so on. The writing concept lessons are meant to spark ideas and help students expand on their writing and evaluate their own and others' compositions.

Most of the writing and language arts period is spent with students writing their own compositions while the teacher circulates among the teams and confers with individual students. Students draft many compositions and then choose a smaller number they would like to carry through all the steps to publication. The steps are as follows:

1. *Prewriting.* Students discuss with their teammates a topic they would like to address and an audience for their writing. They then draft a plan, using a "skeleton planning form," an "idea net," or other forms to organize their thinking.
2. *Drafting.* After preparing a plan in consultation with teammates, the student writes a first draft, focusing on getting ideas on paper rather than spelling and mechanics, which will come later.
3. *Revision.* Students read their drafts to their teammates. The teammates are taught to rephrase the main idea of the story in their own words, to mention two things they liked about the story, and to note two things they'd like to hear more about. The teacher may also confer with students at the revision stage to applaud students' ideas and to suggest additions and changes.
4. *Editing.* Once the author is satisfied with the content of the writing, the mechanics, usage, and spelling must be corrected. Students work with a

partner to go through an editing checklist. The checklist starts with a small number of goals (such as correct capitalization and end punctuation), but then adds goals as students complete language arts lessons. For example, after a lesson on subject-verb agreement or run-on sentences, these may be added to the checklist. First the author checks the composition against the checklist, then a teammate does so, and finally the teacher checks it.

5. *Publication.* Publication involves the creation of the final draft and celebration of the author's writing. Students carefully rewrite their work, incorporating all final corrections made by the teacher. They then present their compositions to the class from a fancy author's chair, and may then contribute their writing to a team book or a team section of a class book. These books are proudly displayed in the class or library. In addition, students can be asked to read their compositions to other classes, or to otherwise celebrate and disseminate their masterpieces!

Language Arts Instruction. About 2 days each week, the teacher teaches structured lessons on language mechanics skills. These are presented as skills for revision and editing, because their purpose is to directly support students' writing. The teacher determines the order of lessons according to problems students are experiencing and skills they will need for upcoming writing. For example, the teacher might notice that many students are having problems with complete sentences, or anticipate that since students are about to write dialogue they might need to learn how to use quotation marks.

Students work in their four-member writing teams to help one another master the skills taught by the teacher. The students work on examples, compare answers with each other, resolve discrepancies, explain ideas to each other, and so on. Ultimately students are quizzed on the skill, and the teams can earn certificates or other recognition based on the average performance of all team members. As noted earlier, immediately after a revision and editing skills lesson the new skill is added to the editing checklist, so language arts skills are immediately put into practice in students' writing.

Eight-Week Assessments

Shifts in assessment practices have been as critical to the project as changes in instruction. At 8-week intervals, reading teachers assess student progress through the reading program on curriculum-based measures developed for the program. The results of the assessments are used to determine who is to receive tutoring, to change students' reading groups, to suggest other adaptations in students' programs, and to identify students who need other types of assistance, such as family interventions or vision or hearing problems.

Family Support

One of the basic tenets of the Success for All philosophy is that parents are an essential part of the formula for success. A family support team works in each school, serving to make families feel comfortable in the school as well as providing specific services. In a few schools, social workers, attendance monitors, and other staff are added to the school's usual staff. In others, the family support team consists of the Chapter 1 parent liaison, vice-principal (if any), counselor (if any), facilitator, and any other appropriate staff already present in the school. The family support team works to involve parents in support of their children's success in school. It contacts parents whose children are frequently absent to see what resources can be provided to assist the family in getting their child to school. Parenting education is provided for interested families. Family support staff, teachers, and parents work together to solve school behavior problems. Also, family support staff are called on to provide assistance when students seem to be working at less than their full potential because of problems at home. Families of students who are not receiving adequate sleep or nutrition, need glasses, are not attending school regularly, or are exhibiting serious behavior problems receive family support assistance.

Connections to the community are also made through the advisory committee, which is composed of the building principal, program facilitator, teacher, and parent representatives. This group meets regularly to review the progress of the program and to identify and solve any problems that arise.

Preschool and Kindergarten

Many of the Success for All schools provide a half-day preschool and/or full-day kindergarten for eligible students. The preschool and kindergarten programs focus on providing a balanced and developmentally appropriate learning experience for young children. The curriculum emphasizes the development and use of language. It provides a balance of academic readiness and nonacademic music, art, and movement activities in a series of thematic units. Readiness activities include use of the Peabody Language Development Kits and STaR, in which students retell stories read by the teachers (Karweit, Coleman, Waclawiw, & Petza, 1990).

Special Education

Every effort is made to deal with students' learning problems within the context of the regular classroom, as supplemented by tutors. Special education resource services are still provided for students assigned to special education in previous years, but no new assignments to resource services are made for reading problems, on the assumption that tutoring services available to all students will be more appropriate. Self-contained services for seriously handicapped students are maintained for students whose needs cannot be met in the regular class.

Facilitators and Professional Development

A primary mechanism for making the changes in a school is the program facilitator. This individual, usually an experienced and highly skilled teacher from within the school, works full time at each school to oversee (with the principal) the operation of the Success for All model. The facilitator helps plan the Success for All program, helps the principal with scheduling, and visits classes and tutoring sessions frequently to help teachers and tutors with individual problems. Program facilitators work directly with the teachers on implementation of the curriculum, classroom management, and other issues, help teachers and tutors deal with any behavior problems or other special problems, and coordinate the activities of the family support team with those of the instructional staff.

The addition of the program facilitator is not the only way in which changes are set into motion in a school. Teachers and tutors, who all have teaching credentials, receive detailed teacher's manuals supplemented by 3 days of in-service at the beginning of the school year. For teachers of grades 1 through 3 and for reading tutors, these training sessions focus on implementation of the reading program, and their detailed teacher's manuals cover general teaching strategies as well as specific lessons. Preschool and kindergarten teachers and aides are trained in use of the STaR and Peabody programs, thematic units, and other aspects of the preschool and kindergarten models. Tutors later receive an additional day of training on tutoring strategies and reading assessment.

Throughout the year, additional in-service presentations are made by the facilitators and other project staff on such topics as classroom management, instructional pace, and cooperative learning. Facilitators also organize many informal sessions to allow teachers to share problems and problem solutions, suggest changes, and discuss individual children. The staff development model used in Success for All emphasizes relatively brief initial training with extensive classroom follow-up, coaching, and group discussion.

OUTCOMES OF SUCCESS FOR ALL

The effects of Success for All on students who begin the program in preschool, kindergarten, or first grade are extremely positive on individually administered tests of reading. Figure 7-1 shows the results (in average grade equivalents) in 15 schools in 7 districts, all in different states. The schools range from

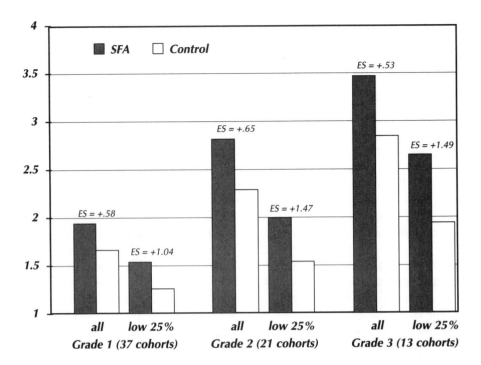

Figure 7-1   Cumulative Mean Reading Grade Equivalents and Effect Sizes in Success for All Schools, 1988–1993

Includes all students in Success for All or control schools since first grade (N=15 school pairs). Schools are in Baltimore, Philadelphia, Charleston (SC), Memphis, Ft. Wayne (IN), Caldwell (ID), and Montgomery (AL).

42% to 100% in free lunch eligibility. Ten of the schools are entirely African-American, 5 are integrated. Effect sizes (the proportion of a standard deviation separating experimental and control groups) are also presented. Note that while Success for All students in general are far outperforming their counterparts in the control group, the effects are particularly dramatic for the students who started out in the lowest quarter of the sample in pretest scores. Significantly, only 2.2% of Success for All third graders who were in the program since first grade are currently performing 2 years below grade level, one traditional indicator of learning disabilities in reading. In contrast, 8.89% of matched control students were 2 years or more below grade level (see Slavin et al., 1992, for more on the research design and findings).

Similar findings have been obtained for schools in Baltimore, Philadelphia, Memphis, Fort Wayne, Indiana, Charleston, South Carolina, Montgomery, Alabama, and Caldwell, Idaho (Slavin, Madden, Dolen, Wasik, Ross, &

Smith, 1993). Special education referrals and assignments for learning disabilities have been reduced by about half in the five Baltimore schools. At a rural Maryland school where the main focus on the program was on providing alternatives to special education, referrals to special education fell from 22 to 6, and assignments fell from 12 to 3 in the first 2 years of Success for All (see Slavin & Madden, 1991). In addition to increasing achievement and decreasing special education assignments, retentions in grade were reduced to near zero in all schools. In the Baltimore city schools, this reduction was from a preprogram mean of about 11% per year in grades K through 3.

The findings to date of the Success for All evaluations illustrate the potential of prevention and early intervention to keep students from falling far behind their agemates, to keep them from failing, and to keep them from being assigned to special education for learning disabilities. All of the Success for All schools serve very disadvantaged student populations; in particular, the Baltimore city schools experience problems with truancy, inadequate health care, parental poverty, drug involvement, and other problems at a level that is unusual even among urban schools. Yet in these schools, students are performing at or near national norms, and even the lowest achievers are well on their way to reading, are being promoted, and are staying out of special education.

Expansion to New Sites

The practical or policy consequences of research on Success for All would be minimal if the program depended on conditions unlikely to be replicated in schools beyond our pilot sites. As of this writing, the program is being implemented in 82 schools in 36 districts in 19 states. These efforts indicate that successful implementation of the program does not depend on the existence of hand-picked staff, charismatic principals, or proximity to Johns Hopkins. The schools are highly diverse and are located in all parts of the country, from California to Idaho to Texas to Alabama to Indiana. This is not to say that every school serving disadvantaged students can successfully implement the program. It does require a clear commitment from the district, principal, and staff to a very different way of organizing their schools. However, it is our belief and experience that with adequate support from their central administrations, the majority of elementary schools serving disadvantaged students will want to implement a program like Success for All and are capable of doing so.

Cost Efficiency

The effectiveness of Success for All in ensuring that students succeed in the early grades is clear, but this success is not gained without commensurate investments. The most important impediments to the widespread use of Success for All are not lack of willingness or skill on the part of school staffs but rather revolve around the cost of the program. Success for All is an expensive program. School districts that concentrate their Chapter 1 funds in their poorest schools can afford the program in such schools without additional expenditures. Bringing in special education, state compensatory education, funding from settlements in desegregation or school finance suits, or bilingual education or English as a second language funding can also help support the program, and these funding sources are in fact supporting Success for All in almost all of its sites around the country. Thus, there are usually few *additional* costs incurred in adopting the program; most costs are simply reallocations of existing dollars. Further, costs need to be weighed in relation to the accomplishments of students and to the long-term costs to society such as welfare, police, prisons, and so on. The link between school success and life success, and between these and the need for expensive social services, is well established. To the degree that Success for All ultimately reduces delinquency, dropout, teen pregnancy, or other problems strongly associated with school failure in low-income communities, its savings to society could far outweigh any costs of implementation (see Berrueta-Clement, Schweinhart, Barnett, Epstein, & Weikart, 1984).

ISSUES RELATED TO SUCCESS FOR ALL

From all indicators, Success for All appears to be a practical, replicable, and effective program for improving the performance of disadvantaged elementary students. None of the major alternatives to Success for All are as effective in increasing reading performance throughout the elementary grades, and only the preschool studies have any evidence of reduced retentions or special education placements. It is expensive, but with recent increases in Chapter 1 funding, most school districts serving many disadvantaged students should be able to afford a credible form of the model, especially if preschool and extended-day kindergarten are provided by funds other than Chapter 1. Immediate and long-term savings introduced by Success for All can ultimately offset most of the program's cost.

The effectiveness of this intervention, and others described in this volume, raises some critical issues related to compensatory education, special education, and school reform—to which we now turn our attention.

Interventions and Compensatory Education

All too often in its 25-year history, the attention and resources of Chapter 1 and its predecessor, Title I, have mostly gone into identifying and remediating the damage sustained by individual children. Yet the fault lies not in the children, but in the system that failed to prevent the damage in the first place. Chapter 1 can be much more than it is today. It can ensure the basic skills of virtually all children. We have argued (see Slavin, 1991) that Chapter 1 must move away from remediation toward prevention and early intervention to see that students do not fall behind in the first place, and should greatly increase its role in staff development for all teachers in Chapter 1 schools.

Current traditions and policies require attention if the necessary changes are to be made. One of the most fundamental principles of Chapter 1 and Title I has been that compensatory funds must be focused on the lowest achieving students in qualifying schools. In principle this makes sense, in that it avoids spreading Chapter 1 resources too thinly to do low achievers any good, but in practice this requirement has led to many problems, including a lack of consistency or coordination between regular and Chapter 1 instruction, disruption of children's regular classroom instruction, labeling of students who receive services, and unclear responsibility for children's progress (Allington & Johnston, 1989; Stein, Leinhardt, & Bickel, 1989).

It is time to recognize that the best way to prevent students from falling behind is to provide them with top quality instruction in their regular classrooms. A substantial portion of Chapter 1 funds (e.g., 20%) should be set aside for staff development and adoption of programs known to be effective by teachers in Chapter 1 schools. For example, by hiring one less aide, schools could instead devote $20,000 per year to staff development, a huge investment in terms of what schools typically spend but a small one in terms of what Chapter 1 schools receive. No one could argue that the educational impact of one aide could approach that of faithful and intelligent implementation of effective curricula and instructional practices in regular classrooms throughout the school; research on the achievement effects of instructional aides finds that they make little or no measurable difference in achievement (see Slavin, 1994). For this amount of money, a school could pay for extensive in-service, in-class follow-up by trained "circuit riders," and release time for teachers to observe each other's classes and to meet to compare notes, as well as purchase needed materials and supplies. The achievement benefits of effective classroom instruction all day would far outweigh the potential benefits of remedial service.

Success for All provides one demonstration of how a schoolwide emphasis on staff development and adoption of effective practices could be implemented under Chapter 1 funding and could greatly affect the learning of all students. There are other examples of programs that have been much more successful for low-achieving students than remedial services. In a review of the literature on effective programs for students at risk (Slavin, Karweit, & Madden, 1989), we identified several such programs, including a variety of continuous progress models, cooperative learning, and peer tutoring. Programs directed at improving classroom management skills also often increase achievement. Many of the exciting innovations in curriculum currently being discussed are not affecting poor schools, but could do so with the support of Chapter 1 funds. In addition to particular classroom methods, schoolwide change programs such as James Comer's (1988) model, Theodore Sizer's (1984) Re: Learning Approach, and Henry Levin's (1987) Accelerated Schools model (as well as Success for All) could be funded by Chapter 1 if it focused on staff development.

To bring about a situation in which schools can choose from among effective programs, several initiatives are needed. Chapter 1 should be funding development and evaluation of promising practices, including third-party evaluations of programs that already exist. It should also be funding research on processes of disseminating effective practices to individual schools. It should be helping to establish training centers around the country that are able to help schools implement effective practices. It should be examining its funding and accountability requirements to see that they support rather than inhibit schools from using Chapter 1 funds to improve their overall instructional practices.

Interventions and Special Education

For more than 20 years, the most important debates in special education research and policy have revolved around the practice of mainstreaming, particularly mainstreaming of students with mild academic disabilities, such as those identified as learning disabled. From early on, most researchers and policy makers have favored mainstreaming academically disabled students to the maximum extent possible (e.g., Leinhardt & Pallay, 1982; Madden & Slavin, 1983), and the passage of Public Law 94-142 in 1975 put the federal government squarely behind this effort. Since that time, students with academic disabilities have certainly spent more time in general education classes than they did before, but the number of students identified for special education services has risen dramatically. Since 1975, the proportion of students categorized as learning disabled has risen more than 250%, while the category of educable mental retardation has diminished only slightly (Office of Special Education and Rehabilitative Services, 1989).

Despite the increase in mainstreaming, significant proportions of both special and general education teachers have never been comfortable with the practice. The Success for All model proposes a markedly different approach to the education of students who are likely to become academically disabled. The key focus of this model is an emphasis on prevention and on early intensive, and untiring intervention to bring student performance within normal limits. We call this approach *neverstreaming* because its intention is to see that nearly all children remain in the mainstream by intervening to prevent the academic difficulties that would lead them to be identified for separate special education services.

One key concept underlying neverstreaming is that instructional programs must help students start with success and then maintain that success at each critical stage of development. First, all students should arrive in kindergarten with adequate mental and physical development. This requires investments in prenatal and infant and toddler health care, parent training, early stimulation programs for at-risk toddlers, effective preschool programs, and so on. Intensive birth-to-5 programs such as the Milwaukee Project (Garber, 1988) and the Carolina Abecedarian Project (Ramey & Campbell, 1984) show that virtually every child can arrive at the school door with normal IQ and language skills. The next critical juncture is assurance that all students leave first grade well on their way to success in reading and other critical skills. This requires effective kindergarten and first-grade instruction and curriculum, family support programs to ensure parental support of the school's goals, and one-to-one tutoring or other intensive interventions for students who are having difficulties in reading. Actually, success in passing from each grade level to the next might be considered a critical requirement for neverstreaming at all levels; programs and practices must be directed toward doing whatever it takes to see that all children make it each year. As students move into second and third grade and beyond, this would mean continuing to improve regular classroom instruction, to monitor student progress, and to intervene intensively as often as necessary to maintain at-risk students at a performance level at which they can fully profit from the same instruction given to students who were never at risk.

The idea here is to organize school and nonschool resources and programs to relentlessly and systematically prevent students from becoming academically disabled from their first day of school (or earlier) to their last (or later). Rather than just trying to adapt instruction to student heterogeneity, neverstreaming attacks the original problem at its source, attempting to remove the low end of the performance distribution by preventing whatever deficits can be prevented, intensively intervening to identify and remediate any remaining deficits, and maintaining interventions to keep at-risk students from sliding back as they proceed through the grades.

Interventions and the School Reform Movement

We are in a time in American society where there is tremendous pressure to reform our schools. Reform efforts range from modest supplements to traditional classroom instruction to radical break-the-mold approaches to school change. Success for All has many components that have been implemented in isolation in many educational environments. It benefits from past research that documents effective instructional programs for children at risk. One does not have to dig too deeply to recognize how the model has benefited from the development and research of others. For example, our tutoring model has benefited from the research on Reading Recovery (see chapters 4 and 8, this volume), our family support team from Comer's (1988) School Development Model, and our cross-grade regrouping from research in the Joplin Plan (Slavin, 1987). Of course our own instructional approaches draw extensively on our earlier research on the benefits of cooperative learning (Slavin, 1990). We have not tried to reinvent the educational wheel. However, we have put together many existing wheels to create a vehicle to optimize success for every child.

We have learned, as have others, the characteristics of successful replication of educational reform. First, we require that central administration, building leaderships, and school staffs want to become involved in the program. At this stage of program maturity we insist that school staffs vote with 80% affirmation that they want the model. This is critical at the early stage of an innovation. Second, our staff development model continues over multiple years once the initial training is completed. The model is comprehensive, and staff need continual support and feedback regarding the quality of implementation. Finally, we have consistently found the critical importance of an onsite facilitator. A facilitator who is knowledgeable about the teaching process, earns the respect of the staff, and is well organized makes all the difference in the quality of the program. With a committed site, a long-term staff development plan, and a talented facilitator, we know we can make a substantial difference in the lives of children.

CONCLUSION

More than a decade ago, Ronald Edmonds (1981, p. 23) put forth three assertions: (1) We can, whenever and wherever we choose, successfully teach all children whose schooling is of interest to us; (2) we already know more than we need to do that; and (3) whether we do it must finally depend on how we feel about the fact the we haven't so far. Edmonds' conclusions were based on his studies of effective and ineffective schools serving poor and minority children. His key assumption was that if the characteristics of effective schools could be implanted in less effective schools, all children could learn. Yet this transfer turned out not to be an easy one. Making a run-of-the mill school into an outstanding one takes much more than telling staffs the characteristics of outstanding schools.

The greatest importance of the research on Success for All and other efforts described in this volume is that they bring us closer to making Edmond's vision a reality. The findings of research on Success for All and related prevention and early intervention programs make it impossible to continue to say that the problems of education in the inner city cannot be solved. The Success for All schools, which include some of the most disadvantaged schools in such cities as Baltimore, Philadelphia, Memphis, and Montgomery, Alabama, do not have unusual staffs or principals. If they can achieve success with the great majority of at-risk children, so can most schools serving similar children. It takes money, but increasingly the money is already in place as Chapter 1 funds increase for high-poverty schools, or can be found from other sources. What is most needed is leadership—a commitment at every level of the political process to see that we stop discarding so many students at the start of their school careers.

There is much more we need to learn how to do and much more we need to learn about the effects of what we are already doing, but we already know enough to make widespread reading failure a thing of the past. Next September, another 6 million children will enter kindergarten. If we know how to ensure that all of them will succeed in their early schooling years, we have a moral responsibility to use this knowledge. We cannot afford to let another generation slip through our fingers.

REFERENCES

Adams, M.J. (1990). *Beginning to read: Thinking and learning about print.* Cambridge, MA: MIT Press.

Allington, R.L., & Johnston, P. (1989). Coordination, collaboration, and consistency: The redesign of compensatory and special education interventions. In R.E. Slavin, N.L. Karweit, & N.A. Madden (Eds.), *Effective programs for students at risk.* Boston: Allyn & Bacon.

Beck, I.L., Ringler, L.H., Ogle, D.M., Raphael, T.E., Armbruster, B.B., & McKeown, M.G. (1989). *Reading today and tomorrow.* Austin, TX: Holt, Rinehart, and Winston.

Berrueta-Clement, J.R., Schweinhart, L.J., Barnett, W.S., Epstein, A.S., & Weikart, D.P. (1984). *Changed Lives: The effects of the Perry preschool program on youths through age 19:* Ypsilanti, MI: High/Scope.

Calkins, L.M. (1983). *Lessons from a child: On the teaching and learning of writing.* Exeter, NH: Heinemann.

Comer, J. (1988). Educating poor minority children. *Scientific American, 259,* 42–48.

Edmonds, R.R. (1981). Making public schools effective. *Social Policy, 12,* 56–60.

Garber, H.L. (1988). *The Milwaukee project: Preventing mental retardation in children at risk.* Washington, DC: American Association on Mental Retardation.

Graves, D. (1983). *Writing: Teachers and children at work.* Exeter, NH: Heinemann.

Karweit, N.L., Coleman, M.A., Waclawiw, I., & Petza, R. (1990). *Story Telling and Retelling (STaR): Teacher's Manual.* Baltimore: Johns Hopkins University, Center for Research on Effective Schooling for Disadvantaged Students.

Leinhardt, G., & Pallay, A. (1982). Restrictive educational settings: Exile or haven? *Review of Educational Research, 52,* 557–578.

Levin, H. (1987). Accelerated schools for disadvantaged students. *Educational Leadership, 44,* 19–21.

Lloyd, D.N. (1978). Prediction of school failure from third-grade data. *Educational and Psychological Measurement, 38,* 1193–1200.

Madden, N.A., & Livermon, B.J. (1990). *Success for All beginning reading: A manual for teachers* (3rd revision). Baltimore: Johns Hopkins University, Center for Research on Effective Schooling for Disadvantaged Students.

Madden, N.A., & Slavin, R.E. (1983). Mainstreaming students with mild academic handicaps: Academic and social outcomes. *Review of Educational Research, 53,* 519–569.

Madden, N.A., Slavin, R.E., Stevens, R.J., & Farnish, A.M. (1987). *Beyond the basics in reading: Teacher's manual.* Baltimore: Johns Hopkins University, Center for Research on Effective Schooling for Disadvantaged Students.

Madden, N.A., Wasik, B.A., & Petza, R.J. (1989). *Writing From the Heart: A writing process approach for first and second graders.* Baltimore: Johns Hopkins University, Center for Research on Effective Schooling for Disadvantaged Students.

Mullis, I.V.S., & Jenkins, L.B. (1990). *The reading report card, 1971–88.* Washington, DC: U.S. Department of Education.

Office of Special Education and Rehabilitative Services (1989). *Annual report to Congress on the implementation of the Handicapped Act.* Washington, DC: U.S. Department of Education.

Ramey, C.T., & Campbell, F.A. (1984). Preventive education for high-risk children: Cognitive consequences of the Carolina Abecedarian project. *American Journal of Mental Deficiency, 88,* 515–523.

Sizer, T. (1984). *Horace's compromise: The dilemma of the American high school.* Boston: Houghton Mifflin.

Slavin, R.E. (1987). Ability grouping and student achievement in elementary schools: A best-evidence synthesis. *Review of Educational Research, 57,* 293–336.

Slavin, R.E. (1990). *Cooperative learning: Theory, research and practice.* Englewood Cliffs, NJ: Prentice Hall.

Slavin, R.E. (1991). Chapter 1: A vision for the next quarter-century. *Phi Delta Kappan, 72,* 586–592.

Slavin, R.E. (1994). School and classroom organization in beginning reading: Class size, aides, and instructional grouping. In R.E. Slavin, N.L. Karweit, B.A. Wasik, & N.A. Madden (Eds.), *Preventing early school failure: Research on effective strategies.* Boston: Allyn & Bacon.

Slavin, R.E., Madden, N.A., Dolan, L.J., Wasik, B.A., Ross, S., & Smith, L. (1993, April). *"Whenever and wherever we choose. . .:" The replication of Success for All.* Paper presented at the annual meeting of the American Educational Research Association, Atlanta, GA.

Slavin, R.E., Karweit, N.L., & Madden, N.A. (Eds.). (1989). *Effective programs for students at risk.* Boston: Allyn & Bacon.

Slavin, R.E., & Madden, N.A. (1991). *Success for All at Buckingham Elementary: Second year evaluation.* Baltimore: Johns Hopkins University, Center for Research on Effective Schooling for Disadvantaged Students.

Slavin, R.E., Madden, N.A., Karweit, N.L., Dolan, L., & Wasik, B.A. (1992). *Success for All: A relentless approach to prevention and early intervention in elementary schools.* Arlington, VA: Educational Research Service.

Slavin, R.E., Madden, N.A., & Stevens, R.J. (1989–1990). Cooperative learning models for the 3 R's. *Educational Leadership, 47*(4), 22–28.

Stein, M.K., Leinhardt, G., & Bickel, W. (1989). Instructional issues for teaching students at risk. In R.E. Slavin, N.L. Karweit, & N.A. Madden (Eds.), *Effective programs for students at risk.* Boston: Allyn & Bacon.

Stevens, R.J., Madden, N.A., Slavin, R.E., & Farnish, A.M. (1987). Cooperative integrated reading and composition: Two field experiments. *Reading Research Quarterly, 22,* 433–454.

Wasik, B.A., & Slavin, R.E. (1990, April). *Preventing early reading failure with one-to-one tutoring: A best-evidence synthesis.* Paper presented at the annual convention of the American Educational Research Association, Boston.

▶ 8

Interactive Writing
A Transition Tool For Assisting Children in Learning to Read and Write

GAY SU PINNELL   **ANDREA MCCARRIER**

Over a 4-year period the authors and kindergarten, first-grade, Chapter 1, and Reading Recovery teachers in Columbus, Ohio, designed a new approach to initial literacy instruction for their kindergarten, first-grade, and Chapter 1 classes in which literacy experiences for children were rich, meaningful, and enjoyable. In this chapter, the authors focus on one part of this new approach, interactive writing. This technique was found to be particularly effective in helping young children understand how written language works as well as how to use it. In interactive writing, the teacher and children collaborate in the construction of a written text, usually in response to a story that has been read aloud. The teacher takes advantage of opportunities in the writing to teach children about concepts of print and sound-letter relationships. Creative drama related to a story also helps to make the literary experience enjoyable. By the end of the kindergarten year, most of the children in the classes in which the interactive writing program was used were already reading. Only a few were judged to be in need of Reading Recovery the following year in first grade.

One issue of *Teacher to Teacher* newsletter, published by a teacher study group of primary teachers, began by asking, "What is interactive writing?" The answer said, "Interactive writing is a way to show children *how* written language works so that they can do it by themselves." As part of their work in university-school study groups, these teachers tried and refined a group writing process designed to help young children develop important concepts about reading and writing. All of these teachers worked in an urban school system. Some taught first grade, others kindergarten or Chapter 1 pull-out groups. Some taught Reading Recovery (a one-to-one intervention) for half the day and classroom or Chapter 1 groups during the other half.

Their assignments varied; but all had worked with a large number of children who were having difficulty learning to read. They knew it was necessary to provide a rich literacy experience in the first years of school. They wanted to help children deal with the features of print in an enjoyable manner that made sense and connected with their oral language knowledge. By and large, the children had no extensive preschool experiences with print prior to kindergarten entry. Letter knowledge was low as were scores on assessment of concepts about print; however, immersion in written language through hearing stories and reading and writing activities enabled children to learn enjoyably and use these important concepts.

This chapter reports teachers' implementations of a framework for literacy lessons and focuses on one approach, interactive writing, that a group of university- and school-based teacher researchers found to be particularly effective in helping young children learn about and use written language.

TEACHER STUDY GROUPS

The teacher study groups, in collaboration with The Ohio State University (OSU), worked for a period of 4 years, meeting weekly to examine theoretical ideas, plan classroom activities, and share children's responses and progress. Although the membership overlapped, four different groups from Columbus Public Schools were involved. Beginning in 1987, the first study group continued for 2 years and was composed of trained Reading Recovery teachers who were concerned about becoming more effective as Chapter 1 and kindergarten teachers. Two other groups worked from 1989 to 1991, and a group of 10 kindergarten teachers, none of whom had been trained in Reading Recovery, volunteered to participate in a study group that worked for 2 years to develop first-year school experiences in literacy. In addition, a small group of experienced Reading Recovery teachers, most of whom had participated in the first study group, worked together weekly for a year to develop both group models and implement school change. This group originated *Teacher to Teacher* and gave the name *interactive writing* to their variation of shared writing because they wanted to emphasize the role of oral conversation as well as the sharing of the mechanics of the task. As OSU teachers, we, the authors of this chapter, were members of all four study groups. All links between study groups were forged by district personnel, including the coordinator of reading, the director of Chapter 1, and by faculty from OSU.

Initially, the central questions addressed by the groups emerged from 3 years of experience in implementing the Reading Recovery program. Our goal as teachers and researchers was to construct knowledge by bringing together what we had learned about teaching young children to read, particularly those who were having difficulty in the beginning stages. These young children needed a great deal of support, but they also needed to become independent (i.e., to learn how to learn reading and writing). Our general agreement was that the problem lay not so much in cognitive development but in the need for children to gather the meaningful literacy experiences that would enable them to participate fully in school-based literacy activities.

Constructing a Foundation

During 4 years of deliberation, we attempted to bring together four basic frameworks. We examined research related to how young children learn to read and write. A body of research, largely qualitative in nature, has focused on young children's literacy development (e.g., Goodman, 1984, 1986b; Teale & Sulzby, 1986). This research has provided evidence that most children acquire critical concepts about reading and writing long before they enter formal schooling. The assumption is that they learn through functional experiences in their daily lives (Harste, Woodward, & Burke, 1984; McGee, Lomax, & Head, 1988). They learn about stories, the way print works, and important relationships such as sound-letter correspondence. This learning appears to be natural because no formal curriculum exists and, generally, caregivers are not consciously trying to teach concepts of literacy. The concepts seem to emerge from experience; thus, the term *emergent literacy* has been used (Clay, 1991).

In preschool experiences, children have *teachers*, their caregivers, and friends, who support literacy development through informal interactions. Research on language learning supports the idea that the quality of interaction is a critical factor in the process. Through interaction with others, children learn language as a system of rules for expressing meaning. They develop knowledge of language systems that are generative in nature because these systems enable them to generate language and to communicate the range of meanings needed in the social context. By the time young children enter school, they have developed this complex, self-generating language system, which is a testimonial to their ability to learn.

Clay (1991) described literacy learning as the development of a self-extending system in which systems of knowledge, gained through experience in the social context, operate together in a way that provides for more learning. Learners construct self-extending systems for themselves; but they are assisted through their interactions with adults who help them take on complex tasks that they could not accomplish alone. This experience leads to independent performance of those same tasks and contributes to the development of the internal strategies that build the system.

For most children, these adult-child interactions take place on an informal basis at home and in the community. Adults are not consciously trying to teach children; nevertheless, they provide a combination of demonstration, support, and direct teaching that helps children develop a foundation of knowledge about literacy that serves them well when they enter school. While learning to read, children must use their ability to respond to decontextualized language (speech that extends to events that are not in the present social context) and to link this language to the visual information presented on the printed page. They must simultaneously deal with what Clay (1991) calls the "twin puzzles" of reading, which are (1) *the hierarchical nature of language*, which is organized in levels from phonemes to words, to sentences, and to larger texts; and (2) *serial order*, which means that the order of language figures critically in the communication of meaning. Oral language is presented serially in time; in English, print is presented in sequence, left to right and top to bottom on the page. To construct meaning from text, the young reader must learn how to selectively adapt to the needed level of the language hierarchy while moving through print in serial order.

Reading is a complex, problem-solving activity that takes place in the reader's mind. Meek (1982) said that "one of the greatest problems for the beginner is that he cannot tell by watching them what [other] readers are actually doing" (p. 20). Children depend on what they can observe others doing and on what they are told to do. In every interaction surrounding literacy events, parents and teachers are demonstrating and indirectly or directly telling children something about the complex activities that make up reading. The assistance of an adult provides the opportunity for the child to enter literacy activities to a far greater extent than he or she could do alone (Clay & Cazden, 1990).

All of this research indicates that school environments should provide rich opportunities for interaction with print. The teacher, like the home caregivers, provides opportunities and support but more consciously provides modeling, scaffolding, and direct teaching while involving children in meaningfully structured activities related to literacy, such as hearing stories, writing messages, reports and stories, and engaging in massive amounts of reading.

Selecting Curriculum Options

In designing the approach to initial literacy instruction for kindergarten, first-grade, and Chapter 1 classes, our teacher researcher group examined several popular frameworks. We knew that children needed opportunities to hear written language read aloud in order to develop implicit knowledge of syntactic patterns that differ from oral language, so a heavy emphasis on children's literature seemed appropriate. The Ohio State University had long been involved in promoting literature-based reading programs as well as the study of literature as an important element of the curriculum even in the early school years (see Huck, Hepler, & Hickman, 1987; Pinnell & McKenzie, 1989).

We assumed that the language arts, including reading, writing, and oral communication were integrated language activities and best learned in concert (Pinnell & Jaggar, 1991). We also knew that young children are active, exploring learners and drew our ideas from the integrated curriculum of the British tradition (King, 1975) as well as from the more recent whole-language models (Goodman, 1986a). Finally, we knew that it was essential to find ways to help children read for meaning to understand the details of print, such as the use of letters, the concept of words, the relationships of sounds and letters, and word-by-word matching while reading left to right. Instructional approaches developed in New Zealand (Holdaway, 1979) provided helpful direction.

All of these models, or adaptations of them, provided a beginning framework for planning and organizing instruction and a rich source of recommendations for books and activities. Using the identified frameworks, teachers engaged children in activities and then turned their attention to the way they interacted with children during those periods, attempting to find the most powerful ways to help children construct knowledge about the processes of reading and writing. In other words, teachers tried to develop the instruction at two levels: (1) how they planned and organized the general activities used; and (2) how they interacted with individuals and groups during those activities.

The Contribution of Reading Recovery

Three years before the first study group began, the district and university had been involved in the Reading Recovery project. Reading Recovery is an early intervention program that places emphasis on involving young children in extensive, holistic reading and writing activities. As described by Smith-Burke and Jaggar (Chapter 4), Reading Recovery is aimed at first graders who are having difficulty learning to read. A specially trained teacher conducts daily, individual lessons with each selected student. During the 30-minute lessons, the child reads and rereads little books, increasing the difficulty level while gaining strategic power in reading and then composes a message with the teacher's help. The entire lesson helps the child engage in reading and writing so that they learn about the underlying processes involved. The emphasis is on independence; children learn the kinds of strategies that good readers employ and they begin to solve their own problems from the beginning of their lessons. Research on the program indicates that the model is highly effective for young, at-risk students (see Pinnell, 1989; Pinnell, Lyons, Deford, Bryk, & Seltzer, 1991). The key is not materials or activities per se, but the teacher's ability to engage in supportive conversation that helps the children make leaps in learning.

District involvement in Reading Recovery contributed to the project in several ways. Through Reading Recovery, many teachers took a fresh, close look at young children learning to read, especially those who did not seem to pick it up naturally. They also took a close look at teaching. While engaged in conversation with children during reading and writing, Reading Recovery teachers had to select the most powerful, memorable examples that helped children understand the underlying processes and develop effective cognitive strategies.

Teachers also experienced a powerful model for staff development, one built on observation and decision making. This model suggests that rather than hearing about and then performing a set of teaching activities step-by-step, teachers must develop and use their analytic skills to adjust and frame instruction for children. Reading Recovery teachers' interactions with students come out of a knowledge base that is established through observation and experience and is constantly checked with evidence from children's responses. Project teachers' learning processes were supported by observation, analysis, and group discussion, processes that were used by all study groups (Deford, Lyons, & Pinnell, 1991). Teachers in these study groups were prepared to enter a long development process rather than relying on materials or quick solutions.

Through Reading Recovery, we developed a new appreciation for the need to skillfully and sensitively teach children who were confused or inexperienced. These children could not be left to pick up the concepts alone. The teacher who could intervene, support, and show children how to learn reading and writing could make the critical difference, especially for those children who appeared to be at a disadvantage as they entered school. Literature-based and whole-language approaches flourished in suburban areas but made little impression in urban areas of our state. With few exceptions, these approaches had been tried several times and discarded by curriculum directors or teachers because children were perceived to need more direct instruction in phonics. The direct approaches tended to include ordered and systematic practice. Some children profited; but the problems were not eliminated because many children, those with little literacy experience, found the activities to be meaningless drills, disconnected from their own knowledge of language. Through Reading Recovery, we worked successfully in urban schools that served large numbers of economically disadvantaged students. Could the observational techniques and instructional rigor of Reading Recovery be used to inform the progressive approaches so that they could meet the needs of inexperienced readers and writers? We were determined not to transfer Reading Recovery as an instructional approach but to examine the theoretical foundation, drawing information that would assist the design of instruction.

CREATING A FRAMEWORK FOR INSTRUCTION

Using the theoretical framework and drawing from descriptive literature on whole-language and literature-based approaches, the teacher groups developed, tested, and refined a lesson framework for small-group and whole-class instruction. The framework consists of a loosely connected range of activities adaptable for primary school children of various ages and levels of experience. Interactive writing, the focus of this chapter, is a key component; but all elements of the framework are interrelated in an integrated curriculum that links reading and writing with meaningful and interesting activities that are surrounded by lively discussion.

Instruction within the lesson framework is based on the premise that, at any point in time, teachers and children have a complex range of options for attention. Learning opportunities of various kinds are inherent within each activity. For example, in a shared reading activity, children might enjoy repeating a story in unison or they might notice words that begin with the same letters as their names. In interactive writing, the teacher might ask children to write words by saying them slowly and using sound-to-letter relationships. Within the experience or activity, the teacher may guide children to focus at any level of the language hierarchy, including meaning, text structure, words, letters, or print conventions. A guiding principle is that the children's sense of meaning and purpose must be sustained at all times. Decisions are based on the teacher's knowledge of what children know and bring to the process, as well as their ability to observe and follow children's attention. The effectiveness of the instruction depends on these moment-to-moment decisions.

Elements of the Lesson Framework

The framework includes six recommended elements; however, the order of these components is not specified. Teachers established routines that suited them and their students, varying according to student day-by-day response. It was not necessary to use every component each day. Longer periods of concentrated time might be required for activities such as interactive writing or extensions through drama or art; but teachers generally agreed that they should provide time for reading aloud and familiar rereading every day. Within a 1-week period, teachers made sure that every component was included in an integrated way. In this section, we describe the six elements we used. We will then highlight interactive writing with an example from a kindergarten classroom.

Reading Aloud

Teachers read to the children daily, often several books each day. Some books were new; others were favorites that the children wanted the teacher to read again. Reading aloud provided a way to help children increase their knowledge of language patterns and the structure of stories. Rereading stories strengthened the process (Martinez & Roser, 1985; Martinez & Teale, 1986; Schickendanz, 1978). The teacher provided a model of oral reading and children often joined in on predictable phrases. The books were carefully selected to support the children's ability to connect one text with another and build knowledge of how stories are written. In a reflective piece of writing, one teacher said:

> *After reading many different variations of* The Gingerbread Boy *to my group of children, I read Joanne Oppenheim's* You Can't Catch Me. *In this story, a pesky black fly goes around boasting to all of the animals on the farm that "no matter how hard you try, try, try, you can't catch me." When I read that the fly came to a fox, the children all went in unison, "Uh, oh." I asked them why they responded that way and they told me about other stories with the fox as a bad character (Henny Penny, Gingerbread Boy, Chicken Licken). They were thinking that the fox would be evil in this story as well. They were making predictions based on prior knowledge of story structure and characterization.*

Familiar Rereading: Collaborative and Independent

In each classroom, there was a wide ranging collection of books, including many that children could read themselves. These books had been carefully introduced to children; some had been read to them. They were familiar enough with the format, language, and meaning to make them their own. The classroom collection included literature that had been read aloud to children and some that was too hard for them to read. They could, however, approximate the texts and read some of the familiar refrains. Other reading materials included very simple *transition texts* (see Clay, 1991) that children could achieve control over. These were predictable, natural language texts. Some were purchased in sets; others were written by children. The collection also included big books that teachers and children collaboratively constructed through interactive writing.

In familiar rereading, children have a chance to use searching and checking strategies "on the run" while reading extended text. They can work out problems for themselves because the reading is at a very easy level. This element provided the opportunity to use their knowledge of letter-sound relationships, language structure, words, etc., as they used their own knowledge of the story to check whether it made sense. Every child had a chance to read fluently with phrasing, in other words, to behave like a good reader.

Reading Challenging Material: Observing and Teaching

To make progress in reading, children must encounter new material that provides challenge and the chance to do reading work, the in-the-head problem solving that builds the self-extending system. Teachers introduced new books to children individually and in groups. Children read these new books with some support but were encouraged to work out the problems they encountered. Periodically, teachers took Running Records of individual children's reading behavior. Running Records involve using a shorthand technique to capture reading behavior. The records are analyzed so that the teacher can make hypotheses about children's development of reading strategies. On a regular basis (every 2 or 3 weeks), teachers tried to plan an individual conference time with each child to take a Running Record and do some quick, individual teaching on the text read. They kept charts of children's reading and, in some classes, children kept their own tapes of reading, adding samples at regular intervals.

Shared Reading

Shared reading, in which teacher and children read in unison, offered an opportunity for children to participate in a highly supported way. Books for shared reading are usually commercially published big books; however, in this project, we found that it was not necessary to purchase these items. Many regular-sized children's literature books (e.g., *Going on a Bear Hunt* by Helen Oxenbury) had print that could capture the attention of a group of children clustered around the teacher who was reading aloud. The most effective big books were often based on children's literature, and produced by the teachers and children through interactive writing. Teachers had a budget of $500 per classroom and they spent it on an excellent collection of literature that supported interactive writing, which provided material for shared reading. The list of books that teachers compiled included many categories of books such as: concept books (alphabet, counting, colors), nursery rhymes and songs, poetry, folk tales, cumulative tales, predictable pattern books, read-aloud books, and books to use across the curriculum (science and social studies). An important criterion for the selection of these books was the representation of multicultural contexts and characters.

Big books, recipes, lists, letters, story maps, and other materials were used for shared writing. Children often used a pointer to read the walls because so much writing was displayed in classrooms. The texts were more complicated than children could be expected to read alone; but they were socially supported by the group. As children became competent in reading a particular text, teachers could use opportunities to promote predicting, searching, checking, and self-correcting, using any appropriate sources of information. One teacher described the process:

> As in reading aloud, both the teacher and children model good reading behaviors. Fluency and phrasing are easily demonstrated as students can use their voices to imitate particular characters. This process helps children understand that the text they read must sound right and make sense. . . . Although a range of reading ability exists within the group, each member is learning at an individual level. The teacher has a wide variety of teaching opportunities during a shared reading experience. For example, knowledge of the conventions of print, such as where to start, left to right directionality, the return sweep, and one-to-one matching of text are easily taught. During shared reading children will increase their ability to use visual information, their vocabulary, and their ability to use and read new sentence structures.

Extending Texts

Texts were grouped thematically and related through a variety of activities that helped children bring more background knowledge to reading and writing and to connect texts. These activities included drama, painting and drawing, music, story mapping, cooking, growing things, and a range of art projects. Often teachers read aloud from more complex texts than the children would be expected to read or use for writing. These complicated texts extended their ideas and knowledge base (Strong, 1986). Extensions contributed greatly to the children's enjoyment and their understanding of reading and writing as well as providing genuine purposes for these activities. For example, in making a story map, children would be required to revisit a story in order to check their information. At other times, children would be required to go beyond the story by writing letters to story characters. As one teacher wrote:

> While working on extensions, group collaboration is a powerful tool to the children's learning. Children discuss what parts of the story should be included, how they feel about particular characters, similarities and differences between one story and another, how words are spelled, where to find information, etc. They show each other where many sources of information can be located. Many times the children answer each others' questions. It is amazing what these "at risk" children are able to discuss and what solutions to problems they are able to come up with when given the opportunity. These children are helping each other learn.

Interactive Writing

Interactive writing is a form of shared writing (see McKenzie, 1988) that supports young children's active involvement in literacy processes. Teachers in our group found it especially helpful for young children who come to school with few opportunities to interact with and notice the details of print. It is a dynamic process that involves teachers and children in: (1) negotiating the composition of text, either narrative or informational; (2) constructing words through analysis of sounds; (3) using the conventions of print; (4) reading and rereading texts; and (5) searching, checking, and confirming while reading and writing. Interactive writing usually grows out of classroom experiences or favorite selections from children's literature. Teachers found that interactive writing was a way of providing powerful demonstrations of the degrees of problem solving necessary to become an independent reader and writer.

In interactive writing, the teacher and children collaborate to construct a written text. The process grows out of the oral language of the classroom as children want to write down important messages and information; but it is different from the traditional language experience approach in several ways. The teacher carefully structures the process to create a readable text for children; planning and organization take place over a relatively long period of time; and, teachers and children "share the pen" in the actual recording of composed messages. Interactive writing can be a message, the morning news, a recipe, a letter, the retelling of a story, or an alternative text. In our project, it usually involved the creation of an extended text, based on a piece of children's literature that had been read aloud many times. Interactive writing offers many opportunities for teaching. For example, in the service of constructing a text, the teacher can direct children's attention to using left to right directionality and spacing of words, or to the construction of a word using knowledge of sound-to-letter relationships.

Interactive writing may begin by hearing a book read several times and then planning and writing a story retelling or alternative test. One class revisited the book *The Fat Cat* (Kent, 1971) by producing an alternative text entitled *The Fat Cat at Big Boy* (a favorite local restaurant). They began planning by listing what the Fat Cat could eat at Big Boy. The teacher who implemented this activity wrote this description:

> *While developing the list, I kept in mind the strengths of each child. For example, Harry, who had just joined our group, knew the letter sound s so he wrote the letter when the children suggested we include the word sign in our list. Miranda understood how to use a known word to generate unfamiliar words. When she suggested that the fat cat could eat men, I said, "You know how to write ten . Can you use ten to help you write men?" Miranda wrote ten on another chart and then immediately wrote men on the chart with the Big Boy story.*

We worked on our list for several days. When it was finished, the list was taped to the wall for the children to use as a resource during independent writing. Some children used the chart as a reference when they wrote their stories. Others used it to verify and monitor their spelling when they reread their stories.

Independent Writing

Children had the opportunity to write independently. There were several types of independent writing, including "balloon writing" on wall displays or in student-made big books, letters to characters, recipes, lists, and individual stories. Once an innovative text had been created by the group, children wrote their own versions. Journals were a regular part of the classroom work and the powerful demonstrations provided in interactive writing contributed to the children's work in their journals. Often daily journal writing was scheduled so that teachers could meet with each child at least once each week, occasionally intervening to help with a word or idea. Children used invented spelling in their individual writing but had opportunities to see and participate in the production of standard spelling in the group writing situation. Teachers' opportunities for instructing are illustrated in the comment below (previously described):

The children's own writing became a powerful source for learning how to work simultaneously on elements of story structure, letter-sound relationships, punctuation, and other components of writing. As in Reading Recovery, the child's behavior provides a guide for teacher decisions. We observe and analyze what the child does and then make teaching points based on that information. With one student, we may be working on hearing the sounds in words in sequence; another may be ready for hearing one sound and representing it with a letter. A third child may be able to use a known word to generate a word needed in the story. Providing time for independent writing helps the teacher focus on each child as an individual learner.

Monitoring Student Progress

Components of the literacy lesson are used flexibly. Within the framework, teachers attempt to gather knowledge about children's strengths and through their interactions and directions, allow children to use knowledge in group settings. They used diagnostic techniques learned in Reading Recovery (but not exclusive to that program, as explained in Clay, 1985) to provide baseline information and they set up systematic, manageable monitoring systems to track children's progress. Running records, story retellings, and writing samples were collected at least every 2 weeks. In addition, teachers kept individualized notes on children. There was emphasis on collecting information on every child. A regular schedule was followed so that each child was noticed and his or her reading behavior analyzed to provide information for teaching.

Shared Writing in a Kindergarten Classroom

In this section, we provide an extended example of the work of one teacher, Ms. Ida Pattacca, and the children in her kindergarten class. The children in Ida's classroom had been selected because they were low scorers on standardized selection tests. The school is in an urban environment where high proportions of children are eligible to receive free lunch. In this example, Ida incorporated five elements of the lesson framework as her students and she revisited the book, *The Turnip* (Domanska, 1969).

Book Selection

One outcome of the study groups' deliberations was an understanding of the importance of selecting books for particular purposes. At times, books were selected to be read aloud because their rich book language extended the child's language. At other times, books with highly patterned text were chosen (e.g., Wildsmith's *Cat on the Mat*, 1982) so that children could use the predictable language structure.

Ida chose to read *The Turnip* for several reasons. First, it was a story she enjoyed reading to the children and her previous experiences indicated that there would be a positive response. Second, the book combined rich book language with a predictable narrative structure and a repetitive language pattern. Third, Ida felt that she could extend the book through shared reading and writing activities.

There were two versions of the tale in the classroom library (*The Great Big Enormous Turnip* by Alex Tolstoy, 1968; and *The Turnip* by Janina Domanska, 1969). Ida chose the Domanska version because it lent itself to the book extensions that she was planning. The author included a larger number of characters in the story, which could then become individual roles in the dramatic reenactment.

Reading Aloud

The first element of the literacy lesson is reading aloud to the children. In her introduction, Ida provided a framework for listening to the story. She began the book introduction by asking the children to name some vegetables they liked to eat. She then brought out a turnip and had the children taste it and told them that in the new book she was going to read, the people loved eating turnips. Then, she read the book aloud several times in order to thoroughly familiarize the children with the story's plot, structure, and language. Familiarity with the story was essential for doing the book extensions. By the end of the first reading, a few children had already picked up the repetitive language pattern in the text and were joining in on the refrain. In the readings that followed, children demonstrated increasingly that they had internalized more of the language from the book. They began to join in the reading of the predictable parts of the text.

Dramatic Reenactment

The teacher chose to do a dramatic reenactment of the story for her first extension of this book for four reasons. First, dramatic reenactment capitalizes on children's enjoyment of dramatic play. Second, dramatic reenactment gives children the opportunity to be actively involved in the extension. Third, these activities let children see the structure of the story as the line of characters, who are trying to pull up the turnip, continues to increase in length. This was a concrete representation of the story that she could draw on when the children engaged in the next extension. Fourth, Ida could demonstrate how to use the book (in this case, the illustrations) as information to decide what characters were needed and when to add them to the line.

Because she recognized the value of repeated readings in helping children internalize story structure, she read the story to them again the next day. Ida then introduced the first book extension, telling them that she would like them to dramatize the story. The children were familiar with the activity because they had dramatized several nursery rhymes earlier in the year.

Before they reenacted the story, Ida had the children list all of the characters involved in helping to pull up the turnip. Although the list could have been done as a shared writing experience, the teacher decided to act as the scribe. She wanted the children to focus on the story's plot. After the children generated their list, Ida demonstrated how they could use the book to check for accuracy. She asked the children to check the list of characters against the illustration in which all of the characters were pulling up the turnip. In the process of checking, the group discovered that they had not included the hens. After the hens were added to the list, they were ready to dramatize the story.

Ida, in the role of Grandfather, modeled trying to pull the turnip. The children quickly added the repetitive text pattern, "but the turnip did not move." They reenacted trying to pull up the turnip with the addition of each new character. Each time, they framed the new segment with the words, "One . . . two . . . three . . . PULL!" and "but the turnip did not move." The reenactment ended with everyone falling down. Afterwards, one of the children brought the group back to the text. In the story, the final character, a magpie, is amazed at his strength and says, "Look what I did." Michael, who remembered this part of the text and wanted it to be part of the dramatization, said, "Rayshawn, you forgot to say 'Look what I did.'" The children agreed and they revised the last bit of the dramatization to include Michael's suggestion.

The dramatic reenactment of *The Turnip* provides several examples of the instructional principles teachers in the Early Literacy Project use in framing their literacy lessons. The first is the importance of selecting a book to suit the purpose for which it is intended. In this case, the teacher wanted to engage the children in a dramatic reenactment that would require them to chronologically recall the sequence of events in the story. She felt that a cumulative tale would provide just enough challenge for them. She could also use the dramatization to show them how they could refer to the book as a source of information or confirmation.

Second, Ida realized the importance of multiple readings of a story prior to beginning an extension based on it. Multiple readings allowed the children the opportunity to remember various aspects of the story or one aspect more deeply. In this particular instance, the children's ready knowledge of the order in which characters appeared in the story seemed to demonstrate that

they had assimilated the sequence of events in the story. They also demonstrated that they had acquired some of the language of the book when they began to chant lines from the text during their reenactment. Third, the teacher followed the lead of the children. When Michael suggested that they revise the ending of the reenactment, she was open to his suggestion.

Shared Reading and Writing

Shared reading and writing were incorporated into the literacy lessons that were derived from *The Turnip*. Shared reading occurred within different contexts. It began with the first reading of the book when the children began to join the teacher as she read those parts of the text that were repetitive. The children also shared in reading the list of characters they constructed for the dramatic reenactment. The second book extension was purposely designed to emphasize shared reading.

Another reason Ida chose *The Turnip*, was because the cumulative nature of the story could be represented in a story map. Before they began this extension, she read the book to them another time. She then used the last illustration, which included all of the characters in the story, as a resource for deciding what they needed to draw.

Each student chose and illustrated one of the characters from the story. Evidence that the children had been paying close attention to the illustrations came when the child who was drawing the magpie said that he thought the magpie was blue and white in the book. When he was asked how he could be sure those were the colors that Domanska used, he immediately went to look at the illustrations in the book. Several other children followed his example to choose the colors for their drawings. These children demonstrated that they had learned that books can serve multiple functions. In this instance, the book was a reference tool.

After the illustrations were completed, the children gathered around a 6-foot long piece of mural paper and began to place their illustrations on the paper. All of the children agreed on the order of the first five pictures but disagreed as to whether the geese or the rooster came next. Immediately, one of the children, Jeules, suggested that they get the book and check the illustrations. From that point on, the children checked the book before placing their illustrations on the mural. At least with this book, they seemed to have learned how to use a picture storybook as a reference tool.

Ida demonstrated flexibility in her teaching during the assembly and shared writing of the mural. She decided not to do any writing until the next day. After all of the pictures had been placed on the story map, she asked the child holding the book if the illustrations were in the correct sequence, reinforcing the use of the book as a reference. Although his answer surprised her, she followed his lead:

Ida: Now, Jordan, have you kept track of this? Have we been doing this right?

Jordan: (Shakes head 'yes.')

Ida: OK. We've been doing this right?

Jordan: We got one more.

Ida: What do you mean, 'we've got one more.' We don't have any more pictures.

Jordan: We need to count.

Ida: The cat? We did the cat.

Jordan: No, count. Grandpa needs to count.

Ida: Oh! Grandpa needs to count! Well, all right. Where's Grandpa? Here's what I'm going to do. Watch. I'm going to put a bubble right near where his mouth is because I want to put something in that bubble that tells what he is saying. I'm going to put this bubble coming right out of his mouth and you know what Grandpa's saying, don't you?

Nate: Yeah.

Terry: Counting.

Ida: He's said . . . .

Ida and the group: One . . . two . . . three . . . pull.

Ida: OK. Now, I'm going to write just what you said.

Ida and the group: One . . . two . . . three . . . pull . . . (as she writes the text in the speech bubble). Now, pull starts with a *p.*

Paul: That's like in my name.

Ida: Now, look. It looks just like Grandpa said that.

Ida and the group: (reading as the teacher points) One . . . two . . . three . . . pull.

Nate: Oh, oh, we messed up.

Ida: Now wait a minute. What do you mean we messed up? You did great!

Nate: I can't find *pull* (as he visually searches the print).

Ida: Don't worry. It's in there a lot. One, two, three, pull (pointing). Now, do you remember?

Nate: I found it.

Ida: OK. Did we do it right, Jordan?

Jordan: (nods head)

Ida: OK.

Following the lead of the child, the teacher found that she had an opportunity to introduce the concept of using speech bubbles to represent dialogue.

Evidence of Ida's tendency to follow children's lead was provided again the next day when the group began to add text to the story map. She thought a brief, repetitive language pattern would be the most productive text for the shared writing activity and later, the shared or independent reading. She decided that the text ought to include the name of each character and the word *pulled*. When she took out the fourth strip with the word *dog* on it, the children responded, "His name is Ringo." As soon as she realized that they were not satisfied with her more generic label, the children and she revised the text to read, "Ringo pulled."

The same sequence of events reoccurred when the children insisted that they change bird to magpie. This time, Ida revised the text quickly. In both instances, the changes the children made reflected their knowledge of the story and their internalization of the author's language. They preferred a more complex text.

In the previous two examples, children learned how to revise a text within the context of a shared writing activity. The teacher gave them an opportunity to construct a text. As they were finishing writing and reading the patterned text, Michael added, "And the turnip came out." Ida immediately picked up on his lead.

Ida: "And the turnip came out." Is that what I should write now, Mark?

Terry: "They go upside down." (derived from the illustration)

Ida: Mark says I should write, "And the turnip came out."

Several children: (talking at once).

Ida: Is that what I should write? "And the turnip came out"?

Several children: (nod their heads).

During the actual writing, the children revised the text again, adding the words *of the ground*. The focus of child talk then shifted away from the message itself to the conventions of print. Once again, the teacher used the children's comments as a springboard from which to discuss early reading strategies (see Clay, 1985) and to attend to the visual details of print. For example, one child's spontaneous comment dealt with the uses of directionality.

Jordan: Start on the left.

Ida: Start on the left, Jordan? That's what I've got to do. I've got to go all the way over here to the left.

Just a few moments later, she began representing sounds in words.

Ida: Turnip. What do I start turnip with?

Mark: t

Ida: You write it in, OK? ". . . And the turnip . . ." What's the next word?

All children: "Came." "Come."

Ida: "Came." Oh, you are good!

All children: k

Ida: It sounds like it starts with a *k*; but we write it with a *c*.

As Ida wrote, she emphasized directionality and the concept of word. She also paid attention to how to graphically represent the initial sounds of words. Children contributed to the writing of the text, not just by suggestions but by coming up to the chart and writing the letters.

Continued Enjoyment of a Text

Throughout the year, *The Turnip* continued to provide opportunities for the children. Initially, it helped them use information derived from hearing written language read aloud. Through retelling, dramatization, and art, the children made the story their own. As they constructed their own written version, they attended to the details of print and letter-sound relationships. They reread while constructing the text. When the writing was complete, the teacher and children read it together as a shared reading experience. Ida then placed it on the wall so that the children could use it as a text during familiar reading time. As soon as *The Turnip* was placed on the shelf, children began selecting it for familiar rereading. Two of the children chose it to take home overnight. The entire sequence of activities focused on the reading and writing of a meaningful text. Within that context, children were provided with opportunities to work on a number of skills. They talked about story structure, put characters in sequence, used the storybook as a reference tool, and controlled some of the visual details of print.

THE POTENTIAL OF INTERACTIVE WRITING

For these young children, language and literacy experiences offered a context in which they could explore important ideas related to literacy. Most of them could read by the end of their kindergarten year; others had a great deal of knowledge to use as a foundation for further learning. While we have no controlled studies to document the effectiveness of the literacy model we used, we did collect evaluation data to guide the development of the project. Our systematically applied observational measures indicated gains in the inventory of knowledge related to reading ability. Project children moved from 8.69 to 48.76 in letter identification. On a dictation task (maximum score = 37), which measured the children's ability to represent sounds with letters, children moved from .31 to 18.27. On writing vocabulary, they gained from .53

TABLE 8-1   End-of-Year Mean Scores for Kindergarten, Reading Recovery, and Early Literacy Groups*

Group	Letter identification	Concepts about print	Writing vocabulary	Dictation	Text reading level
Kindergarten spring scores 1990	48.5	13.5	13.4	18.2	1.9
Reading Recovery entry scores—1987	34.3	7.4	2.9	4.7	.4
Reading Recovery entry scores—1988	28.4	7.2	2.9	4.2	.4
Reading Recovery entry scores—1989	33.1	8.4	3.5	5.3	.5
Early literacy group entry scores—1988	34.8	2.6	2.6	5.7	.7

*The groups represented above are by no means comparable; therefore, no conclusions can be drawn from these data. For kindergarten classrooms, student gains could be attributed to the extra 1/2 day of instruction. It is also important to point out that, notwithstanding the average scores, within each of the 12 kindergarten classes, there were several children who scored low enough to qualify for Reading Recovery.

words to 13.51 words within the 10-minute maximum period. By the end of the year, the average text reading level was 1.94, indicating that children could read simple-patterned texts. The concepts about print assessment (Clay, 1985), which measures children's basic knowledge of concepts such as left-to-right directionality and word-by-word matching, indicated a change from 4.48 to 13.99 (maximum score = 24).

One interesting comparison was between our end-of-year kindergarten children and those who had been historically selected for Reading Recovery at the beginning of first grade. While the groups are not necessarily comparable, this comparison had heuristic value. After all, one of our goals was to enrich the children's entry year in a way that would better sort out those who needed Reading Recovery. We wanted to see whether a rich kindergarten experience would make a difference. Remember that, potentially, all children in our Chapter 1 kindergarten classrooms were candidates for Reading Recovery. For some children, this exceptionally rich experience may have made the critical difference. By achieving high levels of literacy learning, they would not need Reading Recovery. Indeed, the class averages on several measures were considerably higher than scores that historically qualified children for Reading Recovery. Table 8-1 shows end-of-year scores for the children in our kindergarten project as well as average entry scores for Reading Recovery children in the same school district.

These data indicate that a rich entry-year experience can help children with initially low literacy scores move into reading and writing. For those children, Reading Recovery is not needed. Examination of the range of scores, however, reveals that Reading Recovery is still needed for some. For example, for children in Ida's classroom, the range of end-of-year scores on dictation was from 13 to 20 and on text reading level was A (essentially no reading) to 8. In our judgment, 2 to 3 children from the group needed Reading Recovery. They had accumulated some item knowledge, which could serve them well in the highly supportive Reading Recovery context; but they were not yet orchestrating the information in ways that would help them be strategic readers. While more research is needed, our conclusions are as follows:

1. Upon entry to school, children (especially those who have not had extensive preschool literacy experiences) need massive immersion in meaningful reading and writing experiences within a print-rich environment.
2. This rich entry-year experience in literacy learning needs to be followed with Reading Recovery for children who do not engage extensively in reading and writing.
3. A restructuring effort for entry-year literacy education is needed to assure rich literacy support in beginning reading and writing experiences and a safety net to help students who are having most difficulty.

REFERENCES

Clay, M.M. (1985). *The early detection of reading difficulties.* Portsmouth, NH: Heinemann Educational Books.

Clay, M.M. (1987). Implementing educational Reading Recovery: Systematic adaptations to an educational innovation. *New Zealand Journal of Educational Studies, 22,* 351–358.

Clay, M.M. (1991). *Becoming literate: The construction of inner control.* Portsmouth, NH: Heinemann Educational Books.

Clay, M.M., & Cazden, C. (1990). A Vygotskian interpretation of Reading Recovery. In L. Moll (Ed.), *Vygotsky and education: Instructional implications and applications of sociohistorical psychology* (pp. 206–222). New York: Cambridge University Press.

Deford, D.E., Lyons, C.A., & Pinnell, G.S. (Eds.). (1991). *Bridges to literacy: Insights from the Reading Recovery program.* Portsmouth, NH: Heinemann Educational Books.

Goodman, K.S. (1986a). *What's whole in whole language?* Portsmouth, NH: Heinemann Educational Books.

Goodman, Y.M. (1984). The development of initial literacy. In H. Goelman, A. Oberg, & F. Smith (Eds.), *Awakening to literacy.* Portsmouth, NH: Heinemann Educational Books.

Goodman, Y.M. (1986b). Children coming to know literacy. In W.H. Teale & E. Sulzby (Eds.), *Emergent literacy: Writing and reading* (pp. 1–14). Norwood, NJ: Ablex.

Harste, J.C., Woodward, V.A., & Burke, C.L. (1984). *Language stories and literacy lessons.* Portsmouth, NH: Heinemann Educational Books.

Holdaway, D. (1979). *The foundations of literacy.* Sydney, Australia: Ashton Scholastic.

Huck, C.S., Hepler, S., & Hickman, J. (1987). *Children's literature in the elementary school* (4th ed.). New York: Holt, Rinehart, & Winston.

King, M. A. (1975). *Informal education.* Bloomington, IN: Phi Delta Kappa.

Martinez, M.G., & Roser, N. (1985). Read it again: The value of repeated readings during storytime. *The Reading Teacher, 38,* 782–786.

Martinez, M.G., & Teale, W.H. (1986). Classroom storybook reading: The creation of texts and learning opportunities. *Theory Into Practice, 28,* 126–135.

McGee, L.M., Lomax, R.G., & Head, M.H. (1988). Young children's written language knowledge: What environmental and functional print reading reveals. *Journal of Reading Behavior, 20,* 99–118.

McKenzie, M.G. (1988). *Journeys into literacy.*

Meek, M. (1982). *Learning to read.* London: The Bodley Head.

Pinnell, G.S. (1989). Reading Recovery: Helping at-risk children learn to read. *The Elementary School Journal, 90,* 161–183.

Pinnell, G.S., & Jaggar, A.M. (1991). Oral language: Speaking and listening in the classroom. In J. Flood, J.M. Jensen, D. Lapp, & J. Squire (Eds.), *Handbook of research on teaching the English language arts* (pp. 691–720). New York: Macmillan.

Pinnell, G.S., Lyons, C.A., Deford, D.E., Bryk, A.S., & Seltzer, M. (1991). *Studying the effectiveness of early intervention approaches for first grade children having difficulty in reading.* Educational Reports, Martha L. King Language and Literacy Center. Columbus: The Ohio State University. Technical Report available from The Ohio State University, Ramseyer 200, 29 W. Woodruff, Columbus, OH 43210.

Pinnell, G.S., & McKenzie, M.G. (1989). Changing conceptions of early literacy. In B. Cullinan & J. Hickman (Eds.), *Children's literature in the classroom: Weaving Charlotte's web.* Portsmouth, NH: Heinemann Educational Books.

Schickendanz, J.A. (1978). "Please read that story again!" Exploring relationships between story reading and learning to read. *Young Children,* July, 48–55.

Strong, E. (1986). *Nurturing early literacy: A literature based program for at-risk first graders.* Unpublished doctoral dissertation, The Ohio State University, Columbus.

Teale, W.H., & Sulzby, E. (Eds.). (1986). *Emergent literacy: Writing and reading.* Norwood, NJ: Ablex.

Children's Books:

Domanska, J. (1969). *The turnip.* ill. by Janina Domanska. New York: MacMillan.

Rosen, M. (1989). *We're going on a bear hunt.* ill. by Helen Oxenbury. New York: Margaret K. McElderry.

Galdone, P. (1975). *The gingerbread boy.* New York: Clarion.

Oppenheim, J. (1986). *You can't catch me.* ill. by Andrew Schachat. New York: Houghton Mifflin.

Kent, J. (1971). *The fat cat.* New York: Scholastic.

Tolstoy, A. (1968). *The great big enormous turnip.* ill. by Helen Oxenbury. New York: Watts.

Wildsmith, B. (1982). *The cat on the mat.* Oxford, England: Oxford University Press.

▶ 9

Promoting Early Literacy Development Among Spanish-Speaking Children
Lessons From Two Studies

CLAUDE GOLDENBERG

Two studies are described in this chapter. First Goldenberg describes his attempt to develop Spanish-speaking children's reading readiness in kindergarten by developing a program in which predictable Spanish story books were read with the children at school and at home. While this approach led to higher scores on early literacy measures than in traditional kindergarten classrooms, the children had the highest scores of all in two kindergartens in which the teachers had a structured reading program and were teaching their children to read in Spanish. In a second study, the author helped first-grade teachers modify their reading instruction. Teachers began to stress meaning and comprehension to a greater extent, along with the traditionally heavy emphasis on phonics; teachers began to send reading books and activities home to get the parents more involved in their children's reading; and teachers increased the pace of their reading instruction substantially. Second-grade standardized reading scores increased from the 33rd to 53rd percentile at the school where this program was implemented. Goldenberg concludes the chapter with a discussion of issues related to promoting and sustaining the literacy development of Spanish-speaking children.

How do we improve the literacy attainment of children from Spanish-speaking homes? This is surely one of the most urgent questions U.S. educators face. Children from Latino families are more likely to be poor and have a greater chance of failing in school, achieving lower levels of literacy, falling behind in their learning, and dropping out of school altogether than their English-speaking, nonminority peers. Although some educational trends are modestly encouraging (e.g., the proportion of Hispanics who completed 4 years of high school, for example, increased from 46% to 51% in the 1980s; U.S. Bureau of the Census, 1991), Hispanic children nevertheless begin school behind their white, non-Hispanic peers, and the variance increases throughout the grades. Language of instruction is not the issue—or at least, it is not the only issue: These children's academic achievement in early elementary school is the same whether they are in a native-language program (i.e., Spanish bilingual education) or in a structured immersion program using only English (Ramirez, Yuen, & Ramey, 1991).

The rapid growth of the Latino population in the United States suggests that the challenge to the educational system will intensify. Currently at least 2.2 million limited English-proficient (LEP) students are in U.S. schools (U.S. Department of Education, 1991), with some estimates going much higher (Crawford, 1989). Approximately three fourths of these students have Spanish as their home language. California alone has more than 750,000 Spanish-speaking, LEP students, and the number is expected to continue rising well into the 21st century (California Department of Education, 1992). By the year 2000, at least 35% of California's students will be Hispanic. Now, more than ever, U.S. schools must try to reverse the pattern of persistent underachievement among this population.

Where to begin? We can make plausible arguments for different intervention points—early childhood (e.g., Lazar, Darlington, Murray, Royce, & Snipper, 1982), the beginning of elementary school (e.g., chapters 4 and 7, this volume), or sometime in middle school (e.g., Stevenson, Chen, & Uttal, 1990). One logical place to begin is when children begin their formal schooling, which in most cases is kindergarten. Although earlier intervention is unquestionably desirable, only one third of the 3- and 4-year-olds most in need and only 22% of Hispanic 3- and 4-year-olds presently attend preschool in this country (Committee for Economic Development, 1991; National Center for Education Statistics, 1991). In contrast, virtually all children in the United

This chapter is a revised version of a paper presented at the symposium *Teaching children to read: The state of early interventions*, American Educational Research Association, San Francisco, CA, April 1992. The research reported here was made possible by a Spencer Fellowship from the National Academy of Education and a subsequent grant from the Spencer Foundation. My thanks to the children, teachers, parents, and colleagues who made this work possible. Special thanks to Ronald Gallimore.

States attend kindergarten; in the case of Hispanics, 93% of Hispanic 5- and 6-year-olds in the United States are enrolled in school (National Center for Education Statistics, 1991). Although there is a growing need to make quality prekindergarten experiences available to all children, we should also consider the plausibility of concentrating efforts from the time schooling is virtually universal, that is, when almost all children enter kindergarten at age 5.

THEMES AND ASSUMPTIONS

This chapter describes the results of two related efforts undertaken in a southern California school district to try to improve the early native-language (i.e., Spanish) literacy attainment of Spanish-speaking children. One project was aimed at improving emergent literacy activities in kindergarten, and the other project focused on improving reading instruction in first and second grade. Several themes—perhaps assumptions is more accurate—run throughout this chapter.

The first is that children who come to school speaking a language other than English are better served in programs that capitalize on their native language and use it to promote academic and cognitive development for as long as possible during their school careers. The studies reported here involved helping Spanish-speaking students acquire high levels of literacy achievement in Spanish. Children must of course also acquire high levels of linguistic and academic competence in English, but there is no need to accomplish this by quashing the first language. To the contrary: The first language should be seen as a resource to be nurtured and developed rather than squandered (Crawford, 1989).

Many advocates of bilingual education, of course, argue that high levels of literacy in the home language will also help promote high levels of competence in English. The issue is, to say the least, controversial, with numerous ideological and political questions involved. Evaluations of bilingual education programs are complex and sometimes contradictory; partly as a consequence, discussions become mired in politics and ideology (see, e.g., Crawford, 1989; Porter, 1990). Nevertheless, counter-intuitive though it might be, use of the home language in school does not appear to interfere with the acquisition of English skills. Instead, use of the home language in school might lead to superior achievement in English and academic content areas, as many bilingual education proponents argue (see, e.g., U.S. General Accounting Office, 1987), and its use certainly leads to higher levels of achievement in the home language (see studies cited in Baker & deKanter, 1981). Ideally, therefore, we should be able to produce bilingual and biliterate students, as many countries around the world do, particularly in the case of children who come from homes where another language is spoken. We are still far from accomplishing this important educational goal, however, and the acrimony, vituperation, and politics of the bilingual education debate make it all the more difficult to reach.

Second, despite differences in English and Spanish orthographic systems (particularly the greater orthographic regularity of Spanish) and differences in various structural aspects of the two languages, learning to read in Spanish is probably very similar to learning to read in English. Both are alphabetic languages with predictable spelling patterns. Perhaps more important, in both Spanish and English the key task for the reader is to associate or construct meaning based on written alphabetic symbols. It is highly likely, therefore, that the same grapho-psycholinguistic processes will be involved in both languages, and what we know about how to help children acquire literacy in English is probably relevant for helping children acquire literacy in Spanish.

Third, and despite these similarities, Spanish-speaking children learning to read in Spanish in the United States face a far different sociolinguistic context—both with respect to written and oral forms of language—than children learning to read in English do. Whereas written texts of many types are easily accessible to the English-speaking child, Spanish speakers have fewer such opportunities, despite the existence of Spanish-language periodicals and books. Far fewer Spanish books, magazines, environmental print, activity books, or alphabet books—which all form an important part of the context for successful literacy development (Teale, 1978)—are available in the United States. Educational programs such as *Sesame Street* offer token segments in Spanish, but again, these literacy learning opportunities are scarce in comparison to the relative abundance of English literacy materials and experiences. Parents with whom I have worked have remarked that they find it virtually impossible to find Spanish children's books or other literacy materials in neighborhood markets, even in an area that has a more than 90% Latino population and with many Latino businesses and grocery stores. Some families either have brought books from Mexico or Central America or have them sent by friends or relatives; but they are exceptions.

Finally, the perspective reflected in this chapter is that creating effective programs to help at-risk children (or to help any group of children) cannot be seen as merely a matter of implementing research findings at particular sites. As important as research is in helping inform decisions, frame questions, and suggest practices, meaningful educational change can take place only through intensive local efforts that are informed not just by research but also by a detailed understanding of the local site and the local issues framing the thinking of teachers and administrators (Goldenberg & Gallimore, 1989; 1991). Although a discussion of the process of educational change and the relationship between rational, scientific knowledge and school improvement is beyond the scope of this chapter, the studies described here should be seen within this framework: School improvement requires the constructive but complex interplay of local and research-based knowledge.

It follows, then, that to some extent all findings—including the results of program improvement efforts—are local and of limited generalizability. However, this does not preclude transporting successful models from other sites or learning from successful change efforts at those sites. Indeed, many successful and replicable models exist (see, e.g., National Dissemination Study Group, 1989; Slavin, Karweit, & Madden, 1989), as do teaching practices associated with improved student achievement; but we are likely to learn more about how to help children at educational risk, whatever the language they speak, if we have an understanding of the processes leading to successful change at particular sites.

PROMOTING SPANISH LITERACY IN KINDERGARTEN

Our project's efforts to promote early Spanish literacy development in kindergarten began in 1986 when I was teaching first grade in a largely Hispanic, low-income school in metropolitan Los Angeles. The majority of families who send their children to this school are Latino and come from Mexico and Central America. Parents of kindergarten children have been in this country for an average of 9 or 10 years; the range is from 1 to more than 30 years. The highly urban district is in one of the poorest areas of the state, and more than 90% of the children receive free or reduced-price meals at the school.

Prior to teaching first grade I had conducted (at the same school) a study of Spanish-speaking first graders who were at risk for poor reading achievement (Goldenberg, 1989). Then, as a first-grade teacher, I became interested in working with other teachers to find ways to improve early Spanish literacy development. In this effort, I drew from my own research and experiences at the school as well as from previous and ongoing early literacy theory and research (e.g., Anderson, Hiebert, Scott, & Wilkinson, 1985; Chall, 1983), particularly that pertaining to low-achieving minority children (e.g., Kamehameha Schools, 1983).

Simple Spanish Booklets for Kindergarten Children to Read

During the 1985–1986 school year, a kindergarten teacher colleague with whom I was working closely developed some simple booklets in Spanish for her students to learn to read and then take home and share with parents and other family members. The idea generated considerable controversy at the school. Many of the teachers, including the school's instructional specialists, believed that if literacy was to be emphasized in kindergarten—and even this was controversial—teachers should concentrate on children's learning letters, sounds, and phonics rather than reading or pseudo-reading. Other teachers, however, supported language- and meaning-based attempts to help children acquire more knowledge about the forms and functions of literacy, before setting out to teach them to decode.

Despite the local controversy, the idea of providing young children with simple little books even before they could read in a conventional sense was not new and, indeed, is generally accepted. What was new about these booklets was the language in which they were written and the fact that they were easily reproduced and could be sent home for children to keep. Although in English an abundance of materials provides young children with meaning-oriented early literacy opportunities long before they are reading in a conventional sense—e.g., "Instant Readers" (Martin & Brogan, 1971) and "predictable books" (Heald-Taylor, 1987)—in Spanish, there was and continues to be a dearth of readily available, simple books that Spanish-speaking children can hear, learn, and read before mastering the technical aspects of Spanish orthography.

Making such materials available, we thought, might be important because previous research (and our own experiences) suggested that opportunities to deal with age- and development-appropriate texts—e.g., hearing books read and reading or pseudo-reading books—make significant contributions to young children's literacy development. These opportunities are probably the single most important type of prereading experience young children can have, and children who learn to read easily and successfully often come from homes where they have many such experiences (Anderson et al., 1985; Chall, 1983).

Spanish-speaking children in this country rarely have these opportunities. There is a relative scarcity of books in the homes of many U.S. Latino families, and reading to children is relatively infrequent (e.g., Delgado-Gaitan, 1990; Teale, 1986). Ramirez, Yuen, Ramey, and Merino (1986, p. 207, table 146) report that 22% of the parents of Spanish-speaking kindergartners say that they do not read to their children, whereas in a nationally representative sample of parents from a range of socioeconomic and ethnic groups, only 4% reported either never reading to their children or reading only several times per year (West, Hausken, & Chandler, 1991). Consequently, Spanish-speaking children probably receive comparatively few opportunities with extended, meaningful texts at home. At school, their beginning literacy experiences are likely to be almost exclusively weighted toward what are sometimes called "bottom-up" processes—learning letters, sounds, and phonics, rather than having the opportunity to read (or pseudo-read) themselves. The highly regular Spanish orthography leads most teachers to assume that learning to read in Spanish is a straightforward matter of learning the code. For these reasons, the kindergarten teacher with whom I worked decided to develop simple little booklets for her students and to encourage children's participation, both at home and at school, in meaning-oriented reading—that is, top-down experiences with print. Because we wanted the children to be able to take these books home and keep them, it was essential that they be inexpensive and easily reproduced.

1986–87 Pilot Study: Unexpected Results

In 1986–1987, we conducted a pilot study to see whether the teacher-created booklets made any contribution to children's early literacy development. Our objective was not to teach reading per se. Durkin (1974–1975) and Hanson, Siegel, and Broach (1987), for example, had already found that children could be successfully taught to read before first grade. Moreover, Hanson et al. found small but significant effects of learning to read in kindergarten through the end of high school. Our goal was not to attempt to teach reading in kindergarten but to provide Spanish-speaking children with opportunities for interacting with meaningful print and to gauge the effects of these experiences on early literacy growth and knowledge. We predicted that use of the booklets (*Libritos*) at school and at home would lead to increased knowledge of words (sight words), increased ability to derive meaning from familiar print, transfer of knowledge of familiar letters and words to new words, and, in general, greater readiness to learn to read.

To test our hypotheses, two kindergarten teachers in the school used the booklets with the Spanish-speaking children in their classes, and four others served as controls. The latter used the district's reading readiness program (part of the basal series published by Santillana Publishing Co.), supplemented by various other prereading or reading readiness materials. Our measures of literacy development consisted of two group tests in a multiple-choice format, one locally developed for this project and one published commercially, *La Prueba* (Riverside Publishing Co., 1984). Children were tested in the spring of 1987 by instructional aides at the school who had ample experience with young, Spanish-speaking children. Our results were, in a word, disappointing. The experimental and control groups were essentially identical on both measures.

We discovered, however, that our conclusions were premature. When we took a more careful look at the control classrooms, we realized that they did not constitute one group but were instead two distinct pairs of classrooms. Two of the classrooms were indeed standard district kindergartens. Teachers used the district's readiness program, where children learned to trace lines, follow directions, discriminate shapes, sequence events, and so forth. Children heard stories and books read aloud and engaged in a wide range of age-appropriate and developmental activities. However, children's **direct** opportunities with text were quite limited—they learned a few letters and sounds (mostly the vowels and a few consonants) and, toward the end of the year, some of the more advanced children could read some syllables. There was a decidedly nonacademic focus in the classrooms; certainly there were no systematic attempts to teach reading. To the contrary, teachers tried to promote children's acquisition of readiness concepts, and they explicitly disavowed an academic focus.

The other two control classrooms, however, had a very different program. These teachers—both native Spanish-speaking Latinas—supplemented the district's readiness program with an intensive academic focus actually designed to teach the children to read. After perhaps 2 to 3 months of readiness activities at the beginning of the school year, they systematically taught the children the vowels and their sounds, followed by the consonants and their sounds, then how vowels and consonants combine to form syllables (e.g., *ma, me, pu, po*) and words (e.g., *mamá, ama, papa, puma*). Through a combination of drills, practice, and independent seat work, these teachers taught their students to read and write. Furthermore, the teachers stayed in regular contact with parents and sent daily homework beginning in the first week of school with the child's name. Children were expected to complete the homework with the parents' assistance, if necessary, and return it to school the following day.

Instead of a two-group (experimental vs. control) design, by chance we had three groups: The experimental and two distinct controls. We reanalyzed the data, and a different picture emerged. On both the locally developed test and the published readiness test, there were differences among the three groups. This time, there was an experimental effect when the booklets were compared with the standard, general readiness classrooms. However, the classrooms with the strong and direct academic focus scored highest.

Follow-Up Studies: Comparable Results

Because these results were so strikingly unexpected, we conducted a replication in 1988–1989. This time, we knew from the outset that there would be a three-group comparison, and we sampled six children from each of 10 classrooms: four classes at two different schools using the booklets (experimental), four classes at the same two schools with the district readiness program (true controls), and the two highly structured, academic classrooms, which were located at the same school where the original pilot work had been done.

We also revised the booklets because we suspected that the first set was too simplistic. The new booklets (12 in all, renamed *Libros*) began as little more than caption books and became progressively more challenging. They also contained many elements that made them predictable (Heald-Taylor, 1987), such as rhyme, rhythm, redundant words and pictures, and repeating sentence patterns. In addition, we developed two other sets of materials to accompany the booklets—activity sheets with drawings and words from the booklets and an alphabet book, which also contained many of the characters from the booklets (see Goldenberg, 1990, for a fuller description).

Finally, in contrast to previous years, where we had not concentrated on children's learning the alphabet, teachers in the experimental classrooms were encouraged to teach children the letters and sounds of the alphabet. This added component was a direct result of the impressive results we witnessed in the two academic kindergartens as well as a response to the accumulating evidence that knowledge of letters and sounds makes a positive contribution to early literacy development (Adams, 1990; Chall, 1983).

Instead of using the published readiness test, we also developed a set of individually administered early literacy measures tapping a range of early literacy skills and knowledge, grouped into two clusters: (1) a test of giving the name and sound of each upper- and lowercase letter (presented out of sequence) and (2) a range of early literacy skills and knowledge, comprising *Concepts About Print* (Clay 1985; translated into Spanish), comprehension of a story read aloud; identification of rhymes and first syllables, reading phonetically regular words, writing or attempting to write self-selected words, and metalinguistic knowledge about literacy. We also administered the group test of word recognition and sentence comprehension that we had used previously.

For the most part, our results were similar to those of the pilot study: The experimental *Libros* classrooms outperformed the readiness classrooms on the early literacy measures, particularly on the group test of word and sentence reading and on individual subtests of letter names and sounds, identification of first syllables, decoding, and word writing. However, the children from the academic classrooms scored highest on the early literacy measures, except for the letter names and sounds, where scores of the experimental and academic classrooms were essentially the same. There were no differences among the three groups on subtests of oral comprehension, Concepts About Print, identification of rhymes, or metalinguistic knowledge about print.

There was another noteworthy difference among the groups. The testers (native-English bilinguals with extensive experience working with language-minority children) rated each child on his or her word reading ability, and the three groups produced strikingly different patterns: 42% of the children in the academic classrooms were rated fluent readers, whereas only 25% and 4% of the children in the *Libros* and readiness classrooms, respectively, received this rating. In contrast, 75% of the readiness children were rated nonreaders, and almost none of the children in the other classrooms (8% in the *Libros*; 0% in the academic) received nonreader ratings.

In retrospect, the results of the 2 years seem hardly surprising; but because we were working within a local framework that rejected didactic teaching of reading in kindergarten, they were unexpected at the time. The teachers in the academic classrooms actually set out to teach children to read—something we had not envisioned, much less attempted. They did it systematically, efficiently, and effectively. They insisted on—and got—a high degree of "buy-in" from parents and children. Their classrooms were highly disciplined, smoothly running operations with an unambiguous academic agenda. Although children heard stories and had opportunities to paint and go to "centers," the clear priority was learning to read, write, count, compute, and acquire other pieces of important academic knowledge and skills.

Moreover, these two highly dynamic teachers—both of whom were from Mexican families and had grown up in the Los Angeles area—put an explicitly cultural spin on their classroom practices. For example, in discussing the strict discipline they employed, one of the teachers rejected the criticism that they were being unduly and inappropriately harsh with the children:

We're not being mean, that's the way their parents talk to them. When I say ¿*Dónde están tus orejas?* (Where are your ears?) or ¿*Qué, no ves?* (What, can't you see?), it's just an expression. People might say it sounds harsh, but that's just the way we talk. My mother talked to me like that. It's not being mean. (fieldnotes, 3/9/89).

Of course it is impossible to say to what extent these teachers' success is due to their high degree of cultural sensitivity and awareness or their equally high degree of skill and their commitment to Hispanic children's academic achievement. Perhaps both were factors. What is certain, however, were their very impressive results. Additional evidence came from scores on a nationally normed test of Spanish reading achievement given in the fall of first grade (Spanish Assessment of Basic Education, CTB/McGraw-Hill, 1987). These teachers' students had by far the highest scores in the district—at the 70th percentile according to national norms. The other kindergartens at the school scored around the 60th percentile; the rest of the kindergarten classes throughout the district scored below the 50th percentile.

Our results to date seemed quite clear: Compared with the standard readiness program used in the district, which afforded children little direct exposure to written texts, the booklets and the accompanying materials seemed to provide literacy learning opportunities that could lead to enhanced early Spanish literacy development. The effects were considerable, with effect sizes approximately .7–.8, meaning that the average student in a *Libros* classroom scored .7 to .8 standard deviations higher than the average student in a readiness classroom. These results were concentrated on knowledge of letters, sounds, and word reading and writing. However, the two academically oriented kindergartens produced even better results, with effect sizes ranging, incredibly, from 1 to 3 standard deviation units, for knowledge of letters, sounds, word reading and writing, and simple reading comprehension, but not on oral comprehension, *Concepts About Print*, or metalinguistic knowledge about print.

Final Study: Effects on Language and Affect

In our final study in this series, we were interested in addressing two issues that had previously received scant attention: The first was whether the use of the *Libros* had any effects on children's language. This is an important question, given the importance of language for ongoing cognitive development and communicative competence (Feagans & Farran, 1982) and the concerns about how schools afford children, particularly low-income, minority children, inadequate opportunities for language use and development. When we began our studies, we had originally predicted that using and sending home these meaningful texts would have an effect not only on written literacy development but also on oral language. Our hypothesis was that use of these books at home would promote more language use between children and parents and this would then lead to children's greater facility with "book talk." In the course of our home studies, however, we discovered that the *Libros* did not promote more language and meaning-based interactions at home (Goldenberg, Reese, & Gallimore, 1992). We decided, therefore, to see whether a somewhat enhanced intervention with the *Libros* could produce effects on children's language use and production. To test the effect of the enhanced *Libros* intervention, the experimental classrooms (*Libros*-experimental) included two additional components; the readiness classrooms (*Libros*-control) used and sent home the *Libros*, but without these additional components:

1. Teachers in the *Libros*-experimental classrooms were encouraged to provide as many opportunities as possible for children to talk about the booklets (and other books or stories) during school time. Teachers were also given copies of the teacher's manual for an oral language and story comprehension program, Story telling and Retelling (STaR) (see chapter 7, this volume), although we never implemented the program in any formal sense. On two to three occasions during the year, I also went into experimental classrooms and demonstrated a model of teaching known as "instructional conversation" (Goldenberg, 1992–1993), which is specifically designed to encourage children to participate orally in discussion about written texts.

2. We added a last page to each *Libro* in the experimental condition, suggesting to parents that they read and talk about the booklet with their child. The page contained a number of suggested questions to guide possible conversations between parents and children such as why the child

liked the story. (Teachers later reported they used this page during their own classroom lessons.) The experimental teachers also sent home brief notes two to three times per week for parents, reminding them to read and discuss the booklets (or other reading matter) with their children. Parents signed the notes, and children returned them the next day.

The second issue we addressed in our final study was this: Is there any evidence of negative effects of the academic kindergartens on children's attitudes or dispositions? Many recent statements about appropriate learning environments for young children take a strong stand against many of the practices observed in the more academically oriented classrooms (see, e.g., Early Childhood and Literacy Development Committee, 1986; National Association for the Education of Young Children [NAEYC], 1988). The NAEYC specifically warns that "inappropriate instructional techniques are a source of stress for young children." Inappropriate practices include, for example, teacher-directed reading lessons, dividing the curriculum into discrete subjects such as reading and math, and paper and pencil practice exercises or worksheets that children are expected to complete independently (NAEYC, 1988).

Results of Final Year's Study: Something Old, Something New
As happened the previous year, the experimental *Libros* classrooms scored the highest on letter names and sounds, higher, this time, than the academic classrooms. This probably was due to the emphasis we had placed within the project on helping children acquire knowledge of letters and sounds, which served to reinforce further whatever effects the alphabet books had. Again, as before, on the other literacy measures (which we have subsequently found to correlate .73 with standardized reading achievement at the end of first grade), the academic kindergartens outperformed the other classrooms. Except for learning letters and sounds, the academic classrooms were more successful overall in helping children acquire beginning and early literacy knowledge and skills. There were no differences on the early literacy measures (except for letters and sounds) between the experimental classrooms and the control classrooms, both of which were using the *Libros*, although at different levels of implementation. We had two new findings, however.

To permit us to see whether the enhanced version of the *Libros* intervention had any effect on children's productive language, testers showed each child the cover of a book to be read aloud and asked the child to predict what the story would be about. Children's responses were rated from 0 (no response) to 5 (constructs elaborate narrative), then grouped into two response categories—a lower level response (no response or names only a character or an action, but not both—e.g., "*un niño*" "a boy") and a higher level response (one or more characters and one or more actions in a string or sequence of events—e.g., "*Un niño va a encontrar a su mamá. Va a comprar algo a su mamá. Zapatos y una cadena. Es su cumpleaños.*" "A boy is going to find his mother. He is going to buy something for his mother. Shoes and a chain [necklace]. It's her birthday.").

Fifty-two percent of the experimental children gave a higher level response, while only 24% and 27% of the students in the academic and control booklets classrooms, respectively, provided higher level responses. When we combined the academic and control booklets classrooms, the contrast in higher level responses—52% for experimentals vs. 25% for others—was statistically significant ($p < .02$). In other words, children in the experimental classrooms, where we had tried to enhance the *Libros* program to promote more language use and language production by children, were more than twice as likely to make more complex predictions than were the children in the other classrooms.

In a second language measure, after reading the story and asking the child several comprehension questions, testers gave children an overall language rating, from 0 (practically nonverbal) to 3 (quite verbal, fluent, and talkative). We again found a significantly ($p = .05$) different pattern among the groups. Children in the experimental group were approximately three times as likely to receive the highest language rating from the testers (44% for the *Libros* vs. 18% and 14% for the academic and readiness classes, respectively). These results, once again, were consistent with our hypothesis that the enhanced *Libros* treatment, where teachers paid increased attention to oral discussion with the booklets and each booklet contained suggested questions at the back, led to higher language performance by the children. When tested in the fall, the groups had been identical in language and prediction ratings and on the Spanish Bilingual Syntax Measure (Burt, Dulay, & Hernández Ch., 1975), an index of syntactic maturity.

Attitudes Toward Reading and Reading Tests

Finally, results of our inquiry into children's affect and attitudes were also quite clear. Children were first asked (prior to beginning the tests) two questions: "Do you like to read (or have someone read to you)?" and "Do you know how to read?" More than 90% said unequivocally that they liked to read or be read to, and there were no differences among the three groups. Children gave more varied responses as to whether they knew how to read. In both the experimental and the academic classrooms, 77% said they could read or could read a little, while in the booklets control classrooms, 52% said they could read or read a little. The differences were not statistically significant ($p = .07$), but more importantly, there was clearly no evidence that the academic classrooms had negative effects on liking to read or attitudes toward self as a reader.

A second gauge on children's affective dispositions was obtained by having testers rate children on three measures (apparent self-confidence, motivation, and enjoyment of literacy tasks) after 2 days of individual testing. The three scales were highly intercorrelated, so they were combined into one reliable rating of affective disposition. There were again no differences among the groups, indicating no negative side effects of the more structured academic program.

Kindergarten Spanish Literacy: Some Concluding Comments

In a number of ways, the results of the kindergarten studies yielded unexpected findings and led us in some unexpected directions. First, we had originally anticipated that providing kindergarten children with home and school literacy experiences with meaningful little booklets would help promote their early literacy development. The emphasis, in other words, was on *providing opportunities* rather than *directly teaching*. Our expectation turned out to be only partly confirmed. Compared with the standard readiness classrooms, the booklets did have an effect. In several respects, however, our experimental *Libros* and accompanying materials were less effective in promoting literacy than were two structured, academic classrooms where children were directly taught letters, sounds, and how they combined to form words, phrases, and sentences. Two things became clear from the various comparisons of the three studies: Kindergarten children learn more about literacy when they are in classrooms that provide additional and direct opportunities for learning about print. They learn even more when directly taught.

Second, as a result of the consistent findings with the academic classrooms, teachers in the experimental classrooms began to include more direct teaching of letters and sounds. We also developed simple alphabet books that teachers used with children at school and sent home for them to keep and use. Once teachers provided a stronger focus on learning the alphabet, we obtained strong and consistent effects on these measures, as might be expected.

Third, our last study suggested that the booklets, accompanied by appropriate verbal interactions with children, could have some important effects, independent of text-based skills such as reading and writing words, knowing letters and sounds, and so forth. We found that a greater emphasis on discussing the stories, encouraging children to talk about them, and including questions at the back that parents and teachers could use in talking about the books had an effect on children's language production.

Finally, this series of studies suggests there is some basis for rethinking current trends away from academic learning in kindergarten. Although the entire early childhood education establishment appears unanimous in its condemnation of teaching academic skills before first grade, one of the unexpected findings from this series of studies was that children might actually benefit from academic learning and direct academic teaching—if it is skillfully done. Certainly, children's early literacy skills were enhanced in the highly academic classrooms, and there was no evidence whatever of negative socioemotional consequences (Hanson et al.,1987, report similar findings on children they followed to high school). In fact, we have at least anecdotal evidence of positive socioemotional effects on the enhanced academic competence these children experienced. During the 1989 spring testing, one of the testers (who was unaware of the issues and hypothesis in the study) wrote in her notes that the children in these two classrooms "seem quite advanced over [the others tested]—maybe 1 year. Not only did they know much more but their affect was much more positive, i.e., initiated conversation, smiled, appeared higher energy and more confident" (tester fieldnotes, 6/89).

Although I am not necessarily making a case for academic kindergartens, I *am* suggesting that the current, mainstream revulsion at teaching academic skills to 5-year-olds merits reexamination, particularly when there is evidence that children can benefit from such learning while suffering no adverse side effects. A lot depends on the teaching and the context in which academic learning is expected to take place. The last words go to one of the two teachers in the academic kindergartens, who confounded some of my most cherished assumptions about early literacy development:

> Teachers think these kids are so deprived we need to let them play all day here. That really makes me mad because I came from a background like this. [Teachers use assumptions about children's backgrounds] to allow letting kids play all day rather than taking responsibility for teaching them what they need to know so they can be academically successful. These kids can learn, but they have to be taught. If more teachers realized this and did what they were supposed to do, more of these kids would go on to college. (fieldnotes, 8/31/89)

SPANISH LITERACY DEVELOPMENT IN FIRST AND SECOND GRADES

The next part of the project related to improvement of Spanish reading by first and second graders in the same school where the kindergarten study described previously began—a largely Hispanic elementary school in southern California (see Goldenberg & Gallimore, 1991). As with the kindergarten studies, our project's efforts to improve native-language literacy attainment in grades 1 and 2 also began when I was teaching first grade at the school. This first- and second-grade effort was important because it represented an attempt to extend improved literacy learning opportunities in kindergarten on into early elementary school. Previous studies suggest that preschool literacy gains tend to disappear by mid-elementary school if early elementary programs do not extend and build upon achievement prior to first grade (e.g., Durkin, 1974–1975; however, see also Hanson et al., 1987, which challenges this assertion). We were therefore interested in finding ways to produce high levels of native language reading development on into the early years of elementary school.

This effort is also significant because it illustrates one of the themes of this chapter: Successful change did not result from the direct application or implementation of research findings to a particular school site. Instead, it was the result of long-term, cumulative work informed by an understanding of local issues and circumstances, no less than by an awareness of issues and findings generated from research. In many respects, as with the kindergarten studies, the original model envisioned was not the one that eventually emerged. For example, the original emphasis of my efforts to improve early reading achievement assumed that a focus on meaning would essentially displace instruction on letters, sounds, and syllables. This turned out not to be the case, however, and what eventually evolved was a balanced early literacy program where meaning coexisted more or less peacefully with letters, sounds, and syllables.

In fact, a set of fundamental changes evolved in several domains of the early reading program, one of which has already been described for kindergarten. These changes altered considerably the achievement patterns among Spanish-speaking first and second graders at the school. The changes can be grouped into four categories: (1) literacy opportunities in kindergarten; (2) a balanced emphasis on meaning and decoding in first grade; (3) increased home and parent involvement; and (4) improved pacing of instruction.

Changes in School Literacy Program

Increased Attention to Literacy in Kindergarten

The school's kindergarten program went from a readiness orientation prior to 1985 to one that 2 years later placed more emphasis on literacy learning opportunities for children. This was partly the result of the kindergarten studies described previously. Teacher turnover and the arrival of new kindergarten faculty and other personnel also contributed to this shift. The two academically oriented kindergarten teachers transferred from another school and brought with them an explicitly academic focus. On the one hand, this created some tensions with a faculty that was not academically oriented, particularly for kindergarten. On the other hand, it contributed to the emergence of a critical mass of teachers and administrators who shared, at least in this respect, a commitment to changing the early literacy emphasis at the school.

Considerable controversy remained about the early reading curriculum, as reflected by the different orientations of teachers in our kindergarten studies. The controversy mirrored many of the debates in early childhood education; however the issue was no longer whether kindergarten should include literacy learning opportunities. Instead, the question was what kinds of literacy learning opportunities should kindergartners have? The topic of kindergarten literacy, which previously had been associated with an excessively academic orientation that most of the faculty and administration explicitly rejected, became legitimate, in part, because there were different ways teachers could make literacy opportunities available to children. Although the more explicitly academic classrooms continued to produce the highest levels of achievement, the overall levels and expectations for all kindergarten children at the school shifted considerably. This shift signaled a widespread acceptance at the school that (1) kindergarten children were more capable and ready than most people realized, (2) under the right circumstances they could learn a great deal about print and how it functions, and (3) the school had an important role to play in the children's early literacy development.

Balanced Emphasis on Meaning and the Code in First Grade
Spanish reading instruction tends to be excessively weighted toward a phonics-based, bottom-up approach. The predominant focus is on having children learn two-letter syllables comprising a consonant and a vowel, which constitute the basis for Spanish orthography. As a result, early literacy learning experiences Spanish-speaking children have in school are often decontextualized and divorced from meaning. Prior to the changes described here, first-grade teachers at the school required children to learn all of the syllables made from the five vowels and the consonants *m, p, t,* and *l* before they could progress in the reading series and begin to read even the briefest meaningful texts.

This focus is potentially of greatest harm to children who have relatively few authentic literacy opportunities outside of school. For some children at the school, especially those who made the slowest progress in learning letters and sounds, reading instruction consisted primarily of games, drills, and various activities focusing on the sounds letters make and how letters combine to form syllables. Throughout first grade, these students had few opportunities to read meaningful texts, phrases, or in some cases, even words. Even after children got over the hurdle of the syllables, little instruction focused on understanding or deriving meaning from written texts. In a word, the first-grade reading program was unidimensional in the extreme, and the results were very low levels of reading achievement and very slow progress through the reading curriculum.

Gradually, beginning in 1985, meaningful reading began to infiltrate into first-grade reading instruction. For example, short, simple stories—either copied from a book or generated through a language experience approach—were written on charts, and children read and discussed them as whole texts. These activities proved to be valuable, even—perhaps especially—with groups of children that had previously experienced only endless rounds of phonic and syllable drills and exercises. Children learned to read the chart stories through a variety of bottom-up and top-down processes. Individual stories were then copied, and children began to accumulate folders of little stories they could read, take home, illustrate, and so forth. More materials were also introduced, in the form of workbooks and worksheets, that contained more connected text for children to read.

More emphasis on meaning and comprehension also resulted from some informal testing conducted at the school, which revealed that if children were directly taught comprehension skills such as selecting the best title for a simple passage, their performance improved dramatically. Teachers then began to devote more attention to teaching such skills, thereby reinforcing a greater emphasis on the meaning of texts, but also teaching skills that children needed in order to pass end-of-book tests. More attention to meaning might also have resulted from numerous discussions I had with colleagues and several presentations I made about early literacy.

Teachers gradually went from an excessively narrow conception of reading and reading instruction to a broader one, where meaning and reading connected text played more prominent roles. One teacher, in fact, who served on a faculty committee considering reading instruction at the school, successfully argued for a reduced emphasis on phonics as the only means for providing children with literacy learning opportunities. As with the kindergarten program, reading in first grade underwent important changes between 1985 and 1987. Children began reading more connected text, and teachers began to target specific comprehension skills. Phonics and syllables were not banished from the curriculum, but they became part of a more balanced program where children received a wide range of literacy learning opportunities.

Increased Home and Parent Involvement

Prior to 1985, first-grade teachers did not regularly enlist or contact parents to help their children academically. When teachers did contact parents, it was generally for discipline problems. Teachers generally held assumptions that tended to work against promoting the sort of parent involvement that might help children's academic achievement, e.g., parents needed a great deal of training before they could help their children, parents were largely illiterate and deemphasized academic achievement in favor of family or survival values, families were under such economic stress they could not play a meaningful role in children's academic development, or literacy in the home was not a part of the families' culture.

However, research in the school and community suggested that these assumptions were largely inaccurate. For example, children's homes were not devoid of literacy. Although the overall educational levels of parents were indeed low, they had at least rudimentary reading skills, and many actually read at much higher levels. Similarly, although literacy did not occupy a prominent place in many of the homes, neither was it entirely absent. Virtually all homes sent and received letters to relatives in Mexico or Central America; all received printed flyers or advertisements; most parents reported (and subsequent studies have confirmed) that children consistently asked about signs, other environmental print, or the contents of letters to or from relatives, none of which would be possible if literacy did not exist in the homes at least at some level. Perhaps most important, parents placed great value on educational achievement and its importance for social and economic mobility. One mother, for example, told me this:

> *Uno puede abrirse camino teniendo muchos estudios. En cambio así, uno tiene que andar limpiando, pidiendo de gata porque no puede uno hacer otra cosa.* (If you've studied a lot, you can open up opportunities for yourself. Otherwise, you have to clean houses or ask for handouts because you don't know how to do anything else.) (Goldenberg & Gallimore, 1991, p. 9)

Other parents explicitly pointed to their own situations as a kind of negative example for their children: *"Nosotros no estudiamos, y mírenos aquí"* ("We didn't study, and look at us here"), one father responded, when asked why he wanted his child to continue with his schooling.

Although doubts continued to persist among teachers about parents' willingness or ability to help their children academically, gradually a new set of practices emerged. Reading books and other literacy materials began to be sent home regularly. In kindergarten, as we have seen, teachers gave children various materials or literacy-related activities to take home and complete, usually with the help or supervision of parents. In other classrooms, teachers sent more conventional homework, such as materials on which children were to practice writing their names or letters of the alphabet.

The textbook policy—which previously did not permit books to be taken home—was changed, and in first grade, reading books and other materials for practice and enrichment began to go home on a regular basis. In all classrooms there was much more emphasis than ever before on having children read at home, which prior research has shown helps improve reading achievement (e.g., Tizard, Schofield, & Hewison, 1982). Teachers also used a number of simple techniques to facilitate practice and reinforcement at home, such as easily reproducible forms where teachers or students wrote down home assignments. Another technique was a cumulative word list, to which key words from reading books were gradually added over a period of weeks.

In this area, too, the successful practices that eventually evolved were not entirely consistent with my original expectations. Previous research suggested that increased opportunities to interact with print at home should promote higher levels of reading achievement (e.g., Anderson et al., 1985; Teale, 1978). Consistent with this and with my previous studies at the school, I hypothesized that providing parents with the appropriate information— suggestions that they read to children, take them to the library, and engage them in various everyday learning activities—would lead to substantial improvements in achievement. Accordingly, at the beginning of each school year, I met with parents to provide them with this information and other information about what children would be learning at school.

Parents were interested and supportive, but there was little evidence that the mere provision of information had a strong effect on home literacy practices or on achievement. We found, instead, that it was important to follow up regularly in the form of homework assignments, of the sort just described, or notes or phone calls home. When we systematically extended children's learning experiences outside school—by sending home books and other materials on a regular basis and consistently monitoring and following through—achievement started to improve.

Improved pacing of first-grade Spanish reading instruction
In general, and net of other effects, the more material students have an opportunity to learn, the more they are likely to learn (see review in Goldenberg & Gallimore, 1991). The issue of pacing is significant, particularly for lower achieving students, since these are the students for whom teachers are most likely to slow down the pace of instruction inappropriately, thereby greatly reducing children's opportunities to learn additional and more challenging material (Leinhardt & Bickel, 1989).

At the end of the 1983–1984 school year, no one at the school expected children to proceed through the reading curriculum according to publishers' norms. The staff made a sharp distinction between the publishers' norms and what was reasonable to expect at the school with this population. Children were considered on grade level if they completed and mastered the material in the second of three first-grade preprimers. Exceedingly slow progress through the reading curriculum thus did not alarm anyone. The widespread, not unreasonable, assumption was that, as one teacher said, "You have to take the kids from where they are" and get them as far as possible. Although in theory this made perfect sense, in practice it led to passivity in the face of low-achievement levels. This passivity then reinforced very low expectations, which, in turn, further reinforced the absence of any need to do things differently.

Not surprisingly, in 1984, nearly one half (49%) of the first-grade Spanish readers were still in the first of three first-grade preprimers at year's end and only 7% were at grade level, that is, reading in a book that was at least minimally appropriate and sufficiently challenging for children who had been in school since kindergarten. However, 3 years later, at the end of the 1986–1987 school year, the situation was exactly the reverse, and more than 45% of the students were in the final preprimer at the end of first grade with only about 10% in the first one. The following year, the situation had improved even more, with nearly 25% of the first graders reading in a second-grade book, and only 1% still in the first preprimer.

One reason for the improved pacing in the reading curriculum was that the principal and one of the instructional specialists had instituted pacing conferences during the 1986–1987 school year. Each teacher met individually with a specialist to discuss the progress that children were making in math, reading, and language. The specialist reported that although at first some teachers expressed some discomfort with this new procedure, the conferences had been beneficial in helping teachers keep in mind the bigger picture, that academic achievement was an ongoing developmental process.

To a significant degree, the improvement in pacing cannot be seen as independent of the other changes already mentioned—the earlier start in literacy learning during kindergarten; the more balanced, substantive approach to reading instruction in first grade; and systematic, regular efforts to involve children's homes and parents in their early literacy achievement. In fact, the dramatically changed picture of student progress in the reading program, as suggested by the data on first-grade book placement at the end of the year, is best understood as the result of the several factors identified here working in concert. Children were learning earlier and learning more about literacy, both in and out of school. Teachers were able to challenge children more, yet appropriately. As a result, there was no longer any need—whether real or perceived—to spend weeks and months in endless rounds of phonic and syllabic drilling. Improved pacing was thus more than a vacuous exercise in turning textbook pages faster, and it was as much an effect of improved achievement as it was a cause.

Effects on Reading Achievement, 1985–1989

What have been the effects of these changes on the early reading achievement of Benson's Spanish readers? To answer this question, we analyzed second- and third-grade test results in Spanish. Achievement tests are administered within the first weeks of school, so student scores presumably reflect previous years' learning. (Demographic changes and grade retentions around the district were also analyzed to rule out the possibility that achievement changes were due to these extraneous factors.)

We found very clear evidence of improvement in reading achievement at the school, both over time and in relation to the other schools in the district.

Between 1986 and 1987, CTBS-Español reading scores in the beginning of second grade increased by 20 percentile points, from the 33rd to the 53rd percentile. Scores at the other schools remained essentially unchanged during these years. It is particularly worth noting that whereas in 1985 and 1986 Benson was below the other schools in second-grade Spanish achievement, beginning in 1987, Benson scores became—and remained—higher than those at the other schools in the district.

Third-grade achievement scores demonstrate a similar pattern. Until 1986, third graders at the school, just as the second graders, scored considerably below those in the rest of the district. Again, beginning in 1987, third-grade scores improved both in absolute and in relative terms. The differences in 1987 and 1988 between Benson students' scores and those of the rest of the district are not as large as in second grade. Not until 1989—when they surpassed the 50th percentile on national norms—did they reach statistical significance. The more modest changes in third-grade achievement, in 1987 and 1988, suggest an indirect, or spillover, effect from some of the changes that had occurred in the lower grades. The substantial change in 1989 scores, however, are probably the results of direct efforts to improve the substance and focus of literacy instruction in second grade. These efforts were an outgrowth of some of the changes described previously and they represented an explicit attempt to expand the scope of previous work at the school (see Gallimore & Goldenberg, 1989).

Reading achievement improved across the range, but particularly among the lowest achieving children. The rise in mean scores, in other words, was not simply the result of accelerating the learning of higher achieving students. At both grades 2 and 3, students scores at the 10th, 25th, and 50th percentiles were above those of the national sample at those percentile levels. At the 75th and 90th percentiles, second-grade students' scores were virtually indistinguishable from those of the national sample. In third grade, the higher scores dropped off in relation to national norms. At all levels, however, students at the school scored considerably higher than those in the rest of the district (Goldenberg & Gallimore, 1991).

PROMOTING AND SUSTAINING THE LITERACY DEVELOPMENT OF SPANISH-SPEAKING STUDENTS

For perhaps understandable reasons, language *use* and language *instruction* have dominated research and policy considerations in the education of Spanish-speaking children. Yet given the patterns of achievement among Hispanic children—whether taught in English or Spanish—there are clearly many more issues involved.

To be sure, language is important: When and how the native language should be used; when and how English should be introduced; should the native language be phased out once children can benefit from English instruction; does learning that took place in the first language then transfer and become accessible in the second language; if so, what transfers and what doesn't? Each of these language-oriented questions is important in its own right, and, to one degree or another, they have received the attention of practitioners and scholars (e.g., California State Department of Education, 1984; Cummins, 1979; Goldman & Trueba, 1987; Wong Fillmore & Valadez, 1986).

A focus on language is not enough, however. Even the most enlightened *language* policy will falter in the context of an ineffective *instructional* program. Yet little attention has focused on the larger issues of school and classroom effectiveness in bilingual education, independent of language matters. I will close by briefly addressing two of these.

Early Reading Instruction in Spanish

One set of issues that must be examined very closely has to do with Spanish-language reading instruction and the literacy learning opportunities we provide Spanish-speaking children. Although attaining high levels of native-language literacy is central to the theory of bilingual education (e.g., Krashen & Biber, 1988; Wong Fillmore & Valadez, 1986), with rare exceptions (e.g., Edelsky, 1986; Goldenberg & Gallimore, 1991), Spanish language literacy has received very little attention from researchers in this country. Research and descriptions of practice do exist, of course, in Spanish-speaking countries (e.g., Ferreiro & Teberosky, 1982; *Lectura y vida*, a journal published by the International Reading Association), but the different literacy context for the Spanish-speaking child in an English-speaking country might make even this literature problematic for U.S. Spanish-language educators. One clear implication, therefore, is that intensive efforts are needed to develop effective instructional models to help children acquire high levels of literacy knowledge and skills in Spanish.

Results of the studies described here suggest that the provision of increased literacy learning opportunities, both at home and at school, will have a positive effect on Spanish-speaking children's literacy development. Contrary to many professionals' assumptions that these children are generally not ready to learn about literacy when they enter school, we found that they are indeed able and willing learners. As to what kinds of early literacy opportunities are most beneficial, the kindergarten studies described earlier suggest that a strong emphasis on learning letters, sounds, and how they combine to form syllables and meaningful words—that is, a code emphasis—gave kindergarten children an early and valuable start in learning to become literate. This finding is consistent with findings based on research with English-speaking populations (Adams, 1990; Chall, 1983). A code emphasis might be especially pertinent and useful in Spanish, due to the greater orthographic regularity, or, alternatively, because of the relative transparency of Spanish orthography, a code emphasis might be misplaced. Children might instead benefit more from a well-conceived and implemented meaning-based approach in which, essentially, they decipher the code for themselves. The results of our studies seem to lend support for the first hypothesis, but clearly these questions warrant investigation and empirical testing. In any event, experiences other than code-based ones are also important for literacy development. We found that reading and discussing stories probably produced effects on children's oral language production, at least as gauged by our simple assessments.

In first grade, a reading program that combines continued learning of letters and sounds, and how they combine to form syllables and words, together with adequate opportunities for reading (and writing) meaningful and extended texts at school and at home, seemed to help children achieve at higher levels than before. However, what this combination should be—in other words, what the optimum balance is between, on the one hand, learning the code and other technical skills and, on the other, reading for meaning and communicative purposes—is another matter. Again, this seems like a fruitful area for continued research and reflective practice.

Through happenstance, I arrived at a balance in my own teaching that seemed very useful. In my final 2 years at the school, I taught half-time and shared my classroom with a teacher who was code-oriented in contrast to my meaning-based approach. We decided that on the days when she taught, she would emphasize the letters and syllables featured in the lessons or stories that the children were learning. On the days when I taught, I focused on language, meaning, comprehension, and real reading. It was an uneasy alliance at first, but eventually, this 50–50 split seemed to work very effectively. Both of us believed that we had the most successful classes we had ever taught.

Beyond the beginning stages of reading, even less is known about the conditions for promoting sustained reading growth in the native language. Research and theory suggest that the tasks and nature of reading change as children develop as readers (Chall, 1983). Whereas in the early stages of learning to read a certain emphasis on learning the code supports reading development, the focus of reading experiences beyond this early stage must shift if reading development is to continue. In what Chall calls Stage 2 of reading development (typically, late second and early third grades), children need a great many opportunities to read familiar books and stories in order to confirm and consolidate their knowledge about print and its conventions. In

Stage 3 (beginning around fourth grade), there must be more of an emphasis on reading to learn, rather than on learning to read. Expository prose and the learning of new ideas, facts, and concepts from print become important, and children require opportunities to read and learn from more complex, challenging, and less familiar materials. It is likely that native-language literacy—even in a non-native-language context—develops in a similar way. Again, it is an area that would benefit from systematic examination by teachers and researchers alike.

Creating Contexts for Change

Finally, we need to consider the larger context within which any instructional or curricular program must exist. Research during the past 20 years has consistently documented the positive effects of certain school contexts on the achievement of at-risk populations, independent of particular teaching methodologies (e.g, Bliss, Firestone, & Richards, 1991; Lucas, Henze, & Donato, 1990). This body of research has identified a number of characteristics that differentiated more and less effective schools, e.g., strong instructional leadership; high expectations for student achievement; a safe and orderly learning environment, an emphasis on basic skills; continuous monitoring of student progress, and clear and well-understood school goals (Davis & Thomas, 1989).

Clearly, this literature represents a potentially useful knowledge base to help practitioners create conditions in schools that will support meaningful and substantive change. Valuable as it is, effective schools' research is limited in its utility since it is largely retrospective. We know, in other words, that a number of factors distinguish more and less successful schools. With few exceptions (e.g., Peterson & Lezotte, 1991), however, we seem to have little knowledge of the transformation process from its inception—that is, how less successful schools came to be more successful.

This dearth of direct evidence is particularly glaring for schools serving language-minority populations. Ronald Gallimore and I reported a case study of a single school serving a largely Spanish-speaking population and how the early native-language literacy program went from being less to more effective (Goldenberg & Gallimore, 1991). Even here the scope of the study was very limited, and only dealing with native-language reading achievement in grades 1 and 2. No study has examined how an entire school serving a substantially Latino population has gone from ineffective to effective with respect to student learning and achievement. In the context of the rapidly growing Latino population and the persistent underachievement among these students, this is a glaring gap.

There are apparently successful models, however, and no doubt other schools are attempting to replicate successful practices elsewhere. Krashen and Biber (1988) report a number of successful bilingual programs. Crawford (1989) also describes a number of bilingual education success stories, the results of a project ("Case Studies in Bilingual Education") initiated by the California State Department of Education. It would seem extremely useful to attempt to implement these or other models, then to document prospectively the processes schools undergo as they attempt to deal more effectively with the educational challenges they face.

We need, in short, intensive local efforts to improve achievement schoolwide and case studies documenting this effort. Shulman (1986, p. 11) has argued for the importance of knowledge of specific, well-documented and richly-described events as an important component of a professional and theoretical knowledge base. Although context-free research that sets out to test propositions has produced a great deal of useful and important knowledge, the value of cases, according to Shulman, derives from how they can illuminate complex, multifaceted phenomena in particular contexts. Creating school contexts to improve the academic achievement of language-minority children—indeed, to improve academic achievement under any circumstances—is an example of such complex, multifaceted phenomena. We cannot lose sight of this complexity and the serious challenges it poses to practitioners.

REFERENCES

Adams, M. (1990). *Beginning to read: Thinking and learning about print.* Cambridge, MA: MIT Press.

Anderson, R.C., Hiebert, E.H., Scott, J.A., & Wilkinson, I.A.G. (1985). *Becoming a nation of readers.* Champaign, IL: Center for the Study of Reading, University of Illinois.

Baker, K., & deKanter, A. (1981). *Effectiveness of bilingual education: A review of the literature.* Washington, DC: U.S. Department of Education, Office of Planning, Budget and Evaluation.

Bliss, J., Firestone, W., & Richards, C. (Eds.). (1991). *Rethinking effective schools: Research and practice.* Englewood Cliffs, NJ: Prentice Hall.

Burt, M., Dulay, H., & Hernández Ch., E. (1975). *Bilingual syntax measure.* New York: Harcourt Brace Jovanovich.

California State Department of Education. (1984). *Studies in immersion.* Sacramento, CA: Author.

California State Department of Education. (1992). *BEOutreach, 3*(1), 17.

Chall, J. (1983). *Stages of reading development.* New York: McGraw-Hill.

Clay, M. (1985). *The early detection of reading difficulties* (3rd ed.). Portsmouth, NH: Heinemann.

Committee for Economic Development. (1991). *The unfinished agenda: A new vision for child development and education.* New York: Author.

Crawford, J. (1989). *Bilingual education: History, politics, theory, and practice.* Trenton, NJ: Crane.

CTB/McGraw-Hill. (1987). *SABE: Spanish Assessment of Basic Education.* Monterey, CA: Author.

Cummins, J. (1979). Linguistic interdependence and the educational development of bilingual children. *Review of Educational Research, 49,* 222–251.

Davis, G.A. & Thomas, M.A. (1989). *Effective schools and effective teachers.* Boston: Allyn & Bacon.

Delgado-Gaitan, C. (1990). *Literacy for empowerment.* New York: Falmer.

Durkin, D. (1974–1975). A six-year study of children who learned to read in school at the age of four. *Reading Research Quarterly, 10,* 9–61.

Early Childhood and Literacy Development Committee. (1986). IRA position statement on reading and writing in early childhood. *Reading Teacher, 39,* 819–821.

Edelsky, C. (1986). *Writing in a bilingual program: Había una vez.* Norwood, NJ: Ablex.

Feagans, L., & Farran, D. (Eds.). (1982). *The language of children reared in poverty: Implications for evaluation and intervention.* New York: Academic Press.

Ferreiro, E., & Teberosky, A. (1982). *Literacy before schooling.* Portsmouth, NH: Heinemann.

Gallimore, R., & Goldenberg, C. (1989). *Action research to increase Hispanic students exposure to meaningful text: A focus on reading and content area instruction.* Final report to Presidential Grants for School Improvement Committee, University of California.

Goldenberg, C. (1989). Making success a more common occurrence for children at risk for failure: Lessons from Hispanic first graders learning to read. In J. Allen & J.M. Mason (Eds.), *Risk makers, risk takers, risk breakers: Reducing the risks for young literacy learners* (pp. 48–78). Portsmouth, NH: Heinemann.

Goldenberg, C. (1990). Beginning literacy instruction for Spanish-speaking children. *Language Arts, 67,* 590–598.

Goldenberg, C. (1992–1993). Instructional conversations: Promoting comprehension through discussion. *Reading Teacher, 46,* 316–326.

Goldenberg, C., & Gallimore, R. (1989, Autumn). Teaching California's diverse student population: The common ground between educational and cultural research. *California Public Schools Forum, 3,* 41–56.

Goldenberg, C., & Gallimore, R. (1991). Local knowledge, research knowledge, and educational change: A case study of first-grade Spanish reading improvement. *Educational Researcher, 20(8),* 2–14.

Goldenberg, C., Reese, L., & Gallimore, R. (1992). Effects of school literacy materials on Latino children's home experiences and early reading achievement. *American Journal of Education, 100,* 497–536.

Goldman, S., & Trueba, H. (Eds.). (1987). *Becoming literate in English as a second language.* Norwood, NJ: Ablex.

Hanson, R., Siegel, D., & Broach, D. (1987, April). *The effects on high school seniors of learning to read in kindergarten.* Paper presented at the annual meeting of the American Educational Research Association, Washington, DC.

Heald-Taylor, G. (1987). Predictable literature selections and activities for language arts instruction. *Reading Teacher, 41,* 1–12.

Kamehameha Schools. (1983). *Kamehameha Educational Research Institute list of publications.* Honolulu, HI: Author.

Krashen, S., & Biber, D. (1988). *On course: Bilingual education's success in California.* Sacramento, CA: California Association for Bilingual Education.

Lazar, I., Darlington, R., Murray, H., Royce, J., & Snipper, A. (1982). *Lasting effects of early education: A report from the Consortium for Longitudinal Studies. Monographs of the Society for Research in Child Development, 47,* 1–151.

Leinhardt, G., & Bickel, W. (1989). Instruction's the thing: Wherein to catch the mind that falls behind. In R. Slavin (Ed.), *School and classroom organization* (pp. 197–226). Hillsdale, NJ: Erlbaum.

Lucas, T., Henze, R., & Donato, R. (1990). Promoting the success of Latino language-minority students: An exploratory study of six high schools. *Harvard Educational Review, 60,* 315–340.

Martin, B., & Brogan, P. (1971). *Instant Readers teachers' guide, level 1.* New York: Holt, Rinehart and Winston.

National Association for the Education of Young Children. (1988). *Appropriate education in the primary grades.* Washington, DC: National Association for the Education of Young Children.

National Center for Education Statistics. (1991). *Digest of Education Statistics, 1990.* Washington, DC: U.S. Department of Education.

National Dissemination Study Group. (1989). *Educational programs that work* (15th ed.). Longmont, CO: Sopris West.

Peterson, K., & Lezotte, L. (1991). New directions in the effective schools movement. In J. Bliss, W. Firestone, & C. Richards (Eds.), *Rethinking effective schools: Research and practice* (pp. 128–137). Englewood Cliffs, NJ: Prentice Hall.

Porter, R. (1990). *Forked tongue: The politics of bilingual education.* New York: Basic Books.

Ramirez, D., Yuen, S., & Ramey, D. (1991). *Final report: Longitudinal study of structured English immersion strategy, early-exit and late-exit transitional bilingual education programs for language-minority children* (executive summary). San Mateo, CA: Aguirre International.

Ramirez, D., Yuen, S., Ramey, D., & Merino, B. (1986). *First year report: Longitudinal study of immersion programs for language-minority children.* San Mateo, CA: Aguirre International.

Riverside Publishing Co. (1984). *La Prueba Riverside de Realización en Español.* Chicago: Author.

Shulman, L.S. (1986). Those who understand: Knowledge growth in teaching. *Educational Researcher, 15*(2), 4–14.

Slavin, R., Karweit, N., & Madden, N. (Eds.). (1989). *Effective programs for students at risk.* Boston, MA: Allyn & Bacon.

Stevenson, H., Chen, C., & Uttal, D. (1990). Beliefs and achievement: A study of black, white, and Hispanic children. *Child Development, 61,* 508–523.

Teale, W. (1978). Positive environments for learning to read: What studies of early readers tell us. *Language Arts, 55,* 922–932.

Teale, W. (1986). Home background and young children's literacy development. In W.H. Teale & E. Sulzby (Eds.), *Emergent literacy: Writing and reading* (pp. 173–206). Norwood, NJ: Ablex.

Tizard, J., Schofield, W.N., & Hewison, J. (1982). Collaboration between teachers and parents in assisting children's reading. *British Journal of Educational Psychology, 52,* 1–15.

U.S. Bureau of the Census. (1991, October). *The Hispanic population in the United States: March 1991.* Current Population Reports, Series P-20, No. 455. Washington, DC: U.S. Government Printing Office.

U.S. Department of Education. (1991). *The condition of bilingual education: A report to the Congress and the President.* Washington, DC: U.S. Government Printing Office.

U.S. General Accounting Office. (1987, March). *Bilingual education: A new look at the research evidence* (PEMD-87-12BR). Washington, DC: General Accounting Office.

West, J., Hausken, E., & Chandler, K. (1991). *Home activities of 3- to 8-year olds: Findings from the 1991 National Household Education Survey.* Washington, DC: National Center for Education Statistics.

Wong Fillmore, L., with Valadez, C. (1986). Teaching bilingual learners. In M. Wittrock (Ed.), *Handbook of research on teaching* (3rd ed.), (pp. 648–685). New York: Macmillan.

▶ 10

Interventions and the Restructuring of American Literacy Instruction

ELFRIEDA H. HIEBERT   BARBARA M. TAYLOR

*This chapter stresses that first-grade early literacy inter-
ventions are necessary but not sufficient. Preschool and
kindergarten efforts are needed to enhance the literacy experiences of children who enter school with low levels of literacy. For children who did not become proficient readers
by the end of first grade, second-grade interventions are
needed, not as a replacement for first-grade interventions
but as a means of fostering continued growth in reading
fluency. Successful interventions for children in the middle
grades are also urgently needed to help children make the
transition from reading stories for enjoyment to reading informational text with the goal of reading to learn. Issues
pertaining to teacher education, state and national policies,
and the need for broad, diversified schoolwide models of intervention are also discussed.*

This book contains the reports of a number of projects that aim to get children who have often failed in school off to the right start in literacy. A consistent theme rings through all of these reports: The majority of children who enter school with low levels of literacy can leave the primary grades as proficient readers and writers. The descriptions of these projects show that this goal can be achieved by different means. The common denominator across the projects is the expectation that children can become proficient, enthusiastic readers and writers. The success stories from these projects are not the result of vision alone, however. Each project involves an implementation plan that attends to factors like teacher or tutor support, instructional methods that promote particular strategies, and assessment.

The stories of many children who enter school each year are very different from those in this volume. How can the vision and strategies that produced the success stories in this volume become a reality for many more children? Changes are needed in many classrooms but classrooms do not exist in isolation. The vision that all children can become literate and the knowledge base to make that vision a reality originate in the institutional contexts in which schools exist such as schools of education and national and state agencies.

Although the reports in this volume point to things that work, many questions remain about making such instruction accessible to all children who need it, and the kinds of structures that support teachers and children for these practices to become commonplace. For example, the writers of this book have described ways to get children off to the right start, but a critical question that is left unanswered is—"Does getting off to the right start mean that children automatically stay on track ever after?" This chapter addresses several critical issues related to interventions and the classroom and broader educational contexts in which they occur. These issues are by no means the only ones that need to be addressed. Questions can (and should) be asked about each of the interventions described in this volume. For example, the issue of trainer support needs to be raised with regard to the projects of Hiebert (see chapter 5, this volume) and Taylor et al. (see chapter 6, this volume). What happens when the originators of the project are not involved in a hands-on manner? Such issues have plagued other interventions (Palincsar, Stevens, & Gavelek, 1989). The intent here is not to answer all questions but to provide a framework for discussions of early access to supportive literacy instruction.

EARLY INTERVENTIONS AND CLASSROOM PROGRAMS

A question that comes quickly to the fore in discussions with colleagues at conferences and in classrooms has to do with the necessity of early interventions like those that have been described in this volume. Can't (or shouldn't) classroom teachers do the job? While the research literature might not have documented these effects, many communities have a rich case history of teachers who have been successful with all their students. One of the interventions described in chapter 9 of this volume serendipitously located two of these teachers as part of the control group. They may be the exception rather than the rule. Less experienced teachers are often placed in schools with high proportions of poor children. Further, these schools often receive fewer resources. Factors such as these contribute to the lower levels of literacy attainment among children of the poor, those in urban settings, and those of non-Anglo groups that have consistently been found on the National Assessment of Educational Progress (NAEP) during its 25-year history (Educational Testing Service, 1991). Classroom practices affect the success of interventions as well. The classroom assignment of children accounted for as much variation in the achievement of students in a first-grade intensive project as prior knowledge (Hiebert, 1992). In many contexts, much more can be done in classroom settings, but the availability of Chapter 1 funds means additional resources for supporting poor children in their literacy growth. The projects in this volume suggest that using these resources, at least to some extent, for support beyond that of the classroom teacher enhances the literacy learning of low-income students. Collaborative models in which students participate in a classroom literacy community that is carefully orchestrated by the teacher and in small-group and individual contexts with classroom and specialty teachers are probably the best response in schools with high percentages of poor children. Even more pressing than the question of "where should the instruction occur" are questions having to do with "which levels to target" and "what should be taught at different levels."

Again, solutions that consider the configuration of classroom-specialist support at early childhood and middle-grade levels are a better choice than the emphasis on one or the other level. Surprisingly few case studies can be found that describe the nature of configurations that work at different levels in schools with high proportions of children who depend on schools to become literate. Some general directions for such work can be identified.

Interventions and Early Childhood Contexts: Similarities and Uniquenesses

As reflected in this volume, the bulk of work on interventions during the past several years has been on first grade. A strong argument can be made for first-grade interventions. It is at first grade that reading acquisition becomes a societal expectation (Shepard & Smith, 1988). Arguments can be heard frequently among teachers and teacher educators for moving this milestone to grade 2 or higher as in countries like Sweden (Lundberg, Frost, & Petersen, 1988). Until such agreement is reached (a task of no small proportion), the likelihood that a child who is not successful at this acquisition will ever catch up is small (Juel, 1988). This is not to say that most students will not acquire rudimentary literacy proficiency eventually. The majority of students can perform low-level literacy tasks by fourth grade (Educational Testing Service, 1991) but a substantial portion will never become proficient at the higher level literacies.

Several research groups represented in this volume are considering whether this latter group could attain the higher level literacies if interventions were more comprehensive in their scope. Success for All has extended the period of intervention in both directions—earlier to preschool and kindergarten and later to second grade and above. While literacy events in preschools through second grades emphasize predictable books and self-expressive and narrative writing, the literacy tasks of third grade and above increasingly deal with expository text. Interventions at this level would be expected to emphasize different instructional tasks. Further, while early childhood events may revolve around predictable books, shared reading, and emergent writing, the foci, structure, and content of interventions would not be expected to be uniform across the early childhood years.

Preschool Efforts

Pinnell and McCarrier (see chapter 8, this volume) and Goldenberg (see chapter 9, this volume) have initiated interventions in kindergartens. Even earlier projects might be appropriate as preschool efforts that were part of compensatory education projects of the 1960s showed (Lazar, Darlington, Murray, Royce, & Snipper, 1982). The opportunities for extension of literacy events in Head Start and other preschool contexts are great. A preliminary study conducted by Peterman, Stewart, Sinha, Kerr, and Mason (1991) showed that many occasions for language and literacy were not used in Head Start contexts. In some preschools, books are out of reach to children (Hiebert, Stacy, & Jordan, 1985). The chasm between early childhood and literacy has been a wide one, with literacy events rarely included in descriptions of developmentally appropriate curriculum (Spodek, 1988). As Snow and Ninio (1986) and others have demonstrated, literacy events can be a primary context for linguistic and conceptual development. Models for interventions can be found in the work of Mason, McCormick, and Bhavnagri (1986) and Dickinson (1989) where Head Start teachers learned to use a literacy event like a shared reading of a big book in ways to enhance children's comments and questions.

Kindergarten Interventions

Emergent literacy efforts have been more frequent in kindergartens (Allen & Carr, 1989; Kawakami-Arakaki, Oshiro, & Farran, 1989; Martinez, Cheyney, McBroom, Hemmeter, & Teale, 1989). Pinnell and McCarrier's effort (see chapter 8, this volume) illustrates the directions that most of these projects have taken. Children are involved with engaging books. Some of these books are enlarged so that children can participate by following or reading along as a group. The content of books becomes the source for group and individual writing and music and art projects. Mathematics and science extensions are made, for example, as children study the growth of a plant like a turnip after reading *The Great Big Turnip.*

Brown, Cromer, and Weinberg (1986) described the immediate effects on kindergarten children's retellings of stories as a function of participation in book reading projects. Feitelson, Kita, and Goldstein (1986) reported carryover effects from book reading to specific skills such as letter naming, but with first-grade students. Taylor, Blum, and Logsdon (1986) reported higher scores on a variety of measures when teachers implemented emergent literacy activities. However, the extension of these effects beyond kindergarten (or in the case of Feitelson et al., first grade) is less clear. For example, do fewer students require Reading Recovery as a function of participation in a kindergarten project like the one that Pinnell and McCarrier (see chapter 8, this volume) describe?

Most of the kindergarten projects have not been aimed at teaching children to read, but rather are aimed at immersing students in literacy activities. The perspective underlying these emergent literacy programs is that a foundation in literacy participation such as book reading and writing is needed before activities that foster acquisition of independent reading proficiency commence (Teale, 1987). Goldenberg's (see chapter 9, this volume) questions this assumption. An unexpected finding of Goldenberg's project was the superior learning of students in two control classrooms where kindergarten teachers taught children to read quite purposefully. The comments of these two teachers are similar to the comments of Delpit (1986): Are views of developmental appropriateness that call for unstructured approaches with kindergarten children favoring middle-class children and discriminating against poor children who have not engaged in the same kind and amount of interaction around literacy in preschool environments? Goldenberg's follow-up shows that, with continuing adaptation in the school context, the kindergartners who were in the deliberate literacy instruction classrooms maintained their lead as far as fourth grade. For kindergarten students, attitudes did not seem to suffer as a result of this deliberate instruction but there might be some elements that students acquire as a result of rich book reading and writing experiences that activities with too narrow a focus on specific literacy proficiencies do not foster. Goldenberg suggests a compromise similar to the instructional decisions that characterize the first-grade projects. Students are immersed in book reading and writing activities but they are provided with activities that allow insight into features of words. Even the kindergarten teachers who provided the deliberate instruction did not work with young children in small groups on as systematic a basis as the first-grade projects that are described in this volume. Doubtless many different configurations exist in school districts across the country for kindergarten instruction and the question of which contexts are best in the long run could be described more fully.

First-Grade Interventions

The need for intensive, consistent experiences for particular students is a perspective shared by the developers of the projects in this volume. Most of the projects involve ancillary, specially trained personnel who contribute to the literacy learning of poor children. However, it is important to note that most of the contributors to this volume participated first in restructuring regular classroom instruction. For example, Slavin and colleagues examined ways to increase student literacy through cooperative activities (Stevens, Madden, Slavin, & Farnish, 1987). Taylor and colleagues looked at opportunities for independent reading in classrooms and their relationship to student performance (Taylor, Frye, & Maruyama, 1990). Juel conducted a longitudinal study in which the literacy learning and experiences of a cohort of students were documented (Juel, 1988; Juel, Griffith, & Gough, 1986). Hiebert examined student processes in whole-language classrooms (Fisher & Hiebert, 1990a). In schools with histories of failure, especially when a majority of students depend on schools to become literate, thought will need to be given to classroom interventions that accompany the individual and small-group interventions. Models for these interventions at the first-grade level can be found in the work of Reutzel, Oda, and Moore (1989) and Clarke (1988), and argue for structures that allow for extensive book reading and writing.

At the same time, Hiebert's study (see chapter 5, this volume) shows that classroom programs that immerse students in literacy events are not sufficient for some students. The students in comparison Chapter 1 programs that promoted book reading and writing activities but not did not provide guidance in word-level strategies did poorly, as did some of the children who began higher than Chapter 1 students but remained in the regular classroom program. Classroom interventions are needed, but the forms that these interventions can take are by no means defined or limited to the ones that are described in this volume. Particular principles and components (like staff development) cut across the projects. The configurations of interventions in different schools, especially where a majority of students can benefit from support, need to be described.

Second-Grade Interventions

The current emphasis on first-grade interventions is based primarily on Reading Recovery's focus. The theoretical and empirical evidence for the policy of Reading Recovery to terminate instruction at the end of first grade, even forgoing continuation of programs that did not last the entire 60 lessons in first grade, is difficult to establish. Second grade is very much a part of the early childhood grades. Seven-year-olds enjoy the rhymes, rhythm, and repetition of predictable books. For most second graders, patterns of reading failure are not so entrenched that they are unwilling to try on tasks.

While students' standing at the end of first grade is frequently cited as a reason to concentrate efforts on first grade, studies like Juel's (1988), which show an almost perfect correlation between rank in grade 1 and grade 4, described status quo instruction, where no intervening form of instruction occurred. While Slavin et al. (see chapter 7, this volume) conclude from their project that participation in first grade is better than delaying the intervention, children who receive the intervention in second grade appear to do better than students who receive it in third grade.

Slavin et al. and Goldenberg (chapters 7 and 9, respectively, this volume) demonstrate the need to extend intentional instruction, but neither provides substantive descriptions of how the second-grade projects are alike or different than first-grade efforts. To read texts that are appropriate for second grade requires much more attention to multisyllabic words than is the case with first grade. Neither of these projects has provided an indication of the efficacy of a second-grade intervention as a function of students' previous experiences. Some students might not have become proficient readers as first graders and may be continuing in the intervention, while others may begin the intervention as second graders, having fallen behind intervention students during first grade or having moved into a school as second graders. It might also be that second-grade classroom teachers can do much to buttress and extend the effects of a first-grade intervention through small-group and whole-class events.

A preliminary investigation indicates that a second-grade extension of a first-grade intervention can bring the majority of the children who did not attain grade-level literacy as first graders to proficient literacy, both those who received the intervention as first graders and those new to the intervention in second grade (Catto, 1993). However, second-grade interventions are not being suggested here as automatic for all children, nor as substitutes for first-grade interventions. For children who have not had the many hours of one-to-one lapreading and occasions for scribbling and playing with computers and other literacy-related objects, the 30 hours of individual support or 60 to 75 hours of group support that the first-grade interventions in this volume provide might not be enough. As soon as an intervention is extended, however, it is tempting for teachers to think that "there is no rush" and the interventions might come to look much like typical Chapter 1 programs that end only when children's schooling ends. Providing for those children who need more than 30 to 75 hours of intensive support, while simultaneously resisting the temptation to see the intervention as neverending, will undoubtedly be a challenge. Vigilance is needed through assessment and support structures to maintain high expectations and standards.

Early Interventions and Middle-Grade Instruction

Early interventions for the sake of early gains in themselves are not the goal of any of the projects described in this volume. The aim is to foster higher level literacies among students throughout their school careers and beyond. Since the difficulties of American students lie in higher order processing of text, especially expository text (Chall, Jacobs, & Baldwin, 1990), it is likely that even highly successful early interventions will need to be sustained through instructional activities that guide students in strategies, vocabulary, and structures of expository text. Some reports of early interventions in the form of the addition of preschool (Lazar et al., 1982) or kindergarten literacy instruction (Hanson, Siegel, Broach, 1987) have claimed long-term effects. Typically, however, effects have not been extensive. Almost two decades ago, Durkin (1974–1975) reported the results of a follow-up of an early intervention project in which the positive effects for participating children steadily waned when teachers in subsequent years failed to build on children's proficiencies. Whether any of the interventions in this volume has reversed the trend is not yet clear. When Reading Recovery's longitudinal study stopped at fourth grade, the performances of program students on the task of reading narrative text were not significantly different from either the control group or a randomly selected group of classmates who represented the average band (Pinnell, DeFord, & Lyons, 1988). On a standardized measure, the program students and control students did not differ significantly from one another, with the mean levels of both groups significantly below the classmate group.

Unless effective early interventions are accompanied by a restructuring of instructional experiences beyond grade 2, it would be anticipated that the patterns of the NAEP would not be abrogated among 9- and 13-year-olds in cohorts who have had early interventions. The only project in this volume— Slavin et al. (see chapter 7)—that has dealt with a restructuring of the elementary school does not provide much indication of how instruction changes as students move to the middle grades. The kind of literacy instruction in the middle grades that would sustain and extend the effects of early interventions requires deliberate and planful action in many schools since the critical literacy tasks of the middle grades involve texts in social studies, science, and mathematics. The poor performances of American students on tasks that involve interpreting expository writing (Applebee, Langer, & Mullis, 1988) are explained when observers look for instances of instruction in higher level strategies with informational text, or even at the quality of text. In literacy periods as well as during content area periods, students participate in few occasions where ways of thinking about content area text are modeled (Durkin, 1979). The questions of teachers do not challenge students to think about expository text (Alvermann & Hayes, 1989). Further, content area texts are poorly written and make it difficult for students to comprehend (Armbruster, 1984). In whole-language classrooms, the scenario might not be much better. While literacy periods in whole-language classrooms provide more opportunities for student thinking and discussion than skill-oriented classrooms, the bulk of these periods seems to be spent in self-selected reading of narrative text (Fisher & Hiebert, 1990a). Further, the philosophy underlying whole language might not have spilled over into content areas, meaning that content area instruction of whole-language classrooms looks much like that in skill-oriented classrooms (Fisher & Hiebert, 1990b).

The literature is full of examples of the kind of cognitive strategy instruction that has worked well in experimental classroom implementations (Pressley, Johnson, Symons, McGoldrick, & Kurita, 1989). The current problem could well be an overabundance of riches as university courses and content area teachers' manuals suggest too many strategies for instruction. The students who began with a poor match between school and home literacy might be overwhelmed by the smorgasbord of strategies offered in several different content areas (Pearson & Dole, 1987). The interventions that have aimed to foster a handfull of cognitive strategies in initially low-performing students like Palincsar and Brown's (1984) Reciprocal Teaching, and Englert, Raphael, Anderson, Anthony, and Stevens' (1991) Cognitive Strategy Instruction in Writing have reported substantial improvements in students' thinking about text. If a small set of strategies is used consistently, this target group of students appears able to use the strategies independently.

However, since studies have not used control groups where a similar group of students spent the equivalent amount of time reading, writing, and discussing expository text, it is not clear whether the instruction of cognitive strategies or the increased exposure to expository text fosters the growth. For students who have been successful in early interventions (and also those who arrived in schools at third grade or higher and could not benefit from the early intervention), many occasions for reading, talking, and writing about expository text are needed. It is also likely that modeling by teachers of a few strategies like those of Reciprocal Teaching is helpful to students.

Students who exit early interventions as successful readers remain, on average, in the third quartile—even with narrative text. One treatment that has not been conducted with these students involves frequent occasions to read increasingly more difficult texts. At third grade and above, the gap between initially low- and high-performing students increases substantially (Anderson, Wilson, & Fielding, 1988). A source of these differences, Anderson et al. argue, is that the low-performing students read rarely at home and high-performing students read extensively. This research group has proposed that a lack of reading at home for low-performing students might be compensated for by providing similar periods of time in schools. A handful of research projects verifies the difference that independent reading of self-selected trade books can have on initially low-performing middle-grade students (Elley & Mangubhai, 1983). Some structure during independent reading periods may need to be maintained, as well as occasions for brief discussions. For example, independent reading of a shared passage like those from magazines might provide more direction than is the case with the typical independent reading period. Such occasions for reading, interspersed with reading of self-selected text, can go a long way toward creating a pattern of reading for students outside of school. This proposal for independent reading has not been examined but seems to have sufficient grounds for pursuit by both classroom teachers and researchers.

One type of intervention that is brought up immediately by middle-grade teachers are extensions of the first- and second-grade interventions where the aim is to develop basic reading proficiency. The number of children who can't read at all is probably smaller than is often thought to be the case. Approximately 5% of third-grade students answer less than a third of the items on alternative assessments (Hiebert, 1991). The rest are able to do the tasks—even when those tasks are quite different than the tasks of their regular instruction. Even for the students who fail to complete a third or more of the items on a performance assessment with passages of 600 words or more, it is difficult to know if their failure to do so reflects an inability to read at all or an inability to read *automatically*. The solutions that have been described—daily occasions for reading narrative text and short, informational articles—and guidance in the strategies, structures, and vocabulary of expository text should be tried before first- and second-grade interventions are extended to third grade and beyond.

EARLY INTERVENTIONS AND BROADER EDUCATIONAL CONTEXTS

What teachers teach and how they teach reflects the broader contexts within which schools exist. Teachers are the ones who interact with children but their training and the policies surrounding schools influence perceptions of young children and literacy and also the strategies and materials that are used in classrooms.

Teacher Education

When classroom teachers conduct the intervention (see chapter 6, this volume) or collaborate by extending their classroom environments to create matches with the intervention (Hiebert & Almanza, 1993), the manner in which classroom teachers gain the necessary expertise becomes a critical question. Even when the consistent, intensive instruction of the intervention is provided by supplementary teachers, a solid classroom literacy program is necessary if the literacy proficiencies gained through the intervention are to be maintained and extended.

The projects described in this volume provide a forum in which teachers interact with one another and receive guidance and feedback from staff developers. In Reading Recovery, the structures for support are intensive during the training year. In all likelihood, no comparable teacher development efforts exist at either preservice or in-service stages in the United States. Reading Recovery has a maintenance structure for teachers to sustain their fidelity to the instruction. The other projects with shorter histories than Reading Recovery have had a support structure to initiate teachers into the instruction but the means for maintaining participation and integrity of instruction have not been dealt with as systematically as Reading Recovery. Taylor et al.'s (chapter 6, this volume) survey of participation after the training year indicates that approximately 67% maintain the instruction after the initiation year. Teachers who maintain the instruction produce levels comparable to those when the support structure was present.

If interventions are within the domain of in-service, two routes can be taken. The requirement for special endorsements in literacy of some Chapter 1 programs could place some of the demand on universities. Reading Recovery training occurs in universities, and a similar model might be taken for other efforts. Even so, since classroom teachers make a substantial difference, their teacher education programs need to support them in establishing a knowledge base for working in schools with high proportions of children who depend on schools to become literate. A handful of programs across the country are geared to teaching in urban settings, but hardly enough to fill the current context. With movement of teacher education to fifth-year programs, there might be even less time available for courses on literacy and language. Attempts at implementing projects that are either based in classrooms or depend on strong liaisons with classroom programs attest to the belief among many teachers that "it isn't my job" to teach the lowest performing students (Bean, Cooley, Eichelberger, Lazar, & Zigmond, 1991). Perhaps the best that initial teacher education programs could do would be to make clear the vision of literacy learning that underlies the projects in this volume, and to develop an acquaintance with rudimentary components of implementation projects. Berliner (1985) proposed that university-based laboratories where teachers-to-be viewed videotapes and studied transcripts, among other tasks, could create contexts for reflection. In particular, teachers-to-be can reflect on contexts where they might never have experiences, like the second-grade classroom in Harlem of Dawn Harris Martine that is featured in a videotape series (Martine, 1990). Some have proposed extensions of teacher education programs, such as Anderson and Armbruster's (1990) attempt to use elements of the Reading Recovery training with preservice teachers. If teacher education programs gave teachers a basic foundation, school districts and university partnerships could build on this commitment and create the knowledge base that leads to effective instruction.

The mismatch of many teacher education programs and the contexts of the classrooms into which beginning teachers are initiated also requires attention. If teacher education programs emphasize a perspective that works with middle-class children, teachers leave their programs with the expectation that the learning of a 6-year-old child whose experiences with literacy have been few will simulate the learning of some middle-class children who have spent as many as 2,000 hours interacting about literacy at home (Adams, 1990). When literacy events are created in ways that assume that children will naturally move into literacy with little or no instruction, the children who depend on schools to become literate are disenfranchised (Delpit, 1986).

The best scenario would be one where a basic level of expertise in implementing thoughtful, intensive instruction for low-performing students would be laid in preservice teacher education programs, and where districts, universities, and ancillary agencies would collaborate in providing for support structures and networks that extend teachers' expertise. At present, teachers who work with large numbers of low-performing students, as is the case with Chapter 1 teachers' assignments, rarely have contexts where they can share their accomplishments and concerns. The perspective of change that seems to underlie most staff development efforts is one of immediate, one-time, long-standing change. When a small number of dollars was requested to sustain a support structure in an intervention project, the staff development coordinator for one district commented that the teachers should be sufficiently empowered to do the project on their own. Such a perspective on change goes contrary to the constructivist model to which most current restructuring efforts adhere. Schools and districts where change has occurred show that restructuring efforts take time and depend on structures in the institution that sustain the effort (Cuban, 1990; Fullan, 1991).

State and National Policies

Chapter 1, the only sustaining federal program that provides additional resources for poor children, is a morass of policies that, when untangled, do not necessarily benefit the poor children for whom it is intended to support. Chapter 1 should be the context for the additional support to classroom teachers and to children directly that can get poor children off to the right start. Several assumptions that underlie the projects in this volume go contrary to current Chapter 1 policies. These policies of Chapter 1 are not malicious or intentionally aimed at creating obstacles for successful early interventions. The policies reflect a different set of assumptions about how best to help poor children get a leg up.

All of the projects described in this volume are based on the assumption that, by beginning early, a sizable portion of reading difficulties can be prevented. If classroom instruction in succeeding years builds on this early start, large amounts of remedial instruction should not be needed. In contrast, Chapter 1 policy is based on a remedial model. Funds are allocated to sites where need is greatest, and need is based on standardized test results from grade 2 and beyond. A school that has concentrated their Chapter 1 funds on an emergent literacy program in kindergarten such as the one Pinnell and McCarrier describe (see chapter 8, this volume) and an intensive intervention in grade 1 could well find itself no longer in need. That is, if the lowest quartile has learned to read, a district would be out of compliance if funds continued to be given to this school rather than a neighboring school where no early interventions have been conducted and where the bottom quartile continues to perform poorly in grades 2 and above. Routes are available for districts to obtain waivers from state Chapter 1 agencies, and national Chapter 1 leaders likely would argue against the possibility that successful early interventions would be penalized. However, local interpretations of policies often are more rigid than those that might be intended by the national policymakers with whom the policies originated (Brown, 1991).

Current Chapter 1 policies also act against a "sustenance and extension" model for Chapter 1. Once students have moved above the level on the standardized test used for Chapter 1 eligibility they can no longer receive Chapter 1 services. Further, Chapter 1 teachers' loads are determined on working with students over the major part of the year. Current guidelines would not support a model where students who successfully completed an early intervention are sustained in their reading practices by in-class seminars conducted by the Chapter 1 teacher. Again, special waivers can be obtained for innovative programs but the structure of Chapter 1 does not encourage sustaining the gains that have been made. This policy has stood in place despite consistent findings in national evaluations of Chapter 1 that students make gains in

Chapter 1 but lose them soon after leaving the program (Kennedy, Birman, & Demaline, 1986). Policies have not been amended, nor have projects been designed to examine the question of what type of support structures would sustain these gains.

SUMMARY

Many more children can become literate than now is the case. For some children, the length of time might need to be longer than for others (into grade 2 and even beyond), but the majority of children can be facile readers and writers by the end of first grade. While early interventions are necessary, they are not sufficient. While clearly successful, early interventions tell only part of the story. Diversified models of intervention are required, where several different partial solutions work together. Reading Recovery, with its strong preventive perspective and stellar teacher training, could well be the centerpiece of these models. However, a second tier of interventions is also needed. The obligation for designing and administering this second tier should not fall to Reading Recovery trainers and teachers. Teachers, teacher educators, and researchers who have expertise in other areas should assume this responsibility. The other partial solutions are already present. What is needed at this point are efforts to coordinate these partial solutions.

REFERENCES

Adams, M. (1990). *Beginning to read: Thinking and learning about print.* Cambridge, MA: MIT Press.
Allen, J., & Carr, E. (1989). Collaborative learning among kindergarten writers: James learns how to write at school. In J. Allen & J.M. Mason (Eds.), *Risk makers, risk takers, risk breakers: Reducing the risks for young literacy learners* (pp. 30–47). Portsmouth, NH: Heinemann.
Alvermann, D.E., & Hayes, D.A. (1989). Classroom discussion of content area reading assignments: An intervention study. *Reading Research Quarterly, 24,* 305–335.
Anderson, R.C., & Armbruster, B. (1990). *Teachers College Record, 91,* 396–408.
Anderson, R.C., Wilson, P.T., & Fielding, L.G. (1988). Growth in reading and how children spend their time outside of school. *Reading Research Quarterly, 23,* 285–303.
Applebee, A.N., Langer, J., & Mullis, I.V.S. (1988). *Who reads best? Factors related to reading achievement in grades 3, 7, and 11.* Princeton, NJ: Educational Testing Service.
Armbruster, B.B. (1984). The problem of "inconsiderate text." In G.G. Duffy, L.R. Roehler, & J. Mason (Eds.), *Comprehension instruction* (pp. 202–217). New York: Longman.
Bean, R.M., Cooley, W.W., Eichelberger, R.T., Lazar, M.K, & Zigmond, N. (1991).

Inclass or pullout: Effects of setting on the remedial reading program. *Journal of Reading Behavior, 23,* 445–464.

Berliner, D.C. (1985). Laboratory settings and the study of teacher education. *Journal of Teacher Education, 36,* 2–8.

Brown, M.H., Cromer, P.S., & Weinberg, S.H. (1986). Shared book experiences in kindergarten: Helping children come to literacy. *Early Childhood Research Quarterly, 1,* 397–406.

Brown, R. (1991). *Schools of thought.* San Francisco: Jossey-Bass.

Catto, S.L. (1993). *An examination of a second-grade literacy intervention: Patterns of student performance and the relationship of selected factors.* Unpublished dissertation, University of Colorado-Boulder.

Chall, J.S., Jacobs, V.A., & Baldwin, L.E. (1990). *The reading crisis: Why poor children fall behind.* Cambridge, MA: Harvard University Press.

Clarke, L. (1988). Invented versus traditional spelling in first graders' writings: Effects on learning to spell and read. *Research in the Teaching of English, 22,* 281–309.

Cuban, L. (1990). Reforming again, again, and again. *Educational Researcher, 19,* 3–13.

Delpit, L.D. (1986). Skills and other dilemmas of a progressive black educator. *Harvard Educational Review, 56,* 379–385.

Dickinson, D.K. (1989). Effects of a shared reading program on one Head Start language and literacy environment. In J. Allen & J.M. Mason (Eds.), *Risk makers, risk takers, risk breakers: Reducing the risks for young literacy learners* (pp. 125–153). Portsmouth, NH: Heinemann.

Durkin, D. (1974–1975). A six year study of children who learned to read in school at the age of four. *Reading Research Quarterly, 10,* 9–61.

Durkin, D. (1979). What classroom observations reveal about reading comprehension instruction. *Reading Research Quarterly, 14,* 481–533.

Educational Testing Service. (1991). *Trends in academic progress.* Washington, DC: Office of Educational Research and Improvement, U.S. Department of Education.

Elley, W.B., & Mangubhai, F. (1983). The impact of reading on second language learning. *Reading Research Quarterly, 19,* 53–67.

Englert, C.S., Raphael, T.E., Anderson, L.M., Anthony, H.M., & Stevens, D.D. (1991). Making strategies and self-talk visible: Writing instruction in regular and special education classrooms. *American Educational Research Journal, 28,* 337–372.

Feitelson, D., Kita, B., & Goldstein, Z. (1986). Effects of listening to series stories on first graders' comprehension and use of language. *Research in the Teaching of English, 20,* 339–356.

Fisher, C.W., & Hiebert, E.H. (1990a). Characteristics of tasks in two approaches to literacy instruction. *Elementary School Journal, 91,* 6–13.

Fisher, C.W., & Hiebert, E.H. (1990b, April). *Shifts in reading and writing tasks: Do they extend to social studies, science, and mathematics?* Paper presented at the annual meeting of the American Educational Research Association, Boston, MA.

Fullan, M.G. (1991). *The new meaning of educational change.* New York: Teachers College Press.

Hanson, R., Siegel, D., & Broach, D. (1987, April). *The effects on high school seniors of learning to read in kindergarten.* Paper presented at the annual meeting of the American Educational Research Association, Washington, DC.

Hiebert, E.H. (1992, May). *Impact of home, classroom, and prior knowledge factors on the reading performances of intervention students.* Paper presented at the CORR preconvention of the International Reading Association, Orlando, FL.

Hiebert, E.H., & Almanza, E. (1993, April). *Extending an early literacy intervention across Chapter 1 and classroom contexts.* Paper presented at the annual meeting of the International Reading Association, San Antonio, TX.

Hiebert, E.H. (1991, April). *Comparison of student reading performance on standardized and alternative tests in high-stakes contexts.* Paper presented at the annual meeting of the American Educational Research Association, Chicago, IL.

Hiebert, E.H., Stacy, B., & Jordan, L. (1985). *An analysis of literacy experiences in preschool settings.* Unpublished manuscript, University of Kentucky, Lexington, KY.

Juel, C. (1988). Learning to read and write: A longitudinal study of fifty-four children from first through fourth grade. *Journal of Educational Psychology, 80,* 437–447.

Juel, C., Griffith, P.L., & Gough, P.B. (1986). Acquisition of literacy: A longitudinal study of children in first and second grade. *Journal of Educational Psychology, 78,* 243–255.

Kawakami-Arakaki, A.J., Oshiro, M.E., & Farran, D.C. (1989). Research to practice: Integrating reading and writing in a kindergarten curriculum. In J.M. Mason (Ed.), *Reading and writing connections.* Boston: Allyn & Bacon.

Kennedy, M.M., Birman, B.F., & Demaline, R.E. (1986). *The effectiveness of Chapter 1 services.* Washington, DC: Office of Educational Research and Improvement, U.S. Department of Education.

Lazar, I., Darlington, R., Murray, H., Royce, J., & Snipper, A. (1982). Lasting effects of early education. *Monographs of the Society for Research in Child Development, 47* (2-3, Serial No. 195).

Lundberg, I., Frost, J., & Petersen, O. (1988). Effects of an extensive program for stimulating phonological awareness in preschool children. *Reading Research Quarterly, 23,* 263–284.

Martine, D.H. (1990). *Viewers' guide: Teaching reading—Strategies from successful classrooms: Reading-writing connections.* Urbana-Champaign, IL: University of Illinois, Center for the Study of Reading.

Martinez, M.G., Cheyney, M., McBroom, C., Hemmeter, A., & Teale, W.H. (1989). No-risk kindergarten literacy environments for at-risk children. In J. Allen & J.M. Mason (Eds.), *Risk makers, risk takers, risk breakers: Reducing the risks for young literacy learners* (pp. 93–124). Portsmouth, NH: Heinemann.

Mason, J.M., McCormick, C., & Bhavnagri, N. (1986). How are you going to help me learn? Lesson negotiations between a teacher and preschool children. In D. Yaden & S. Templeton (Eds.), *Metalinguistic awareness and beginning literacy: Conceptualizing what it means to read and write* (pp. 159–172). Portsmouth, NH: Heinemann.

Palincsar, A.S., & Brown, A.L. (1984). Reciprocal teaching of comprehension-fostering and comprehension-monitoring activities. *Cognition and Instruction, 1,* 117–175.

Palincsar, A., Stevens, D., & Gavelek, J. (1989). Collaborating with teachers in the interest of student collaboration. *International Journal of Educational Research, 13,* 41–54.

Pearson, P.D., & Dole, J.A. (1987). Explicit comprehension instruction: A review of research and a new conceptualization of instruction. *Elementary School Journal, 88,* 151–165.

Peterman, C.L., Stewart, J.P., Sinha, S., Kerr, B.M., & Mason, J.M. (1991, December).

Linking language and emergent literacy: Observations, interventions, and model building. Paper presented at the annual meeting of the National Reading Conference, Palm Springs, CA.

Pinnell, G.S., DeFord, D.E., & Lyons, C.A. (1988). *Reading Recovery: Early intervention for at-risk first graders.* Arlington, VA: Educational Research Service.

Pressley, M., Johnson, C.J., Symons, S., McGoldrick, J.A., & Kurita, J.A. (1989). Strategies that improve children's memory and comprehension of text. *Elementary School Journal, 90,* 3–32.

Reutzel, D.R., Oda, L.K., & Moore, B.H. (1989). Developing print awareness: The effect of three instructional approaches on kindergartners' print awareness, reading readiness, and word reading. *Journal of Reading Behavior, 21,* 197–217.

Shepard, L.A., & Smith, M.L. (1988). Escalating academic demand in kindergarten: Counterproductive policies. *Elementary School Journal, 89,* 135–145.

Snow, C.E., & Ninio, A. (1986). The contracts of literacy: What children learn from learning to read books. In W.H. Teale & E. Sulzby (Eds.), *Emergent literacy: Writing and reading* (pp. 116–138). Norwood, NJ: Ablex.

Spodek, B. (1988). Conceptualizing today's kindergarten curriculum. *Elementary School Journal, 89,* 203–212.

Stevens, R.J., Madden, N.A., Slavin, R.E., & Farnish, A.M. (1987). Cooperative integrated reading and composition: Two field experiments. *Reading Research Quarterly, 22,* 433–454.

Taylor, B.M., Frye, B.J., & Maruyama, G.M. (1990). Time spent reading and reading growth. *American Educational Research Journal, 27,* 351–362.

Taylor, N.E., Blum, I.H., & Logsdon, D.M. (1986). The development of written language awareness: Environmental aspects and program characteristics. *Reading Research Quarterly, 21,* 132–149.

Teale, W.H. (1987). Emergent literacy: Reading and writing development in early childhood. In J.E. Readence & R.S. Baldwin (Eds.), *Research in literacy: Merging perspectives* (36th Yearbook of the National Reading Conference) (pp. 45–74). Rochester, NY: National Reading Conference.

Index